T0330372

Environmental Pricing

CRITICAL ISSUES IN ENVIRONMENTAL TAXATION

Series Editors: Larry Kreiser, *Cleveland State University, USA*, Hope Ashiabor, *Macquarie University, Australia* and Janet E. Milne, *Vermont Law School, USA*

The *Critical Issues in Environmental Taxation* series provides insights and analysis on environmental taxation issues on an international basis and explores detailed theories for achieving environmental goals through fiscal policy. Each book in the series contains pioneering and thought-provoking contributions by the world's leading environmental tax scholars who respond to the diverse challenges posed by environmental sustainability.

Previous volumes in the series:

Original book published by CCH Incorporated

Volumes I–IV published by Richmond Law Publishers

Volumes V–VIII published by Oxford University Press

Titles in the series include:

Environmental Pricing

Studies in Policy Choices and Interactions

Edited by

Larry Kreiser

Professor Emeritus of Accounting, Cleveland State University, USA

Mikael Skou Andersen

Professor of Environmental Policy Analysis, Aarhus University, Denmark

Birgitte Egelund Olsen

Professor of Law, Aarhus University, Denmark

Stefan Speck

Project Manager, European Environment Agency (EEA), Denmark

Janet E. Milne

Professor of Law, Vermont Law School, USA

Hope Ashiabor

Associate Professor of Law, Macquarie University, Australia

CRITICAL ISSUES IN ENVIRONMENTAL TAXATION, VOLUME XVI

Edward Elgar
PUBLISHING

Cheltenham, UK • Northampton, MA, USA

Published by
Edward Elgar Publishing Limited
The Lypiatts
15 Lansdown Road
Cheltenham
Glos GL50 2JA
UK

Edward Elgar Publishing, Inc.
William Pratt House
9 Dewey Court
Northampton
Massachusetts 01060
USA

A catalogue record for this book
is available from the British Library

Library of Congress Control Number: 2015935904

This book is available electronically in the **Elgar**online
Law subject collection
DOI 10.4337/9781785360251

ISBN 978 1 78536 024 4 (cased)
ISBN 978 1 78536 025 1 (eBook)

Typeset by Servis Filmsetting Ltd, Stockport, Cheshire
Printed and bound in Great Britain by T.J. International Ltd, Padstow

Contents

Figures

Tables

Editorial review board

The 15 chapters in this book have been brought to publication with the help of an editorial review board dedicated to peer review. The 19 members of the board are committed to the field of environmental taxation and are active participants in environmental taxation events around the world.

Chair:
Larry Kreiser
Cleveland State University, USA

Members:
Mikael Skou Andersen
Aarhus University, Denmark

Hope Ashiabor
Macquarie University, Australia

Kris Bachus
University of Leuven, Belgium

Nils Axel Braathen
Organisation for Economic Co-operation and Development (OECD), France

Bill Butcher
The University of New South Wales, Australia

Jacqueline Cottrell
Green Budget Europe (GBE), Belgium

David Duff
University of British Columbia, Canada

Soocheol Lee
Meijo University, Japan

Janet E. Milne
Vermont Law School, USA

Anna Mortimore
Griffith University, Australia

Birgitte Egelund Olsen
Aarhus University, Denmark

Sven Rudolph
Kyoto University, Japan

Stefan Speck
European Environment Agency (EEA), Denmark

Natalie Stoianoff
University of Technology, Sydney, Australia

Rahmat Tavallali
Walsh University, USA

Walter Wang
University of San Diego, USA

Stefan E. Weishaar
University of Groningen, the Netherlands

Yan Xu
The Chinese University of Hong Kong, Hong Kong

Contributors

Antenucci, Marianna, Italian Association of Energy Wholesalers and Traders (AIGET), Italy

Bachus, Kris, Catholic University of Leuven, Belgium

Bubna-Litic, Karen, University of South Australia, Australia

Cottrell, Jacqueline, Green Budget Europe (GBE), Belgium

Fonseca Capdevila, Enrique, Lawyer, Spain

Governatori, Michele, Italian Association of Energy Wholesalers and Traders (AIGET), Italy

Grau Ruiz, María Amparo, Universidad Complutense Madrid, Spain

Guo, Xingjie, Renmin University of China, China

Jarvie, Deborah L., University of Lethbridge, Canada, Monash University, Australia

Kawakatsu, Takeshi, Kyoto Prefectural University, Japan

Kettner, Claudia, Austrian Institute of Economic Research (WIFO), Austria

Kicia, Malgorzata, European Commission, DG ENV, Belgium

Kletzan-Slamanig, Daniela, Austrian Institute of Economic Research (WIFO), Austria

Köppl, Angela, Austrian Institute of Economic Research (WIFO), Austria

Kreiser, Larry, Cleveland State University, USA

Lerch, Achim, Hessian University of Cooperative Education, Germany

Mao, Yujiao, Renmin University of China, China

Mersinia, Ioanna, University of Eastern Finland, Finland

Pirlot, Alice, FNRS Research Fellow, Université Catholique de Louvain (UCL), Belgium

Rosenstock, Manfred, European Commission, DG ENV, Belgium

Rudolph, Sven, Kyoto University, Japan

Sprohge, Hans, Wright State University, USA

Vanswijgenhoven, Frederic, Catholic University of Leuven, Belgium

Villar Ezcurra, Marta, San Pablo CEU University, Spain

Weber, Rolf H., University of Zurich, Switzerland

Wu, Jian, Renmin University of China, China

Foreword

Over the last few decades, it has been proven that environmental taxes can be effective and efficient instruments for environmental policy. Environmental taxation contributes to environmental improvements by introducing a price signal that reduces the demand for environmentally harmful products or helps insure that polluters take into account the costs of pollution on the environment when they make production or consumption decisions. However, in spite of the many advantages of environmental taxes, their use has been relatively limited in many countries.

The limited use of environmental taxes as a policy instrument can partly be explained by the fact that policymakers often fear that environmental taxes have a negative impact on income distribution or on the international competitiveness of the domestic industry; typically the most polluting energy intensive sectors of the economy. In general, there are different ways to address such concerns without compromising the environmental benefits of environmental taxation, for example, imposing similar costs on foreign products through the use of Border Tax Adjustments which are duties charged at the border on imported products.

In practice, environmental taxes are seldom used in complete isolation. They are applied in combination with other regulatory instruments or packages of instruments. Thus, the current picture of national policies on climate change, energy transitions and the environment is often a patchwork of different policy instruments. In general, there is a critical lack of knowledge on how such different policy instruments interact and work together. Therefore, it is important to examine the impact of different policy mixes, including environmental taxation, in order to identify effective and efficient combinations of policy instruments.

Volume XVI of Critical Issues in Environmental Taxation gives a comprehensive discussion of these issues and of recent research on the environmental and economic impact of applying environmental taxes. In particular, it discusses the high potential for a wider use of environmental taxation in combination with other policy instruments, provided that such environmental taxes are well-designed and that their potential impact on international competitiveness and income distribution are properly addressed.

Birgitte Egelund Olsen
Professor of Law
Aarhus University, Denmark

Preface

In recent comments regarding the ravages of climate change, Pope Francis stated that 'humans have slapped nature in the face'. This does not have to be. High quality research on climate change, global warming and environmental sustainability can lead to changes in the way we interact with nature. High quality research on these issues is the mission of Critical Issues in Environmental Taxation.

Volume XVI of Critical Issues contains 15 chapters on environmental issues involving environmental pricing: studies in policy choices and interactions. These chapters have been prepared by environmental experts from around the world. We hope you find these studies to be enlightening and worthy of consideration by policymakers.

Larry Kreiser, Lead Editor
Mikael Skou Andersen, Co-Editor
Birgitte Egelund Olsen, Co-Editor
Stefan Speck, Co-Editor
Janet E. Milne, Co-Editor
Hope Ashiabor, Co-Editor
August 2015

Abbreviations

AB	Appellate Body
ARENA	Australian Renewable Energy Agency
BCA	border carbon adjustments
BEPS	Base Erosion and Profit Shifting
BTA	border tax adjustments
CCGT	combined cycle gas turbines
CCL	Climate Change Levy
CDS	clean dark spread
CFC	chlorofluorocarbon
CJ	Court of Justice
CPH	combined heat and power
CPI	climate policy integration
CSR	Corporate Social Responsibility
CSR	Country-Specific Recommendation
CSS	clean spark spread
CT	carbon tax
DPJ	Democratic Party of Japan
EAP	Environmental Action Programme
EC	European Commission
ECM	Environment-Competitive Matrix
EED	EU Energy Efficiency Directive
EFR	environmental fiscal reform
EHS	environmentally harmful subsidies
EPI	environmental policy integration
ERDF	European Regional Development Fund
ESF	European Social Fund
ET	environmental tax
ETD	EU Energy Taxation Directive
ETR	Environmental Tax Reform
ETS	emissions trading system
EU	European Union
FFS	fossil-fuel subsidies
FIP	feed-in premiums
FIT	feed-in tariffs

GATT	General Agreement on Tariffs and Trade
GBER	General Block Exemption Regulation
GC	green certificates
GDP	gross domestic product
GHG	greenhouse gases
HAP	hazardous air pollutant
IDMET	Integrated Domestic Market of Emissions Trading
IMF	International Monetary Fund
IPCC	International Panel on Climate Change
IPCEI	important projects of common European interest
IRENA	International Renewable Energy Agency
IVM	Institute for Environmental Studies
JVETS	Japan Voluntary Emissions Trading Scheme
kW	kilowatt
LDP	Liberal Democratic Party
MC	marginal costs
METI	Ministry of Economy, Trade and Industry
MFN	most-favoured nation
MoE	Ministry of the Environment
MRET	Mandatory Renewable Energy Target
MW	megawatts
NAS	National Academy of Sciences
NRC	National Research Council
NRP	National Reform Programme
OCGT	open cycle gas turbines
OECD	Organisation for Economic Co-operation and Development
PCA	principal component analysis
PLS	Pollution Levy System
PPA	power purchase agreement
PPP	polluter pays principle
PV	photovoltaic
RAE	National Regulatory Authority
RES	renewable energy sources
SA	South Australia
SAM	State Aid Modernisation
SCM	Subsidies and Countervailing Measures
SME	small to medium-sized enterprise
UNG	unconventional natural gas
WFD	EU Water Framework Directive
WTO	World Trade Organization

PART I

Case studies in policy integration

1. Climate policy integration: evidence on coherence in EU policies*

Claudia Kettner, Daniela Kletzan-Slamanig and Angela Köppl

1.1 INTRODUCTION

Climate change represents the most exigent environmental problem our societies face. Just as much as a wide array of activities are or will be affected by climate change, current production and consumption patterns drive the emission of greenhouse gases (GHG). Many climate-relevant decisions are taken in policy areas other than environmental policy with only little regard to climate change impacts. It has to be recognized that climate policy is a cross-sectoral issue and needs to be firmly integrated in general and sector-specific policy areas that frame economic activity and societal development (Kok and de Coninck 2007; Ahmad 2009; Mickwitz et al. 2009). Experience however shows that there is a divide between the need of addressing climate policy as cross-sectional issue and short-term policy decisions that imply a low hierarchical rank for climate policy. Still a big step is necessary to depart from climate policy as add-on policy area towards comprehensive integration.

Climate policy integration or mainstreaming is not only required for sectoral policies with direct physical interlinkages like energy or transport but also for other policy areas including budgetary, R&D or regional policy. Complementing climate-specific policies with sectoral policies that integrate climate policy objectives ensures that producers and consumers are confronted with coherent signals for investment decision and behavioural changes (Mickwitz et al. 2009).

Climate policy integration (CPI) has experienced increased interest in recent years, which is also reflected in the incorporation of climate policy aspects in various EU policy documents (for example, the Europe 2020 Strategy). This development builds on the experience with environmental policy integration but also stems from the recognition of the urgency of the problem of climate change that requires action to be taken in almost every sector of society and economy. The EU strives for a leading role in international negotiations, underpinning this ambition with domestic action like the introduction of the EU Emission Trading Scheme in 2005 and the adoption of the Climate and Energy Package in 2009. The 20-20-20 targets for energy and climate and the visions for 2050 underline the political commitment on the general EU level and the increased consideration of climate change issues in energy policy.

However, the existence of a wide range of different institutions and departments in the EU, as well as of different levels of governance (EU, Member State, regional, local) represents a major obstacle for policy integration and the development of a coherent climate policy framework. As a number of studies (Kok and de Coninck 2007; Adelle et al. 2009; Dupont and Oberthür 2011; Mickwitz et al. 2009; Medarova-Bergstrom et al. 2011) show, while general political commitment for CPI exists, the actual mainstreaming in sectoral policies still has to be improved. The complexity of the institutional setting in the EU limits a comprehensive analysis of all aspects of CPI into other policy areas in the chapter. The focus here is on horizontal policy integration at the EU level. The chapter contributes to the new research field of CPI concentrating on some selected policy areas by identifying (potential) conflicts and synergies.

1.2   CONCEPTS AND APPROACHES TO CLIMATE POLICY INTEGRATION

Climate policy integration (CPI) can be regarded as a continuation of approaches for environmental policy integration (EPI) in the 1980s and 1990s that aimed at contributing to the reduction of environmental problems and guiding the transition to sustainable development (Adelle et al. 2009; Jordan and Lenschow 2010).

On a general level EPI refers to the integration of environmental aspects and policy objectives into sector policies like energy and agriculture (Adelle et al. 2009). Based on the definition for EPI by Lafferty and Hovden (2003) CPI can be defined as:[1]

- the incorporation of the aims of climate policy objectives into all stages of policymaking in other policy sectors,
- complemented by an attempt to aggregate expected consequences for climate change mitigation and adaptation into an overall evaluation of policy and a commitment to minimize contradictions between climate policies and other policies.

Accordingly climate policy objectives are given priority in decisions in non-environmental policy areas and the integration should be reflected in general and sector-specific policy strategies as well as applied instruments and ideally in policy outcomes (Mickwitz et al. 2009).

Thus policy integration or mainstreaming aims at increasing coherence, minimizing duplications or contradictory policies and identifying trade-offs and synergies between policy areas (Kok and de Coninck 2007). While occasionally there will be obvious synergies that can be exploited – for example, the promotion of renewables that is beneficial for ensuring energy security *and* reducing carbon emissions – in other cases the sectoral and climate policy objectives may be conflicting – for example, increasing cohesion and accessibility by developing road transport infrastructure in peripheral regions. In the latter cases political decisions have to be made regarding the importance that is assigned to climate policy aspects relative to the sectoral objectives. However, sectoral policies in general tend to have a short-term focus, while climate change requires long-term strategies coupled with the requirement to immediately implement measures.

Policy integration can be analyzed from different points of view, in other words, within or across government levels. Horizontal policy integration focuses on mainstreaming climate policy objectives into other sectoral policies on one level of government. Vertical policy integration in contrast takes a top-down approach and focuses on mainstreaming throughout multiple levels of government and policymaking.

The analysis in this chapter focuses on horizontal CPI on the EU level, in other words, the assessment of the extent to which other non-environmental sectoral policies take into account climate policy targets and whether the climate relevance of measures represents a relevant criterion for funding or if funds are provided for specific climate-related activities (for example, for R&D or infrastructure). As the comprehensive assessment of EU policies is an extensive research agenda, the chapter focuses on selected policy areas.

For our analysis we choose a hierarchical approach starting from strategic documents (Lisbon Treaty, Europe 2020 Strategy). We then focus on two sectoral policies – energy and cohesion policy. On the EU level energy policy focuses mainly on target setting (for example, the renewable, energy efficiency targets for 2020) and formulating medium to long-term development paths (for example, by defining infrastructure priorities), while the choice and implementation of policy instruments remains in the competence of Member States. We therefore focus the analysis on strategic EU energy policy documents. In contrast, regional policy makes up a large part of the EU budget and represents an important source of funding for infrastructure projects in predefined priority areas. We therefore assess the thematic priorities of regional policy in two periods (2007–2013, 2014–2020) and the budget allocations for climate related areas.

Our analysis illustrates the evolution of climate policy issues over time, maturing from a secondary policy concern to an acknowledged central policy issue. It furthermore discusses the potential synergies and conflicts between the different policy areas.

1.3 EU CLIMATE POLICY INTEGRATION: TREATY ON THE FUNCTIONING OF THE EUROPEAN UNION AND EUROPE 2020 STRATEGY

With the Treaty of Lisbon (European Union 2008) the Treaty on European Union and the Treaty establishing the European Community that 'organizes the functioning of the Union and determines the areas of, delimitation of, and arrangements for exercising its competences'[2] were amended. Regarding climate and energy issues the Lisbon Treaty implied the inclusion of a specific article on energy (Article 194) as well as the explicit reference to the commitment to sustainable development and the combat against climate change (Articles 11[3] and 191[4]). The introduction of energy into the Treaty – a policy area for which previously no EU competence was defined[5] – provides a legal basis for a more harmonized, common energy policy. The aims of EU energy policy are stated in the Lisbon Treaty as:

1. ensuring the functioning of the energy market,
2. ensuring security of energy supply in the European Union,
3. promoting energy efficiency and energy saving and the development of new and renewable forms of energy and
4. promoting the interconnection of energy networks.

Energy is one of the areas of 'shared competences' between the EU and Member States as defined in Article 4. However, the EU's competence is limited by the requirement included in Article 194 (2), namely that EU measures 'shall not affect a Member State's right to determine the conditions for exploiting its energy resources, its choice between different energy sources and the general structure of its energy supply'. In such cases decisions have to be adopted unanimously, while in general a qualified majority and the cooperation with the EU Parliament are sufficient. This reflects that energy is still widely regarded as a national policy issue although the codification in the Treaty creates better possibilities for a common policy focusing on sustainable structures that are compatible with climate change mitigation. It has to be taken into account, however, that the promotion of energy efficiency and renewables is just one out of four objectives of the EU's energy policy and the energy policy objectives are of equal rank.

With the Europe 2020 Strategy (EC 2010b) a vision for a social market economy was presented defining the kind of growth aspired:

1. Smart growth: developing an economy based on knowledge and innovation.
2. Sustainable growth: promoting a more resource efficient, greener and more competitive economy.
3. Inclusive growth: fostering a high-employment economy delivering social and territorial cohesion.

Five headline targets were defined for employment, social inclusion, research and development and climate and energy. The Europe 2020 strategy has incorporated the targets for (GHG) emission reductions, energy efficiency and renewables set out in the EU's Climate and Energy Package (see below), integrating them at the highest political level. The targets stand alongside the objectives for employment, R&D and social inclusion. The Strategy thus references the legal obligation accepted by adopting the directives under the Climate and Energy Package. But while synergies between resource efficiency, innovation and competitiveness are emphasized, the potential trade-offs between the targets are not explicitly discussed in the Strategy or the related documents. The main conflict can be identified by the need to achieve economic growth in order to ensure employment, social cohesion and fiscal stability, while the climate and energy policy targets require a paradigmatic change and a redefinition of growth in order to ensure the long-term decarbonization of the economies.

1.4 EU CLIMATE POLICY INTEGRATION: ENERGY POLICY

With the recognition of climate change as the most challenging environmental problem and energy use as the main driver for GHG emissions the interdependence of energy and climate policies has gained increased political attention. It is acknowledged that efforts to mitigate climate change support energy policy objectives like increasing energy security and vice versa (de Jong et al. 2010; Adelle et al. 2009).

Although energy issues were one of the reasons for establishing the European Coal and Steel Community,[6] Member States regarded this policy area as their own competence related strongly to national security and energy sovereignty considerations. In recent years the reluctance to agree to a common energy policy has declined in light of rising and volatile oil prices, increasing import dependence, political instability in supplying regions or interruptions in the gas supply from Russia. Last but not least the recognition of environmental impacts, especially GHG emissions, has contributed to the shift of competences to EU level (Dupont and Oberthür 2011; de Jong et al. 2010; Adelle et al. 2009). However, energy policy on the EU level is concerned with strategic aspects and setting medium to long-term goals while instrument choice and implementation remains in the competence of Member States.

In 2006 the Green Paper 'A European Strategy for Sustainable, Competitive and Secure Energy' (EC 2006) was published. Just as the Communication 'An energy policy for Europe' (EC 2007a) it identified the main challenges for energy policy and calls for a balance between:

- combating climate change, in other words, significantly reducing energy-related GHG emissions;
- limiting external vulnerability, in other words, decreasing the reliance on imported energy sources and increasing the security of supply and;
- promoting growth and jobs (competitiveness), in other words, decreasing the vulnerability due to rising and volatile energy prices by completing the internal market and increasing investment in energy savings and renewable energy.

The Communication further outlined the need for a strategic vision, internal action and international cooperation since '[e]xisting measures on areas such as renewable electricity, biofuels, energy efficiency and the Internal Energy Market have achieved important results but lack the coherence necessary to bring sustainability, security of supply and competitiveness' (EC 2007a).

The presidency conclusions from the European Council Meeting in March 2007 (European Council 2007) also emphasized the issues of sustainability, competitiveness and security of supply and called for the development of an integrated European climate and energy policy in order to achieve effective climate protection.

The importance of security of supply in the EU's energy policy was underlined in 2008 by the Communication 'An EU Security and Solidarity Action Plan' (EC 2008b) acknowledging the EU's role in protecting its energy interests beyond Member States' actions, especially in terms of external relations and important infrastructure projects.

In 2007 the EU covenanted to ambitious GHG reduction targets (EC 2007b). The climate and energy targets set for 2020 ought not only contribute to climate change mitigation but also increase energy security and ensure a head start in the development of low carbon technologies. EC (2008a) defined two key objectives for 2020:

- a reduction in EU GHG emissions of at least 20 per cent below 1990 levels and
- a 20 per cent share of renewable energy sources in EU energy consumption.

In January 2008 the EC proposed binding legislation to implement the 20-20 targets. This 'Climate and Energy Package' became law in spring 2009 via four central documents that recognized the interdependencies between the two policy areas:[7]

1. *New EU ETS Directive* (Directive 2009/29/EC)[8]
   While in the first two trading phases national caps were set by the Member States, since 2013 an EU-wide cap applies to the emissions trading system (ETS) sectors. The overall emission reduction target for the ETS sectors amounts to 21 per cent in 2020 compared with 2005 emissions. Allocation of permits is increasingly based on auctioning.
2. *Effort Sharing Decision* (Decision 406/2009/EC)
   Emissions from non-ETS sectors have to be reduced by 10 per cent until 2020 compared with 2005. In the effort sharing decision, this target is split between Member States reflecting their economic welfare. The national emission targets range from −20 per cent for Luxembourg and Denmark to +20 per cent for Bulgaria.
3. *Renewables Directive* (Directive 2009/28/EC)
   The EU target of achieving a share of renewables in gross final energy consumption of 20 per cent by 2020 is distributed among the Member States. The national targets range from 10 per cent for Malta to 49 per cent for Sweden.
4. *Carbon Capture and Storage Directive* (Directive 2009/31/EC)
   The directive provides the legal framework to minimize 'any risk to the environment and human health' related to carbon capture and storage. The provisions cover the selection of sites, permitting, CO_2 stream acceptance criteria (post-)closure obligations and financial issues.

In 2010 two communications were published by the European Commission that defined the challenges for a common European energy policy until 2020. Energy 2020, a strategy for competitive, sustainable and secure energy (EC 2010c), refers to the central energy policy goals laid down in the Lisbon Treaty, in other words, 'to ensure the uninterrupted physical availability of energy products and services on the market, at a price which is affordable for all consumers (private and industrial), while contributing to the EU's wider social and climate goals'.

The second communication 'Energy infrastructure priorities for 2020 and beyond – A Blueprint for an integrated European energy network' (EC 2010d) focuses on providing the physical basis required for reaching the energy policy and economic goals set out in Europe 2020. The efforts for fundamentally restructuring the energy systems, in other words, to make them compatible with the long-term policy objectives, have to be lifted from Member State to EU level requiring a common infrastructure strategy and funding. The main challenges that have to be tackled comprise electricity and natural gas grids and storage, oil transport and refining infrastructure, district heating and cooling networks, CO_2 capture, transport and storage, removing regulatory obstacles and financing gaps.

Summarizing, it can be concluded that although for a long time energy security issues and the creation of an efficient internal market were the main objectives of EU energy policy, an increasing consideration of climate policy concerns can be observed in recent years. Strategic energy policy documents (especially Energy 2020) indicate the integration of climate policy and the emphasis given to synergies, especially between the objectives of sustainability and security of supply. However, pursuing the different energy policy goals can also bring trade-offs. Regarding infrastructure development the continued important role of fossil fuels is underlined. With the agreement on the Climate and Energy Package, however, the interlinkages between the two policy areas seem to have been recognized and are being addressed jointly.

1.5 EU CLIMATE POLICY INTEGRATION: REGIONAL POLICY

In addition to CPI in overarching strategies, and other policy areas with direct linkages like energy, the consideration in terms of defining priorities for expenditure is also called for (Medarova-Bergstrom 2011). In this context not only is funding for climate policy measures of relevance but also spending in other areas that might have counterproductive effects. The need for CPI in other areas like cohesion, agriculture and research of the EU budget is also emphasized in the 2010 EU Budget Review Communication (EC 2010a). In order to illustrate the importance of EU spending for climate policy issues Regional Policy is chosen as an example. The main goal of the EU's regional policy is to improve the economic welfare of regions and to reduce regional disparities

(European Union 2007). This policy area has a share of one third of the EU's total budget at its disposal.[9] Thus the funds for Cohesion Policy are important in quantitative terms. In addition this policy area is relevant in qualitative terms as it affects structural change and long-term development decisions, for example, for transport or energy infrastructure, contributing either to low carbon development paths or carbon lock-ins.

In terms of governance the responsibilities are split between the EU and the Member States. The overarching priorities for regional policy are defined at EU level. The Community Strategic Guidelines represent the framework for all actions that can be supported by the Funds. The Member States develop National Strategic Reference Frameworks which describe their economic strengths and weaknesses and define the respective priorities for regional development. Finally Operational Programmes are developed that account for requirements in individual regions. Operational Programmes and NSRF have to be approved by the European Commission before implementation. The Member States manage the programmes and implement the Operational Programmes by selecting projects and evaluating them.

The Cohesion policy budget is mainly divided into three sources (depending on the kind of measure and the region in which it is funded):

- The European Regional Development Fund (ERDF) focuses its investments on the priority areas innovation and research, the digital agenda, support for small and medium-sized enterprises and the low-carbon economy.
- The European Social Fund (ESF) focuses on improving employment and education opportunities, promoting social inclusion and combating poverty.
- The Cohesion Fund[10] focuses on environmental and transport infrastructure projects (including the Trans-European Transport Networks, TEN-T).

While in the first place targeting economic growth, competitiveness and job creation in the supported regions, regional policy can also contribute to solving long-term challenges like climate change. This was highlighted in the reflection process on the future Cohesion Policy (EC 2008c) and an external report (Barca 2009) recommending climate change as one of the key priorities of Cohesion Policy. Especially in the period 2007–2013 the extent of CPI in regional policy seemed to be limited although on the strategic level it has been emphasized. Under Cohesion Policy about 3 per cent of the total budget was allocated to energy efficiency and renewables (see Figure 1.1). Clean public transport, intelligent transport systems

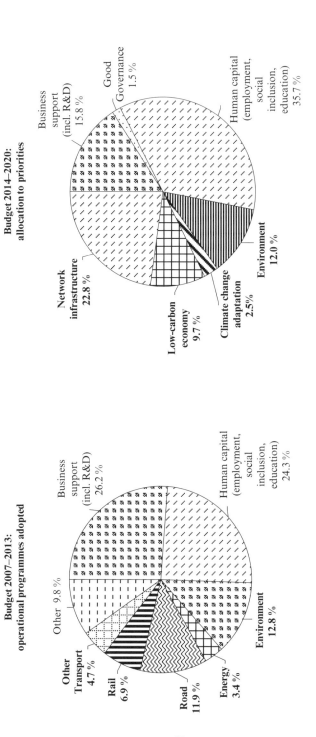

Source: https://cohesiondata.ec.europa.eu/

Figure 1.1 EU regional policy available budget by priorities 2007–2013 and 2014–2020

and rail infrastructure received a further 10.5 per cent of the budget. In contrast 12 per cent has been allocated to road construction and rehabilitation, which improves accessibility of (peripheral) regions but can also be expected to increase GHG emissions and furthermore contributes to locking regions into carbon-intensive structures.

In preparation of the new programme period 2014–2020 a thorough reform of regional policy was discussed and implemented. Generally cohesion policy plays a key role for achieving the EU's 2020 goals. Thus one main aspect of the reform concerned the definition of 11 thematic priorities that reflect the 2020 targets. With respect to CPI the relevant topics are supporting the shift towards a low-carbon economy, promoting climate change adaptation, protecting the environment and sustainable transport. For the shift in thematic priorities and their respective shares in the available budget 2014–2020 see Figure 1.1. While in the period 2007–2013 climate related aspects were included in topics like transport or energy they are now explicitly labelled and funded: More than 12 per cent of the budget are dedicated to climate change adaptation and the shift towards a low-carbon economy. Additional funds are provided under the title of network infrastructure (including sustainable transport) and environment (for projects promoting resource efficiency).

In addition to aligning cohesion policy with Europe 2020 and defining new investment priorities the reform also included procedural aspects aimed at reinforcing the policy's performance via the definition of conditionalities, monitoring and stronger evaluation of results.

The reform shows a stronger integration of climate change issues on the strategic level of regional policy. It has to be evaluated after the end of the current programme period to which extent the thematic concentration of resources was successful and contributed to a real shift towards a low-carbon economy.

1.6   IDENTIFICATION OF SYNERGIES AND CONFLICTS: CONCLUSIONS

Energy and climate policies are highly interrelated policy areas with strong spill-overs. This is increasingly recognized in EU policy documents. In recent years climate policy aspects have been progressively integrated into strategic energy policy as reflected in the main objectives: security of supply, competitiveness and sustainability. With the Climate and Energy Package the two policy areas were finally addressed jointly.

Within energy policy documents there is some ambiguity concerning

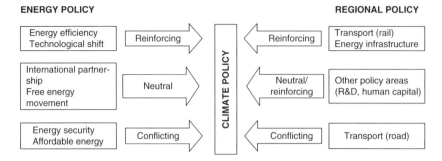

Source: Own illustration.

Figure 1.2   Synergies and conflicts between energy, regional and climate policy

the consistency and synergies/conflicts with climate policy. In the specific policy documents – especially the Climate and Energy Package defining the 2020 targets – climate policy objectives are supported whereas in the basic strategic documents some inconsistencies or conflicts prevail especially given the future role attributed to natural gas and energy security issues.

In general interactions and potential synergies between various policy objectives are recognized (see Figure 1.2). Especially the sustainability objective is regarded as having positive impacts on energy security and climate policy. However, the policies are not all mutually reinforcing. Improving energy security does not necessarily imply reducing GHG emissions. The focus on diversifying the sources for fossil fuel imports and considering carbon capture and storage as viable methods for maintaining fossil electricity generation do not contribute to increasing energy efficiency and decarbonizing the economy.

Regarding an assessment of climate policy concerns being integrated in regional policy and in project funding in particular, the focus has to be put on the ERDF and the Cohesion Fund, as these funds include the programme categories that potentially affect GHG emissions. This is especially the case for energy infrastructure, focusing on renewables, which can be expected to contribute to the climate policy objectives. In contrast investments in the transport infrastructure can result in either positive (in the case of rail networks) or negative (road infrastructure) impacts. While in the period 2007–2013 some reference was made to integrating climate policy concerns into programmes, the regional policy reform for the period 2014–2020 brought major changes. CPI is addressed more explicitly given the alignment of regional policy with the EU 2020 targets and the explicit definition of respective thematic priorities. In addition more weight is given to result monitoring and evaluation.

Our qualitative assessment of EU policies confirms that while there is a high general commitment to climate change action on EU level, evidence on climate policy integration into specific policies analysed here is not clear cut.

The scoping of some EU documents with respect to CPI indicates that in the recent past climate change issues have been recognized in a number of strategic EU documents, even in the Lisbon Treaty. From the examples chosen for our analysis it cannot be concluded that climate policy has widely been acknowledged as a cross-cutting issue along all horizontal policy areas within the EU. However, this chapter only addresses a snapshot of the wide range of EU policies. The research on CPI in the EU thus needs to put further emphasis on a comprehensive analysis of policy integration on the horizontal as well as vertical level.

NOTES

*   This research is based on the project ICPIA that was funded by the Austrian Klima- und Energiefonds.
1. This definition is also followed by Dupont and Oberthür (2011) and Mickwitz et al. (2009).
2. The Treaty on the Functioning of the European Union (Consolidated Version, 2008), Article 1.
3. Article 11 comprises the objective to integrate environmental protection requirement into the definition and implementation of the Union policies and activities, in particular with a view to promoting sustainable development.
4. Article 191 states the following objectives for environmental policy: preserving, protecting and improving the quality of the environment, protecting human health, prudent and rational utilization of natural resources, promoting measures at international level to deal with regional or worldwide environmental problems, and in particular combating climate change.
5. On the evolution of EU energy policy and the interlinkages with climate policy see de Jong et al. (2010) and Adelle et al. (2009).
6. See http://europa.eu/legislation_summaries/institutional_affairs/treaties/treaties_ecsc_en.htm (accessed 4 May 2015).
7. These are complemented by regulations for transport. Energy efficiency is not directly addressed in the legal framework of the energy and climate package. The EU's framework for increasing primary energy efficiency by 20 per cent by 2020 is regulated under Directive 2012/27/EU.
8. For details on the EU ETS see Kettner et al. (2010).
9. For the period 2014–2020 a maximum of €351.8 billion will be available.
10. Available for the Member States whose living standards (Gross National Income per capita) are less than 90 per cent of the EU average.

REFERENCES

Adelle, C., M. Pallemaerts and J. Chiavari (2009), *Climate Change and Energy Security in Europe Policy Integration and its Limits*, Stockholm, June.

Ahmad, I.R. (2009), *Climate Policy Integration: Towards Operationalization*, DESA Working Paper No. 73 Economic and Social Affairs, ST/ESA/2009/DWP/73.

Barca, F. (2009), *An Agenda for a Reformed Cohesion Policy: A Place-based Approach to Meeting European Union Challenges and Expectations*, Independent Report, Brussels.

Decision 406/2009/EC of the European Parliament and of the Council on the effort of Member States to reduce their greenhouse gas emissions to meet the Community's greenhouse gas emission reduction commitments up to 2020.

de Jong, S., S. Sterks and L. Wouters (2010), *The EU as Regional Actor: Energy Security and Climate Change*, Working Paper No. 8, EU GRASP.

Directive 2009/28/EC of the European Parliament and of the Council on the promotion of the use of energy from renewable sources and amending and subsequently repealing Directives 2001/77/EC and 2003/30/EC.

Directive 2009/29/EC of the European Parliament and of the Council amending Directive 2003/87/EC so as to improve and extend the greenhouse gas emission allowance trading scheme.

Directive 2009/31/EC of the European Parliament and of the Council on the geological storage of carbon dioxide.

Directive 2012/27/EU of the European Parliament and of the Council on energy efficiency.

Dupont, C. and S. Oberthür (2011), *Climate Policy Integration into EU Energy Policy: Achievements and Driving Force*, Brussels: Institute for European Studies.

European Commission (EC) (2006), *Green Paper on A European Strategy for Sustainable, Competitive and Secure Energy*, SEC (2006) 317.

European Commission (EC) (2007a), *An Energy Policy for Europe*, SEC (2007) 12.

European Commission (EC) (2007b), *Limiting Global Climate Change to 2 degrees Celsius the Way Ahead for 2020 and Beyond*, COM (2007) 2.

European Commission (EC) (2008a), *20 20 by 2020 – Europe's Climate Change Opportunity*, COM (2008) 30.

European Commission (EC) (2008b), *Second Strategic Energy Review: An EU Energy Security and Solidarity Action Plan*, COM (2008) 781.

European Commission (EC) (2008c), *Regions 2020 An Assessment of Future Challenges for EU Regions*, Commission Staff Working Document.

European Commission (EC) (2010a), *The EU Budget Review*, COM (2010) 700.

European Commission (EC) (2010b), *Europe 2020, A Strategy for Smart, Sustainable and Inclusive Growth*, COM (2010) 2020.

European Commission (EC) (2010c), *Energy 2020, A Strategy for Competitive, Sustainable and Secure Energy*, SEC (2010) 1346.

European Commission (EC) (2010d), *Energy Infrastructure Priorities for 2020 and Beyond – A Blueprint for an Integrated European Energy Network*, COM (2010) 677.

European Council (2007), Presidency Conclusions 8/9 March 2007, retrieved from http://register.consilium.europa.eu/pdf/en/07/st07/st07224-re01.en07.pdf (accessed 20 April 2015).

European Union (2007), Cohesion Policy 2007–2013, Commentaries and official texts, Brussels.

European Union (2008), *Treaty on the Functioning of the European Union*, Brussels, retrieved from http://eur-lex.europa.eu/LexUriServ/LexUriServ.do?uri=OJ:C: 2010:083:0047:0200:en:PDF (accessed 20 April 2015).

Jordan, A. and A. Lenschow (2010), 'Environmental policy integration: A state of the art review', *Environmental Policy and Governance*, **20** (3), 147–158.

Kettner, C., A. Köppl and S. Schleicher (2010), 'The EU Emission Trading Scheme: Insights from the First Trading Years with a Focus on Price Volatility', in Dias Soares, C., J.E. Milne, H. Ashiabor, L. Kreiser and K. Deketelaere (eds), *Critical Issues in Environmental Taxation VIII. International and Comparative Perspectives*, Richmond, UK: Oxford University Press, pp. 205–225.

Kok, M.T.J. and H.C. de Coninck (2007), 'Widening the scope of policies to address climate change: Directions for mainstreaming', *Environmental Science and Policy*, **10** (2007), 587–599.

Lafferty, W. and E. Hovden (2003), 'Environmental policy integration: Towards an analytical framework', *Environmental Politics*, **12** (3), 1–22.

Medarova-Bergstrom, K., A. Volkery, P. Schiellerup, S. Withana and D. Baldock (2011), *Strategies and Instruments for Climate Proofing the EU Budget*, Brussels: Institute for European Environmental Policy.

Mickwitz P. et al. (2009), *Climate Policy Integration, Coherence and Governance*, PEER Report No 2, Helsinki.

2. Tax treatment of the interaction between water and energy

Marta Villar Ezcurra and Enrique Fonseca Capdevila[1]

> A drop of water, a piece of land, or a kilojoule of renewable energy cannot be seen through the single lens of one sectorial policy or management system. What might appear to be an efficient policy in one dimension can be harmful for others . . . an adequate response to emerging challenges, and specifically the linkages between water, energy and land, make it imperative to examine and manage the trade-offs not only among users and uses of the same resource, but also of other related resources.
>
> EU, The 2011/2012 European Report on Development

2.1 THE NECESSARY JOINT MANAGEMENT OF WATER AND ENERGY TO REACH ENVIRONMENTAL OBJECTIVES IN AN EFFICIENT WAY

Water and energy are tightly interlinked and choices made in one domain have consequences on the other, whether positive or negative. However, there is a traditional division between water and energy considerations with respect to the management issues. Therefore despite the clear connection between the two sectors, water and energy planners routinely make decisions that impact on one or the other without adequate understanding of the scientific or political complexities of the other sector.

This miscommunication often hides joint management opportunities to the detriment of budgets, efficiency or environment, and inhibits both sectors from fully accounting for the financial, environmental or social effects they have on each other.

The United Nations qualifies the incentives to increase efficiency facing the two domains as asymmetrical: energy users have little or no incentive to conserve water due to zero or low prices, but water users normally do pay for energy, even though prices may be subsidized. Water and energy prices are strongly affected by political decisions and subsidies that support major sectors such as agriculture and industry. These subsidies often distort the true economic relationship between water and energy. Particularly for water, price is rarely a true reflection of cost – it is often even less than the cost of supply. Although water–energy nexus have led to a growing recognition of such interdependencies, the complex direct and indirect interactions are rarely fully appreciated, let alone incorporated into decision-making processes.[2]

The challenge for twenty-first century governance is therefore to embrace the multiple aspects, roles and benefits of water, and to place them at the heart of decision-making in all water-dependent sectors, including energy.[3] Climate change policy acts as a stressor of the already-intense competition over water and energy resources. The demand for more energy drives calls for more water and vice versa. Climate change also affects energy use: the challenges of climate change and population growth are expected to aggravate the current increasing demand and imbalances in water availability and energy use.

The water–energy nexus hence is also critical for understanding the driving forces, feedback relationships and the water and energy cycles for efficient and sustainable use of these resources. In order to manage both water and energy, decision-makers need to consider ways that can maximize the supply of one while minimizing the over use of the other.[4]

This priority should consider three relations: energy for water, energy from water and water for energy. The potential of energy savings in water treatment processes, or through reduced demands of transporting water in infrastructures, is very significant. In any case, joint treatment of the water–energy appears not only as a logical recommendation but as a practical obligation.

The development and application of information and communication technologies present great potential in both areas. Engineers have identified in the water and energy interactions what are the extent and levels of reversibility and complementarity, highlighting the role of renewable energies.

In the case of Spain, according to hydroelectricity experts, there is still a potential 5000 MW with nearly 300 public dams without exploitation and the potential in the reversibility of the falls of water pumping and energy storage is virtually infinite, including pumping of sea water. Although the strong interrelationship between systems of collection, transport, treatment, irrigation and storage of water and the production, storage, maintenance and distribution of energy has been analysed from the technical, economic, environmental and strategic perspective with particular intensity and progress is recognized in this area, so far issues as important as the incidence of taxation, regulated prices, subsidies and other aspects of economic public intervention in the management of water and energy relations remain virtually unexplored.[5] To move forward in the development of integrated models that allow a better understanding of all the possibilities is a priority.

The importance of addressing in a comprehensive manner the influence of taxation and other charges, parafiscality, public subsidies and public policy pricing which often incorporates a component of compulsory transfer of costs or prices between the different uses of water and energy and between different consumers, is undeniable to properly define the objectives that are intended to be achieved by public intervention and to ensure efficiency in environmental, economic, strategic and social terms.

These considerations – which have general application – are of greater importance in countries such as Spain[6] due to some particularities:[7]

- insufficient rainfall;
- very irregular orography;
- strong importance of the agriculture;
- random distribution over the territory of the consumption of water and energy;
- seasonal consumption pattern;
- weather reasons and importance of the tourism sector both of a seasonal nature;
- sources diversity of electricity power production with a high weight of the non-renewable and emitting CO_2 sources; and
- high possibilities of implementation of electricity production from renewable sources, and fluvial, groundwater, marine and rain water pick up facilities, with structural and temporal limitation in its growth and maintenance problems.

In short, the increasing significance of the joint management of water and energy and the proper assessment of the public interests involved, requires not only the construction of economic models (that allow the best possible knowledge of the way in which taxes and other economic instruments of the public administrations are influencing on the production and use of energy and water and their alternative uses), but also the definition of the best policies and the use of fiscal instruments that serve to get more rational uses of water and energy and its replacement in an environmental perspective.

This chapter aims to identify and analyse the general guidelines of current EU tax legislation for water and energy and also the broad outlines of its Spanish implementation, focusing on the most important aspects about the way in which taxation negatively affects the objective of obtaining the best environmental results in the joint management of water and energy. Our analysis refers only to specific water and energy taxes without taking into consideration many other related taxes but similar conclusions may be applied to them.

2.2   AN OVERVIEW OF THE EU LEGAL CONTEXT

In the absence of more determined actions at a EU level, many of the EU government's statements pointed out the need to move away from the existing silos and work towards an integrated approach for sustainable development. The European Commission recognized that there are existing EU policies which are contributing to adaptation efforts. In particular, the Water Framework Directive (WFD) establishes a legal framework to protect and restore clean water across Europe by 2015 and to ensure the long-term sustainable use of water.[8]

The water–energy–land nexus is a central focus of the Report *Confronting Scarcity: Managing water, energy and land for inclusive and sustainable growth.*[9] In the words of the European Commission certain solutions are important (for example, payments for ecosystem services) and they downplay the appropriateness of others (for example, mandates on biofuel production). The outcome of employing this analytical approach ranges within two possible extremes: (1) that certain policies and actions that seem appropriate in one area are detrimental when viewed from an integrated perspective; and (2) that certain policies that appear to be inefficient in one sector are efficient when viewed from an integrated perspective. The Report also highlights that:

> [T]he public sector should develop legal and regulatory frameworks that are conducive for private-sector development and responsive to concerns of less powerful and more fragmented actors (smallholders, consumers, civil society actors, and so on). This will help to stimulate private investment (for example, in renewable energy or water). It could also strengthen the host-country's capacity to establish the regulatory, legal and implementation capacity to manage investor's interest and bring it into line with the overall development vision (for example, through a strengthening of land-tenure systems that are both cost-effective and protective of customary and collective rights).[10]

EU regulation related to water and energy taxes contemplates incentives for environmental purposes in an isolated way. This means that the link between both areas is not promoted at EU level. Therefore, it seems convenient to start developing incentives on both water and energy taxation addressed to reach joint objectives for a more efficient use in a combined consumption of both water and energy.

2.2.1   The EU Water Framework Directive (WFD)

Community water policy is a competence shared between the Community and Member States where the principle of subsidiarity applies. On 23 October 2000, the WFD was adopted.[11] The concept of 'management of water resources' does not cover every measure concerned with water, but covers only measures concerning the regulation of the use of water and the management of water in its quantitative aspects.[12]

The energy features of the water cycle, although they are not explicitly set out in the articles, are addressed in Recital No. 16, where the need for greater integration between other Community policies and the water policy is pointed out and the energy policy is considered on the first place. Besides, Recital No. 49 recognizes that technical specifications should be laid down to ensure a coherent approach in the Community as part of this Directive.

The need to conserve adequate water supplies is one of the drivers behind what is arguably one of the Directive's most important innovations – the introduction of pricing. Adequate water pricing[13] acts as an incentive for the sustainable use of water resources and consequently helps to achieve the environmental objectives under the Directive. But it is clear that water and energy prices are strongly affected by subsidies that support industry and its competitiveness and these subsidies distort the true economic relationship between water and energy. Particularly for water, price is not a true reflection of cost and may in fact be less than the cost.[14]

Member States will be required to ensure that the price charged to water consumers – such as for the abstraction and distribution of fresh water and the collection and treatment of wastewater – reflects the true costs. Whereas this principle has a long tradition in some countries, this is currently not the case in others. However, derogations will be possible, for example, in less-favoured areas or to provide basic services at an affordable price.

As regards recovery of costs for water services, Article 9 provides that Member States shall take account of the principle of recovery of the costs of water services, including environmental and resource costs, and in accordance, in particular, with the polluter pays principle (PPP).

Member States shall ensure by 2010 that water-pricing policies provide adequate incentives for users to use water resources efficiently, and thereby contribute to the environmental objectives of this Directive; an adequate contribution of the different water uses, disaggregated into at least industry, households and agriculture, to the recovery of the cost of water services and taking into account the polluter pays principle. Member States may in so doing have regard to the social, environmental and economic effects of the recovery as well as the geographic and climatic conditions of the region or regions affected. The problem is that the Directive does not define what environmental costs and costs relating to resources are.

The 2007 Commission Communication on Water Scarcity and Droughts included options related to putting the right price tag on water, allocating water more efficiently and fostering water efficient technologies and practices.[15] The Commission will continue to support work to improve the science–policy interface ad further develop the prototype of the hydro-economic model. This will also help in the assessment of the costs and benefits of the reference scenarios and Member States' programmes of measures, in coordination with other tools at national and/or river basin level.[16]

The third Report from the Commission on the Implementation of the WFD[17] states that:

> [A]n efficient use of water requires measuring the volume of water used. Flat rates, tariffs that rely on the irrigated area or shared bills among users hardly provide any incentive for sustainable water use. . . . Environmental and resource costs are also an essential part of the cost recovery to ensure that externalities generated by the use and disposal of water are adequately recovered. Moreover, the cost of water services should be recovered taking into account the polluter pays principle.

2.2.2 The EU Energy Taxation Directive (ETD)

The EC Treaty confers on the European Community only a limited competence in the field of taxation and is bound by the unanimity rule. Taxation partly determines the price of energy products and electricity. Then, tax harmonization under the ETD[18] sets a minimum level of taxation for a variety of energy commodities according to the use of the energy products and electricity,[19] but Member States should be permitted to apply certain other exemptions or reduced levels of taxation. In particular, Article 15 allows applying exemption or reductions in the level of taxation to electricity – among others, of hydraulic origin produced in hydroelectric installations, of solar, wind, wave, tidal or geothermal origin and energy products and electricity used for combined heat and power generation – and specifically it allows Member States to apply a level of taxation down to zero to energy products and electricity used for agricultural, horticultural or piscicultural works in forestry.[20]

2.2.3 The EU Energy Efficiency Directive (EED)

Regarding the EED,[21] Member States shall set up measures in order to use energy more efficiently at all stages of energy chain, from the transformation of energy and its distribution to its final consumption. These measures include energy efficiency obligations schemes, the exemplary role to be played by the public sector and consumers' right to have exact information on their energy consumption.[22]

According to Article 3(1) each Member State shall set an indicated national energy efficiency target, based on either primary or final energy consumption, primary or final energy savings, or energy intensity. Besides, Article 7 establishes that each Member State shall set up an energy efficiency obligation scheme and as an alternative to setting up this energy efficiency obligation scheme, Member States may opt to take other policy measures to achieve energy savings among final customers, including the following policy measures or combination thereof: energy or CO_2 taxes that have the effect of reducing end-use energy consumption; financing schemes and instruments or fiscal incentives that lead to the application of energy-efficient technology or techniques and have the effects of reducing end-use energy consumption and standards and norms that aim at improving the energy efficiency of products and services, including buildings and vehicles, except where they are mandatory and applicable in Member States under Union law.[23]

2.2.4   Tax Incentives and State Aids

When the Member States establish tax reliefs to better manage water and energy, it is easy to be under the scope of Article 107(1) of the Treaty on the Functioning of the European Union laying down the principle that State aid or other State intervention that distorts competition is prohibited. However, in certain cases, State aid may be compatible and does not need to be notified (in other words, measures that are block exempted) but generally environmental and tax aids need to be notified to the European Commission.

If an aid category is not covered by the General Block Exemption Regulation (GBER)[24] or by the guidelines, it may still be directly assessed under and declared compatible with the Treaty rules. Although Member States may apply for tax exemptions and reductions, according to the current ETD that possibility may be checked under State aid rules and these measures have to be notified following its Article 26. However, the GBER prevents under Article 44 that 'aid schemes in the form of reductions in environmental taxes' fulfilling the conditions of the ETD shall be compatible with the common market and, consequently, shall be compatible with the internal market and shall be exempted from the notification requirement.[25] In this regard, certain categories of environmental and energy aids have been moved to the new GBER, including measures to promote renewable energies, to clean up contaminated sites, to promote district heating and to improve the energy efficiency in buildings. When expenditure in such projects complies with the criteria specified in the Regulation, those measures do not need Commission approval before they can be implemented.[26]

In the State aid context 'energy taxes' are not specially regarded as such. Nevertheless, the GBER links the exemption of notification to the compliance of the requirements on the minimum taxation level under the ETD. In addition, the Guidelines on State aid for environmental protection and energy 2014–2020[27] applying to State aid granted for environmental protection or energy objectives in all sectors governed by the Treaty, have adopted a similar approach when dealing with tax reductions in or exemption from environmental taxes.[28] When environmental taxes are harmonized, the Commission can apply a simplified approach to assess the necessity and proportionality of the aid.[29] For other non-harmonized environmental taxes and harmonized taxes below the Union minimum level of the ETD, a Member State should clearly define the scope of the tax reductions in order to demonstrate the necessity and the proportionality of the aid.[30]

Besides, the Guidelines provide that with regard to aid for the production of hydropower, its impact can be twofold: on the one hand, such aid has a positive impact in terms of low GHG emissions; on the other hand, it might also have a negative impact on water systems and biodiversity. Therefore, when granting aid for the production of hydropower, Member States must respect the WFD and, in particular, Article 4(7) thereof, which lays down criteria in relation to allowing new modifications of bodies of water.[31]

2.3   AN OVERVIEW OF THE SPANISH TAXATION ON WATER AND ENERGY

When we look at the Spanish regulation on water and energy taxation we find a similar situation to the one described at the EU level, because taxes include incentives for certain uses of energy and also the multiple water regulations contemplate special uses of water but there is no a particular consideration for the use of energy in an efficient way vis-à-vis the water consumption and the same apply when we review the incentives on water taxation.

2.3.1   Taxes on the Uses of Water

The different uses of water are financed in Spain with taxes, charges and fees at different levels (State, regional and local). In synthesis, State regulated taxes and water tariffs finance the costs for investment, conservation and exploitation of upstream water supply. Local taxes and tariffs finance both the service of water supply in drinking water, as the sewage system and to a lesser extent the purification due to the assumption by the autonomous regions of competences in this matter. Finally, autonomous regions levy their own taxes on the discharge of wastewater, taking into account the volume of water consumed and its collection covers the costs of construction, maintenance and operation of sanitation and purification infrastructures.

2.3.2 Taxes on Production and Consumption of Electric Energy

The Tax Production of Electric Energy Act[32] established a new tax which levies the production and incorporation into the power system of electric power generated in any type of facility, being the tax base the amount that corresponds to the electric power incorporated to the national electric system and the rate of taxation at 7 per cent.

Concerning nuclear energy, there is also a tax on the production of spent nuclear fuel and radioactive waste from nuclear power generation and another tax on the storage of spent nuclear fuel and radioactive waste from centralized facilities.

For hydroelectric power, the Law on Waters[33] has established a tax on use of inland waters for electrical energy production, which is applied to the concessionaires of hydroelectric exploitations. Tax base is the electric energy value produced on the correspondent facility and the tax rate is 22 per cent. Spanish Law provides 90 per cent tax reduction for power facilities equal to or less than 50 MW, production facilities with power greater than 50 MW pumping technology, and others that may be established by law for reasons of energy policy.

On the other hand, Spain levies the consumption of electric energy under the excise taxes regulation, which applies to energy consumers of any nature. The taxable base is calculated by multiplying the theoretical base of VAT for an equivalent consumption, excluding own tax on electricity, being the tax rate at 5.11269632 per cent with a minimum of 0.5 euros per megawatt-hour (MWh) consumed for industrial uses (agricultural irrigation is included) and 1 euro per MWh consumed for other uses.

The Law includes exemptions for the production for own use in installations of special regimes, the manufacture, import or intra-Community purchase of electricity for self-consumption in production, transport and distribution of electric power facilities. Finally, 85 per cent of the production, importation or intra-Community acquisition of electricity for the chemical reduction processes electrolytic, mineralogical and metallurgical processes and other uses, is exempt.[34]

In short, the relationship between the uses of electricity and water remains out of the taxation of the Spanish taxes on electricity, except for the specific case of the use of continental waters to produce electricity, the application of a minimum level for the electrical consumption for industrial uses like irrigation and for the special treatment for the production of hydroelectric power by pumping techniques.

This setting of the energy taxation does not apply, therefore, any special treatment for the generation of electrical energy to the national electricity system in specific processes of water uses and its manipulation, and neither does it include any tax special treatment for the uses of energy that can generate savings of water, recovery, purification, or rationalization of uses from the most varied points of view. Also, it is not allowed a selective tax treatment of objectives based on zones, times, schedules or any other circumstance related to water consumption.

2.4 INTERFERENCES AND INEFFICIENCIES OF THE CURRENT REGULATION IN THE EU AND SPAIN

In the EU and Spanish legislation, water and energy tax instruments are not integrated. Consequently, their application generates interferences and inefficiencies in taking the most beneficial decisions on production, consumption and treatment of both water and energy, and sometimes the optimal economic and environmental behaviours are excluded.

In addition, water pricing is very much impacted by the different taxes and other charges applied to energy which in many cases far from reflect a correct distribution of costs and environmental related impacts. In turn, water pricing is conditioned by political decisions, regional and local particularities and other issues that influence very much prices paid for different uses of water in the many areas of the Spanish territory.

The way in which price of water is calculated implies that taxes on energy and taxes on water itself are added. If there are no incentives in order to reduce the impact of taxation on water prices when certain uses of water are desirable – in terms of environmental efficiency impacts on water and energy consumption or in terms of sustainable uses of both of them – sometimes the best option may be discouraged. The same analysis applies to taxes on energy when concerned with the water cycle.

All needs have to be addressed in order to design tax incentives for the best joint management of water and energy in an environmental and efficient way, because if they are drafted just taking into consideration the corresponding prices of water and energy and not the real cost of the different factors, neither of their economical interactions will be properly reflected.

According to the United Nations Report,[35] lack of data puts water resources management at a political disadvantage in terms of priority decision-making. While energy may be perceived as 'big business' the central role of water in socio-economic development remains under-acknowledged. As a result, many of the decisions made and implementation mechanisms adopted with respect to energy (for example, improved efficiency, economic growth, enhanced service coverage or benefiting the impoverished) fail to take proper account of the impact of these actions on water resources or the different benefits to other users.

The European Commission remarks that one of the problems of the current ETD is that Member States can compensate differences in production costs by applying favourable tax treatment according to Article 16 of the ETD. The standard tax treatment of renewable fuels is therefore not adapted to their characteristics and any adaptation can only take the form of optional de-taxation to a strict State aid assessment.[36]

With the current tax framework the indirect benefits of the possible actions on water and energy that indirectly generates less consumption or additional production on the other, and the correspondent advantages from the environmental point of view are not contemplated with regard to the tax incentives. In addition, in many cases potential beneficiary actions are penalized by the accumulation of taxes and charges.

Apart from that, the EU State aid regulation creates additional difficulties in order to establish a real selective system of tax incentives conceived for any particular possible action in the combined management of water and energy. This is because there is not enough flexibility in order to accept selective measures, which are justified by environmental objectives, resulting from the joint management of water and energy, due to the fact that these types of actions are not contemplated in the regulation.

To sum up, the driver of the action to promote the better management of the synergies between water and energy has to be the creation of appropriate models, in order to evaluate environmental and economic effects of this desirable target of adapting tax regulations and other related regulations to the needs of water and energy.

2.5 SOME PROPOSALS FOR THE IMPROVEMENT OF TAXATION AS AN INSTRUMENT FOR ENVIRONMENTAL PURPOSES

In the current state of science and technology development, it is accepted as a fact that the integration of the management of water and energy can save significant costs in terms of consumption and avoidance of negative environmental effects. It should be accepted also that the necessary tax measures for this purpose should be driven as quickly as possible.

There cannot be doubts that tax incentives must have a leading role in the promotion of these measures because subsidies, both in its strict concept and as including regulations of prices, cannot exclusively exhaust the scope of incentive policies.

In countries decentralized like Spain, and where in addition there is some tradition of instability in public grants, regulations and prices, tax incentives (especially if its temporary duration is established by law becoming consolidated rights) present a special attraction for investment and financing plans. Moreover, they are often taken with greater simplicity and generality due to the allocation of tax powers to the Central States.

However, the design and implementation of tax incentives required in this matter have a complexity far exceeding those that other types of incentive usually have. Although in some cases general tax incentives could be established for certain actions on energy consumption and water activities that necessarily involve the reduction of other interrelated consumption of greater intensity and environmental efficiency, in most cases, the required incentives are singular, and closer to those related to R&D, which in many countries are undergoing processes of technical evaluation of objectives.

The particularity that shows the incentives for efficiency in the joint management of water and energy is that the objectives to be achieved often may not be identified directly with the use of specific technologies or certain investments, and especially in countries with characteristics as the Spanish ones in which the objectives to be achieved are different in each area of the territory. The design of the incentives often depends – among other factors – on infrastructures already established in each case and also on the pre-existing uses of the water and energy when implementing an action that is considered beneficial. For example, in part of the territory, biomass crops substitution by solar panels can be considered entitled to subsidies and other forest areas can be considered qualified for incentives of biomass cultivations. Also, certain activities that consume energy can be eligible when their consumptions are produced to take advantage of underutilized wind energy production. There are areas of the territory where irrigation via a drip system can be encouraged; this involves power consumption but saving, in turn, electricity consumption in the transport of water, thereby saving water and savings in electricity production, while in other parts of the territory it may be preferable not to encourage the increase of the surface for agricultural use in irrigation.

In summary, tax incentives required in this area may not be general in many cases. They should be established in a case-by-case basis and linked to specific policies in each of the possible numerous actions to improve efficiency in the joint management of water and energy and their environmental effects.

The very concept of 'environmental tax incentive' requires an integrated approach: its main purpose has to be to adapt fiscal incentives on energy to certain production and consumption which, in turn, reach savings in water consumption and indirectly lower consumption and higher energy yields linked to the management of water. In the case of the incentives on taxation of water (and administratively regulated prices) the guiding principle of the integrated approach should be the same.

Water consumption that indirectly creates savings in energy consumption or facilitates greater clean energy production capacities must be also considered for the design of incentives, but in both cases, as we have exposed, eligible proceedings cannot be general but specific to certain areas, agricultural, industrial, climatic, hydraulic situations and a varied set of circumstances which must be taken into account to direct the resources available for environmental incentives to the more efficient actions in this field.

The same lack of generality that deserves special attention in the introduction of tax incentives makes it also necessary on the regulation on State aid. For its efficiency, it is more than convenient that incentives in this area can be established and applied with agility and that are excluded from prior authorization, except in those cases in which the authorities of the Member States deem it necessary in order to ensure legal certainty knowing that the projects comply with the rules on State aid.

2.6   CONCLUSIONS

The interdependence between water and energy is indisputable. Currently, a tax treatment that takes into account the water–energy nexus does not exist in the tax regulation at EU level or in general terms at a national level. No integrated approach of tax policies – exempting a few exceptions related to hydropower and irrigation – exists despite of the reports at international and EU level, claiming that only this perspective will allow the achievement of climate change goals.

The objective of the joint management of water and energy has to be pursued at different levels and the regional and the local objectives are no less important. The definition of the targets has to be addressed at EU level, based on technical and economic models reflecting the real interaction from an environmental point of view, of the different uses of water and energy and without forgetting strategic and macroeconomic considerations.

To assure the compliance of tax incentives in the water and energy nexus, to EU law, it would be desirable that – at least – the guidelines on State aid expressly contemplates the compatibility of tax incentives on a joint water and energy nexus within European Union law, to ensure the legality of the incentives and to promote a greater level of legal certainty. EU Directives should also be aligned towards the encouragement of joint management of water and energy when environmental objectives and integrated strategies for the European Union are in place.

NOTES

1. San Pablo CEU University.
2. See UN WATER, *The United Nations World Water Development Report 2014*: Water and energy, vol. 1 (2014), pp. 6, 14.
3. *The United Nations World Water Development Report 2014*, p. 3.
4. Global Water Partnership Toolbox: Water and Energy Security, http://www.gwp.org/en/ToolBox/CRITICAL-CHALLENGES1/Water-and-Energy/ (accessed 20 April 2015).
5. For a complete analysis on water impact of energy for power and transportation in the USA, see Roberta Mann, 'Like water for energy: The Water–Energy Nexus through the Lens of Tax Policy', *University of Colorado Law Review*, vol. 82 (2011), p. 505, http://ssrm.com/abstract=1792607 (accessed 20 April 2015).
6. In 2007, energy consumption related to the water supply, collection and treatment represented in Spain the 7 per cent of the total energy demand while energy sector uses 25 per cent of the total volume of water (see Laurent Hardy and Alberto Garrido, *Análisis y evaluación de las relaciones entre el agua y la energía en España*, Papeles de Agua Virtual No 6, Fundación Botín, 30 September 2010, pp. 53, 59).
7. See *Libro Verde del Medio Ambiente Urbano*, t. II, Ministerio de Medio Ambiente Medio Rural y Marino-AL21 Red de Redes de Desarrollo Local Sostenible, June 2009, p. 35.
8. See The White Paper 'Adapting to climate change: towards a European framework for action', Brussels, 1 April 2009, COM (2009) 147 final, p. 10.
9. *The 2011/2012 European Report on Development, Confronting Scarcity: Managing Water, Energy and Land for Inclusive and Sustainable Growth*, Overseas Development Institute (ODI), European Centre for Development Policy Management (ECDPM), German Development Institute/Deutsches Institut für Entwicklungspolitik (GDI/DIE) (2012).
10. See p. 9 of the Report.
11. Directive 2000/60/EC, 23 October 2000, of the European Parliament and of the Council establishing a framework for the Community action in the field of water policy (OJ L 327, 22 December 2000).
12. Case C-36/98, *Kingdom of Spain* v. *Council of the EU*, JC of 30 January 2001, para. 55 (EU:C:23001:64).

13. Pricing is a powerful awareness-raising tool for consumers and combines environmental with economic benefits, while stimulating innovation but metering is a pre-condition for any incentive pricing policy.
14. *The United Nations World Water Development Report 2014*, p. 73.
15. These water efficiency measures fit into the overall resource-efficiency objective of Europe 2020.
16. Communication from the Commission, 'A Blueprint to Safeguard Europe's Water Resources', Brussels, 14 November 2012 (COM (2012) 673 final).
17. COM (2012) 0670 final.
18. Directive 2003/96/ EC, 27 October 2003, restructuring the Community framework for the taxation of energy products and electricity (OJ L 283, 31 October 2003).
19. See Recital 17.
20. See Articles 15(1) and 15(3) of the ETD. See also, Articles 16(1) and 16(8).
21. Directive 2012/27/EU, 25 October 2012, amending Directives 2009/125/EC and 2010/30/EU and repealing Directives 2004/8/EC and 2006/32/EC (OJ L 315, 14 November 2012).
22. See Alma-Gabriela Varga, 'The new Directive 2012/27/EU and amendments imposed by it on energy efficiency', *Acta Technica Corviniensis, Bulletin of Engineering*, VI (4) (October–December) (2013), p. 66.
23. Article 7(9) paras (a), (b) and (d) of the EED.
24. Regulation EU No. 651/2014, 17 June 2014, declaring certain categories of aid compatible with the internal market in application of Articles 107 and 108 of the Treaty (OJ L 187, 26 June 2014).
25. For more information see Marta Villar Ezcurra, 'State Aids and Energy Taxes: Towards a Coherent Reference Framework', *Intertax*, 4 (6&7) (2013), p. 341 and 'EU State Aid and Energy Policies as an Instrument of Environmental Protection: Current Stage and New Trends', *EStAL* 4, vol. 12 (2014), number N, p.665.
26. See Recital No 6 of the GBER.
27. Communication from the Commission: Guidelines on State aid for environmental protection and energy 2014–2020 (OJ C 200/1, 28 June 2014).
28. See para. 18(i) and 167–180 of the Guidelines.
29. See para. 172 of the Guidelines.
30. See para. 176 of the Guidelines.
31. See para. 117 of the Guidelines.
32. Law 15/2012, 27 December 2012, tax measures for energy sustainability.
33. Royal Decree-Law 1/2001, 20 July 2001. See the new wording of Article 112 of the consolidated version.
34. Law 38/92, 28 December 1992, on Excise Duties, Articles 97 to 100. In accordance with the wording given by Law 28/2104, of 27 November 2014.
35. *The United Nations World Water Development Report 2014*, Chapter 4, p. 44.
36. See Proposal for amending ETD (COM (2011) 169/3), p. 3.

3. Subsidies to fossil energy consumption in Italy: assessment and interaction with the electricity market

Marianna Antenucci and Michele Governatori

3.1 AIM OF THE CHAPTER

This chapter provides an evaluation of some of the environmentally harmful subsidies in the Italian tax and energy bills system (at least 6 billion[1] €/y in total) and assesses how a carbon tax on fuels would interact with the wholesale electricity market. Such interaction allows then to evaluate how a carbon tax will impact revenues of electricity generation from renewable sources, which currently receive in Italy subsidies for over 10 billion €/y. This allows us to argue to what extent a carbon tax would make a reduction of such green subsidies possible with no harm to profits or competitiveness of green power generators.

3.2 INTRODUCTION: THE *POLLUTER PAYS PRINCIPLE* (PPP) IN THE RULES APPLYING TO ITALY

In the following sections we will recap some of the major supranational, European and Italian rules which provide for the PPP.

3.2.1 PPP in Supranational Guidelines and Treaties

According to the Organisation for Economic Co-operation and Development (OECD 1972) applying PPP to allocate costs of pollution prevention and control encourages rational use of scarce resources and avoids distortion in international trade and investment, provided it is not offset by subsidies to the subjects who bear their costs.

In fact, PPP was conceived as a principle of economic policy (Munir 2013) and as a 'non-subsidization' principle[2] consisting of the internalization of the cost of pollution prevention measures and of the avoidance of state subsidies in favour of polluting activities.

This principle is mentioned in several international declarations on sustainable development or related to climate change such the Rio Declaration[3] (Principle 16), Agenda 21[4] (Chapter 8), the Kyoto Protocol[5] (Article 2), the Implementation Plan of Johannesburg[6] (Chapter III) and the recent outcome document[7] of the 'Rio + 20 Conference (paragraph 224).

3.2.2   PPP in the EU Ruling

In 1973, the European Commission (EC) approved the first Environmental Action Programme (EAP) where it stated that costs of preventing and eliminating nuisances must be borne by the polluter.

PPP is adopted in the subsequent EAPs too and the fifth EAP (1992) states that charges and levies should aim at discouraging pollution at source and encouraging clean production.

In 1987, with the Single European Act the PPP became a pillar of the EU's environmental policy (Article 130) and then it was frequently reaffirmed both in the newer versions of the Treaties (Articles 170–176 of Treaty Establishing the European Community and Article 191 of Treaty on the Functioning of the European Union[8]) and in the legislation.[9]

The Lisbon Treaty provides for a legally binding[10] PPP for the EU legislator (De Sadeleer 2012), although it allows regional exceptions that may weaken the principle.

Recently, the European Commission has reaffirmed the PPP through a set of initiatives[11] to monitor[12] and phase out by 2020[13] all environmentally harmful subsidies (EHS). However the new EU Commission headed by Mr Juncker has put the proposal of revision of the Energy Taxation Directive, whose draft includes a carbon tax on fuels,[14] out of the agenda.

3.2.3   PPP in the Italian Rules

Recommendations to Italy by supranational bodies
In 2013, the OECD recommended Italy to remove environmentally harmful tax provisions and to restructure energy and vehicle taxes to internalize environmental costs, including GHG emissions through a carbon tax component aimed at complementing the EU Emission Trading System and providing a consistent price of carbon across the economy.

In 2013, the National Energy Strategy announced that the government would consider a review of the energy excise taxes also according to their CO_2 content, which could finance the subsidies to renewable energy sources in place of the energy billing system. (Instead, we argue that a carbon tax might substitute some of the subsidies to renewables.)

Article 15 of Law no. 23 of 11 March 2014 commits the government to introduce a CO_2 tax on energy products in accordance with the new (pending at the time of the Law) Energy Taxation Directive. According to the law, new revenues from the carbon tax should be used for reducing labour taxation, supporting clean technologies and renewable energy sources. However, since the revision of the Energy Taxation Directive is de facto abandoned, the Italian government is actually not committed anymore to a carbon tax.

In 2010, the Ministry of Economy initiated a review of the tax expenditure also aimed at identifying inefficient subsidies, and in February 2014 the Ministry of Environment proposed a draft law to Parliament to set a list of EHS, to be updated annually.[15]

3.3   ENVIRONMENTALLY HARMFUL SUBSIDIES IN ITALY: EXEMPTIONS TO EXCISES ON FOSSIL ENERGY PRODUCTS

Italy is aligned[16] to the average of the EU countries in terms of overall amount of environmental taxation. However, the way its burden is distributed through a system of huge exemptions delivers large amounts of environmentally harmful subsidies (EHS)[17] based on the OECD's definition: *a result of a government action that confers an advantage on consumers and producers in order to supplement their income or lower their costs, but in doing so, discriminates against sound environmental policies.*[18]

Data from financial reports of the government's general accounting department[19] show that discounts to excises on energy products in Italy were estimated at 5.8 billion € in 2014. This is based on fuel consumption forecasts and the estimation of revenue forgone does not take into account any behavioural changes resulting from the removal of the tax expenditure.

In Table 3.1 column 3 we estimate what share of these tax exemptions relates to consumption or production of fossil energy products/sources, based on average electricity production mix/import[20] and on average fuels consumption mix.[21] Figures in column 3 should be considered as an EHS based on our findings in section 3.2.

Table 3.1   Excise exemptions on fuels, Italy 2014[22]

Industry	Tax discount (million €)	Of which to fossil energies (million €)
Transport	3,943.3	3,757.7
Energy	0.8	0.6
Agriculture	1,016.5	975.8
Secondary sector	71.5	71.5
Others	827.6	586.0
Total	5,859.7	5,391.6

3.3.1   Commercial Heavy Road Transport

Trucking companies[23] in Italy get refunds on fuel excises since the budget law for 2006[24] imposed a freeze on their fuel excise at the 2005 level,[25] with an overall discount cost which more than quadrupled from 2005. In fact, in 2014, tax revenue loss was estimated as high as 1519.3 million €, with trucks paying[26] in July 2014 0.403 €/L for diesel compared with 0.620 €/L applying to non-subsidized consumers. Earlier discounts from 2005 to 2013 amount to about 6.1 billion €[27] in total.

3.3.2   Shipping

Fuel used for navigation and fishing (transport of passengers and goods) along national waterways and within the EU waters is exempted from the excise tax on fuels. The cost of the exemptions is expected at 615.4 million € in 2014.

3.3.3   Aviation

The use of fuel in commercial airlines and flight school is exempted from the excise tax. This provision does not apply to private pleasure crafts. Annual cost for 2014 is estimated at 1539.4 million €.

3.4   THE NON-MARKET PORTION OF ITALIAN ENERGY BILLS

About half of a standard household electricity bill in Italy relates to general system costs (subsidies to electricity producers, network costs and other system costs). Of these, subsidies to energy intensive manufacturers are estimated by the energy Authority for 2014 at 600 million €/y.

Moreover, system costs are spread unevenly among consumers, with discounts to the smallest and to the largest customers paid by medium-sized non-intense consumers. This provides users connected to very high voltage sections of the power grid (who usually are the largest electricity consumers) with an advantage (subsidy) of about 500 million €/y.[28]

Such cross-subsidy to large and intensive energy users clearly contravene the aim of promoting efficiency, which is set as the top objective in the government's Italian Energy Strategy.[29]

On the other hand, the major part of the non-market portion of Italian energy bills relates to subsidies to renewable energy sources (approximately 11 billion €/y in 2013). The policy debate on affordability of energy bills in Italy is investigating the opportunity for a reduction of subsidies to green energy sources. Below we argue that a carbon tax provides some renewable electricity producers with extra income and can therefore be associated with a reduction of some of the subsidies without negative effects on the competitiveness of the green electricity producers.

3.4.1 Interaction of a Carbon Tax with the Electricity Day-Ahead Market and with Support Policies to Renewable Electricity Sources: Basics of Electricity Spot Markets

Short term competition in power generation is provided mainly through organized market platforms (energy exchanges). Such platforms allow power production plants to place offers to sell their capacity and usually include a day-ahead commitment to sell/buy capacity on an hourly/zonal basis. This day-ahead market is the most liquid short-term exchange for electricity in Italy and hereafter we will refer to it. Demand in this market is set by large buyers who directly access the platform and by system aggregators which calculate the expected demand of smaller or residual power users and/or based on the Transmission System Operator's load forecast.

The supply curve collects all the reserve prices of producers. Equilibrium price is then set in order to meet the demand and applies to all plants and buyers.

In the short-term, if the market is competitive, the reserve price of every plant equals its marginal costs for generation. Since same combinations of technologies and fuels share similar variable costs, a competitive power supply curve is then shaped like in Figure 3.1.

Typically, the Italian merit order electricity supply curve shows on the left (high merit side) the renewable plants (hydro excluding storage, wind, solar) which have fixed-only costs but no variable costs since they do not need any fuel. Moving right, the graph shows: low-variable cost plants

Suppliers behave competitively, no carbon tax (in section 3.4.1)

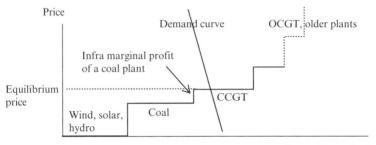

Effect of a carbon tax on fuels (in section 3.4.3)

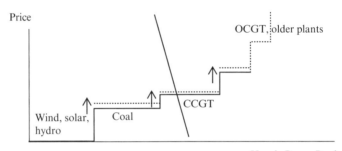

Figure 3.1   Merit order curve in power production

like biomass or coal fired plants; combined cycle gas turbines (CCGT); 'peaker' plants like open cycle gas turbines (OCGT) designed to cover peaks of demand at relatively high variable costs and low fixed costs, and old inefficient plants.

3.4.2   Competitiveness of Day-Ahead Electricity Exchanges – the Italian Case

Evaluation of the competitiveness of generators' behaviour: definitions
One way of showing how competitive is a day-ahead electricity market is evaluating how the equilibrium price tends to be close to marginal costs (MC) of the marginal technology. To show this we need to model MC of power production technologies like coal-fired power plants (C) and combined cycle gas turbine (CCGT). In the Italian case CCGT is still the

marginal technology in the majority of the hours in the period considered in our dataset (mid-2013 to mid-2014).

MC of a coal-fired power plant at time t can be calculated as:

$$MCc_t = Ec * Pc_t + ETSc * Pets_t + GC * Pgc_t \qquad (3.1)$$

Where Ec (*measured as* $\frac{T}{MWh}$) is the amount of coal needed to produce 1 MWh of electricity (inverse of conversion efficiency ratio); Pc_t (*measured as* $\frac{€}{T}$) is the CIF coal price (overall cost in the place of consumption) at time t; $ETSc$ (measured as $\frac{T}{MWh}$) is the amount of allowances for CO_2 needed for 1 MWh of electricity production with this technology under the Emission Trading System (ETS) rules; $Pets_t$ (*measured as* $\frac{€}{T}$) is the price of ETS allowances for 1 T CO_2 emissions at time t; GC is the amount of green certificates (GC) that a non-renewable producer must buy per MWh; Pgc_t (*measured as* €) is the price for a GC at time t.

Similarly, MC of power production for a CCGT natural gas plant at time t will be:

$$MCg_t = Eg * Pg_t + ETSg * Pets_t + GC * Pgc_t \qquad (3.2)$$

Where Eg (*measured as* $\frac{m^3}{MWh}$) is the gas quantity needed to produce 1 MWh of electricity (inverse of conversion efficiency ratio) and Pg_t (*measured as* $\frac{€}{m^3}$) is the gas price at time t.

It is useful to define as clean dark spread (CDS) the difference between the electricity market price at a certain time t (hour) and market zone (z) and overall marginal costs of a coal-fired plant:

$$CDS_{t,z} = MP_{t,z} - MCc_t \qquad (3.3)$$

And clean spark spread (CSS) the difference between the electricity market price at a certain time t (hour) and market zone (z) and overall marginal costs of a CCGT:

$$CSS_{t,z} = MP_{t,z} - MCg_t \qquad (3.4)$$

In a competitive spot market like the one described above we expect the clean spreads of the marginal technology to be close to zero in hours where the technology is marginal (makes the price), while infra marginal technologies (left of the marginal technology in the merit curve) get an infra marginal profit even if they bid at MC.[30]

Table 3.2   Description of dataset referred (July 2013 to June 2014)

Description	Symbol in section 3.4.2	Measured as	Frequency (Value if fixed)	Source	Remarks
Electricity equilibrium zonal price	$MP_{t,z}$	€/MWh	Hourly	GME[31]	Relates the day-ahead electricity market (Mercato del Giorno Prima) run by the GME[32]
Index of the marginal technology		(String)	Hourly	GME	Indicates what generation technology is setting the price for every hour/zone
Quantity	$Q_{t,z}$	MWh	Hourly	GME	Energy sold through the day-ahead market in the hour/zone
ETS allowance price	$Pets_t$	€/tCO$_2$	Daily	Alba Soluzioni[33]	
Price of green certificates	Pgc_t	€/MWh	Weekly	Alba Soluzioni	
Green certificates quota obligation		%	Yearly 2013: 5.03% 2014: 2.52%		Share of energy that must be covered with GC by non RES electricity producers
Coal price	Pc_t	$/t	Daily	Alba Soluzioni	Coal type/location: API#2-CIF ARA
Coal plant inverse efficiency	Ec	t/MWh	Fixed = 0.3771	Alba Soluzioni	Coal plant efficiency supposed 38%, calorific value: 25.12 (MJ/kg)
Gas price	Pg_t	€/MWh	Daily	GME	Gas price in the PB gas market[34] (balancing gas) run by GME
Gas plant inverse efficiency	Eg	m³/MWh	Fixed = 1/49%	Alba Soluzioni	
€/$ exchange rate		€/$	Daily	Italian Central Bank – Banca d'Italia[35]	

Evaluation of the competitiveness of electricity generators' behaviour: results in Italy

Based on the dataset described in Table 3.2, we have evidence that the day-ahead electricity market has behaved pretty competitively in Italy, with zonal spikes in price (zone Sicily) due to lack of interconnection and subsequent higher market power by producers in the island.

Here are some findings:

- Clean spark spread (index of margin for combined cycle gas turbines which have been overall the marginal technology about 60 per cent of the hours) has been on average[36] 7.9 €/MWh (1.2 excluding Sicily) in the hours where this technology is marginal (sets the price). Energy-weighted average clean spread in all hours is 1.3 €/MWh and −1.1 €/MWh including/excluding Sicily.
- Clean dark spread in hours when coal plants are marginal is on average[37] 11.5 €/MWh, while the energy-weighted overall average in all hours is 29.5 €/Mwh. This indicates that coal-fired plants get a normal infra marginal profit, plus a premium even when they are the marginal technology. This might have two reasons: (1) occurrences of the demand curve crossing the supply curve where the latter is vertical (reserve price of demand higher than MC but not high enough to switch on the CCGT plants, so the demand rations itself through a premium price); or (2) coal plants benefit from high concentration of coal plants in the power supply (a few coal plants operated by a few companies).

3.4.3 Effects of (Additional) Carbon Tax on the Italian Day-Ahead Electricity Market

Types of support to renewable electricity production

The European Union with a decision taken in the Council of 8 March 2007 and then implemented with the Directive 28/2009/28/EC set a target of penetration of power production from renewable energy sources (RES) of 20 per cent in 2020 at EU level to be met with compulsory Member States' targets.

Since renewable power plants tend to have higher overall costs than conventional ones, support mechanisms have been developed to provide them with higher income. Such mechanisms include feed-in tariffs (FIT), feed-in premiums (FIP) and green certificates (GC).

FIT are designed to provide RES producers with a comprehensive remuneration per unit of electricity produced. They may be subject to a decay in time but the price received by the operator does not depend on the electricity market price (while the subsidy does), so the RES producer subject to a FIT regime is not exposed to the market fluctuations in the electricity price.

FIP are additional to the market price and aimed at covering the extra cost of RES producers. Therefore, unless FIP are designed to complement the market price of electricity (for instance: inversely linked to it), they do not take exposure to this market out of the RES producer's payoff.

GCs are certificates issued by an institutional body and granted to producers on the basis of their actual electricity production from RES sources. They usually operate in bundle with quota obligations on the demand/supply side and are marketed, so producers or suppliers must buy a certain amount of certificates to meet their obligations. They are then in principle similar to market-based FIP.[38]

Interactions between types of support to renewable electricity production and environmental taxes on fuels

Environmental taxes (ET) on fuels like a carbon tax (CT) have an impact on the electricity market price. As described later, CT affects the payoff of a RES power producer in different ways depending on the support mechanism applied to the plant.

The effect of an additional CT which covers coal and gas is an increase in the variable costs of a non-renewable production plant due to higher total cost of the fuel. As described in section 3.4.2, in competitive day-ahead electricity markets this entails a surge in the price offered by the plant, with a shift up of the supply curve which depends on the impact of the CT. As shown in Figure 3.1, the shift up is proportional to the fuel's carbon intensity and the consequence on average market price depends on the frequency of every technology making the price. In our dataset we observe[39] CCGT as marginal technology in approximately 2/3 of the hours/zones, coal in 1/6 and RES in 1/7.

Effects of a CT on the economics of power production technologies in the Italian day-ahead electricity market

The following is what we can expect in terms of economic payoff for the various generation technologies in a competitive day-ahead electricity market from an additional CT:

- RES with a FIT (including FIP inversely linked to the market price of electricity) are not affected since they have a predefined remuneration for their energy.
- RES with a FIP or GC profit from the surge in the market price of electricity; this is not entirely the Italian case though (see note 32).

- Fossil-fired plants[40] also sell electricity at a higher price but have higher costs too due to the CT. Since the coal-fired mid-merit plants are the most carbon intensive (with CO_2 emissions about twice those of CCGT plants per unit) with a CT they lose more infra marginal profit than they gain from higher sale prices, so they have a negative overall effect, which is consistent with the environmental aim of a CT.
- CCGT is the technology that more frequently sets the price (about two-thirds of the hours[41]) and rarely gets an infra marginal profit, since rarely (less than 2 per cent of the hours) lower merit technologies (like OCGT – peaker plants) set the price. This implies that the effect of an (additional) CT for a CCGT should be almost neutral, with marginal costs rising together with the electricity market price in almost all the hours when CCGT is in operation.

Effects of a carbon tax on the spot price of electricity (Italy)

Based on the results of the Italian day-ahead power market in our dataset and on the findings above, we can assess what effects an additional 1 €/tCO_2 CT (or an increase of 1 €/tCO_2 in the ETS allowances' price) in coal and natural gas would have[42] on electricity prices in Italy. Based on ETSc and ETSg,[43] MCc and MCg would rise respectively by approximately 0.91 and 0.40 €/MWh. Assuming all thermal units bidding at marginal costs and neglecting marginal technologies others than CCGT, coal and RES which cover the vast majority of the hours, the average spot price would increase by 0.42 €/MWh. As seen in section 3.4.2, coal plants might not bid at marginal costs in all the hours when they are marginal. However, there is no reason to expect this to allow a higher CT pass-through than in a marginal bidding situation. In fact, it is rational assuming that plants which can, in some cases, bid higher than MC are already doing it at large, so additional costs cannot be passed through in those hours.

Opportunity for a reduction of support to RES plants following a carbon tax

As seen above, coal power plants can expect a reduction in profits following an additional CT, while the effect on CCGT would be approximately neutral. Some RES plants get an advantage (higher sale price) depending on the type of support scheme they get (plants with FIT, or FIP inversely linked to the electricity price, whose share currently accounts[44] for 65 per cent in energy in Italy, do not get any higher remuneration with higher electricity price). Therefore 35 per cent of the electricity produced by RES plants (about 20 TWh – approximately 7 per cent of total electricity demand) would benefit from an extra margin of approximately 0.4 €/MWh as seen in section 3.4.3 every 1 € of additional CT.

Therefore, our policy recommendation is to lower the support to such plants in order to extract their carbon tax rent, which would reduce the non-market portion of electricity bills of approximately 0.03 €/MWh for every 1 €/tCO$_2$ of additional CT.

3.5 CONCLUSIONS

Current energy tax designs and electricity bills in Italy have counterproductive features in terms of decarbonization and energy saving policies, and they distort competition. Moreover, they infringe rules at supranational and national levels.

A reduction of the environmentally harmful subsidies (EHS) in Italy can both benefit the environment and the economy. A reduction of tax discounts to fossil energies (estimated at 5,400 million € in 2014!) would benefit the State budget and should be used to reduce income taxes.

A carbon tax on energy products allows a reduction of the non-market portion of the energy bills. In fact, it may have a substitution effect on some of the support systems to the renewable electricity sources, thus allowing a reduction of their budget with no harm to the competitiveness of the renewable sources.

ACKNOWLEDGEMENTS

The authors wish to thank Marco Ballicu, Simona Benedettini, Cosimo Campidoglio, Claudia Checchi, Simone Corbo, Aldo Ravazzi, Massimo Ricci and Mark Salzillo for their opinions, suggestions, contributions and corrections.

NOTES

1. 'Billion' is always meant as 10^9 in this chapter.
2. OECD (1995).
3. 'Report of the United Nations Conference on Environment and development' (UN, 1992).
4. 'Agenda 21' (UN, 1992).
5. 'Kyoto Protocol to the United Nation Framework Convention on Climate Change' (1998).
6. 'Plan of Implementation of the World Summit of Sustainable Development' (Johannesburg, 2002).
7. 'The future we want' (UN Conference on Sustainable Development, Rio de Janeiro in 2012).

8. 'The Union policy on the environment shall aim at a high level of protection taking into account the diversity of situations in the various regions of the Union. It shall be based on the principle that . . . the polluter should pay'.

9. PPP generally taken up in directives on waste and on environmental policies.

10. See De Sadeleer, N. (2012) and http://ec.europa.eu/environment/legal/law/pdf/princi ples/2%20Polluter%20Pays%20Principle_revised.pdf (accessed 20 April 2015).

11. http://ec.europa.eu/environment/enveco/taxation/index.htm (accessed 20 April 2015).

12. 7th Environmental Programme.

13. European Commission (2010) and European Commission (2011b).

14. COM (2011) 169 Final.

15. Article 24 of the Bill C/2093 on provisions to promote green economy and to avoid over-use of natural resources.

16. Eurostat   (2014)   http://epp.eurostat.ec.europa.eu/statistics_explained/index.php/ Environmental_tax_statistics (accessed 20 April 2015).

17. Hogg et al. (2014).

18. OECD (2005).

19. State revenue forecast 2014–2016 http://www.rgs.mef.gov.it/_Documenti/VERSIONE-I/ Attivit--i/Bilancio_di_previsione/Bilancio_finanziario/2014/DisegnodiBilancio/Allega toaldisegnodiBilancio/01-Allegato_tecnico-Entrata.pdf (accessed 20 April 2015). (According to Law No. 196 of 31 December 2009 Art. 21 the government's financial plan must detail tax discounts/exceptions and calculate all lost revenue).

20. Italian fuel mix for electricity production in 2013: 57.8% from fossil sources and 42.2% from non-fossil sources (RES and nuclear imported energy). Source: GSE.

21. Italian fuels' consumption 2013–2014: 96% fossil and 4% of biofuels. Source: Unione Petrolifera (2013) http://www.unionepetrolifera.it/it/CMS/pubblicazioni/get/2013/UP %20previsioni%202013.pdf (accessed 20 April 2015).

22. See note 24.

23. Companies that run commercial trucks weighting more than 7.5 tonnes.

24. Law 58/2005.

25. From 2005 to 2012 every increase in the fuel excise rate has been refunded to trucking companies (Law 58/2005, Law 286/2006, Legislative Decree 26/2007, Determination 21102/RU of the 05.04.2011, Determination 77579/RU of the 28.06.2011, Determination 127505/RU of the 28.10-2011, Law 214/2011). In 2012, with Article 61 of Law 27/2012, such reimbursement became automatic, in other words, with no need of further laws.

26. Data from Ministry from economic development (2014) and State toll agency (2014).

27. Data from annual financial statements of the Ministry of Economy and Finance.

28. Based on our estimations on Authority's data.

29. http://www.sviluppoeconomico.gov.it/images/stories/normativa/20130314_Strategia_ Energetica_Nazionale.pdf (in Italian, accessed 20 April 2015).

30. In fact, unless an operator has got reasonable expectation of being the marginal bidder, with a System Marginal Price (SMP) setting a bid at marginal costs doesn't make the bidder give up any opportunity of receiving an infra marginal profit.

31. GME, MGP Historical data: https://www.mercatoelettrico.org/en/download/Dati Storici.aspx (accessed 20 April 2015).

32. Italian state operator of energy exchanges www.mercatoelettrico.org.

33. http://www.albasoluzioni.com/files/GeEO%20Metodologia%20gennaio%202012-2014 0416-142228.pdf see also http://www.albasoluzioni.com/geeo-data.php (accessed 20 April 2015).

34. https://www.mercatoelettrico.org/en/download/DatiStoriciGas.aspx.

35. https://www.bancaditalia.it/banca_centrale/cambi/cambi/cambi-giornalieri.

36. Not weighted with respect to the energy actually produced.

37. Not weighted with respect to the energy actually produced.

38. However, in the Italian system GCs can be bought back by the issuer at a price which is inversely linked to the market price of energy, which makes the overall income of a RES producer supported with GCs similar to a FIT's income.

39. The share of some minor technologies not included in the list has been spread over the included technologies.
40. We assume here that the (additional) CT is lower than the amount needed to change the merit order between plants, including between GGCT and coal fired plants. This assumption does not reduce the significance of our conclusions, since current (very low) CO_2 price is far from triggering a technology switch.
41. The dataset indicates a generation technology as marginal when it sets the price for the observed zone, including cases where the plant is located in a different zone.
42. Assumption: the new/additional CT is not high enough to change the merit order.
43. See definitions in section 3.4.2.
44. Based on our calculations on data by Gestore dei Servizi Energetici (www.gse.it state-owned agency which deals with most support mechanisms to RES power plants in Italy).

BIBLIOGRAPHY

Council of the European Union (1973), 'Programme of Action of the European Communities on the Environment', *Official Journal of the European Communities no. C 112/1*, http://eur-lex.europa.eu/legal-content/EN/TXT/PDF/?uri=OJ:C:1973:112:FULL&from=EN (accessed 20 April 2015).

Council of the European Union (1993), 'A European Community Programme of Policy and Action in Relation to the Environment and Sustainable Development', *Official Journal of the European Communities no. C 138/1*, http://eur-lex.europa.eu/legal-content/EN/TXT/PDF/?uri=OJ:C:1993:138:FULL&from=EN (accessed 20 April 2015).

De Sadeleer, N. (2012), 'The Polluter-pays Principle in EU Law – Bold Case Law and Poor Harmonisation', Social Science Research Network, http://papers.ssrn.com/sol3/papers.cfm?abstract_id=2293317 (accessed 20 April 2015).

European Commission (2010), 'Europe 2020 A Strategy for Smart, Sustainable and Inclusive Growth', COM(2010)2020/Final, http://eur-lex.europa.eu/LexUriServ/LexUriServ.do?uri=COM:2010:2020:FIN:EN:PDF (accessed 20 April 2015).

European Commission (2011a), 'Proposal for a Council Directive amending Directive 2003/96/EC Restructuring the Community Framework for the Taxation of Energy Products and Electricity', COM(2011)169/Final, http://eur-lex.europa.eu/LexUriServ/LexUriServ.do?uri=COM:2011:0169:FIN:EN:PDF (accessed 20 April 2015).

European Commission (2011b), 'Roadmap to a Resource Efficient Europe', COM(2011)571/Final, http://eur-lex.europa.eu/legal-content/EN/TXT/PDF/?uri=CELEX:52011DC0571&from=EN (accessed 4 May 2015).

European Commission (2013), '*Environmental Taxes – A Statistical Guide, Eurostat*', Edition 2013, http://ec.europa.eu/eurostat/documents/3859598/5936129/KS-GQ-13-005-EN.PDF (accessed 4 May 2015).

European Parliament and the Council (2013), 'General Union Environmental Action Programme to '2020 Living Well within the Limit of our Planet', *Official Journal of the European Communities no L 354/171*, http://eur-lex.europa.eu/LexUriServ/LexUriServ.do?uri=OJ:L:2013:354:0171:0200:EN:PDF (accessed 20 April 2015).

Hogg. D., et al. (2014), 'Study on Environmental Fiscal Reform Potential in 12 EU Member States', No 07.0307/ETU/2013/SI2.664058/ENV.D.2 Final Report to DG

Environment of the European Commission, http://ec.europa.eu/environment/integration/green_semester/pdf/EFR-Final%20Report.pdf (accessed 20 April 2015).

Italian Government, Bill C 2093 (2014), Annex of Budget Law 2014 'Disposizioni in materia ambientale per promuovere misure di green economy e per il contenimento dell'uso eccessivo di risorse naturali' http://www.camera.it/leg17/126?idDocumento=2093 (accessed 20 April 2015).

Munir, M. (2013), 'History and Evolution of the Polluter Pays Principle: How and Economic Idea Became a Legal Principle', Social Science Research Network, http://papers.ssrn.com/sol3/papers.cfm?abstract_id=2322485 (accessed 20 April 2015).

OECD (1972), 'Recommendations of the Council on Guiding Principle concerning international Economic Aspects of Environmental Policies', C(72)128, http://webnet.oecd.org/OECDACTS/Instruments/ShowInstrumentView.aspx?InstrumentID=4&InstrumentPID=255&Lang=en&Book (accessed 20 April 2015).

OECD (1974), 'Recommendation of the Council on the Implementation of the Polluter Pays Principle', C(74)223, http://acts.oecd.org/Instruments/ShowInstrumentView.aspx?InstrumentID=11 (accessed 20 April 2015).

OECD (1989), 'Recommendation of the Council concerning the Application of the Polluter-Pays Principal to Accidental Pollution', C(89)88/Final, http://acts.oecd.org/Instruments/ShowInstrumentView.aspx?InstrumentID=38&InstrumentPID=305&Lang=en&Book=False (accessed 20 April 2015).

OECD (1991), 'Recommendations of the Council on the use of Economic instrument in Environmental Policies', C(90)177/Final, http://acts.oecd.org/Instruments/ShowInstrumentView.aspx?InstrumentID=41&InstrumentPID=38&Lang=en&Book (accessed 20 April 2015).

OECD (1995), 'Environmental Principle and Concepts', OCDE/GD (95) 124, http://www.oecd.org/trade/envtrade/39918312.pdf (accessed 20 April 2015).

OECD (2001), 'OECD Environmental Strategy for the First Decade of the 21th Century', http://www.oecd.org/env/indicators-modelling-outlooks/1863539.pdf (accessed 20 April 2015).

OECD (2013), 'Environmental Performance Reviews: Italy 2013 Assessment and Recommendations', http://www.oecd.org/env/country-reviews/EPR%20Assessment%20and%20recs%20ITALY%202013.pdf (accessed 20 April 2015).

REF (2014), 'Energy price forecast 2014', Previsivo Osservatorio Energia Anno XI Numero 32 Luglio 2014, pp. 4, http://www.ref-e.com/en/what-we-offer/previsivo (accessed 20 April 2015).

REF (2014) http://energyathaas.wordpress.com/2014/08/18/raising-gas-prices-to-grow-an-economy/ (accessed 20 April 2015).

Tol, R.S.J. (2005), 'The Marginal Damage Costs of Carbon Dioxide Emissions: an Assessment of the Uncertainties', *Energy Policy* (33), 2064–2074.

Tol, R.S.J. (2007), 'The Social Costs of Carbon: Trends, Outliers and Catastrophes', Discussion Papers 2007-44. Economics Discussion Papers.

UN (1992), 'Agenda 21', http://sustainabledevelopment.un.org/content/documents/Agenda21.pdf (accessed 20 April 2015).

UN (1992), 'Report of the United Nations Conference on Environment and Development', http://www.un.org/documents/ga/conf151/aconf15126-1annex1.htm (accessed 20 April 2015).

UN (1998), 'Kyoto Protocol to the United Nations Framework Convention on

Climate Change', http://unfccc.int/resource/docs/convkp/kpeng.pdf (accessed 20 April 2015).

UN (2002), 'Plan of Implementation of the World Summit of Sustainable Development', http://www.un.org/esa/sustdev/documents/WSSD_POI_PD/English/WSSD_PlanImpl.pdf (accessed 20 April 2015).

UN (2012), 'The future we want', A/RES/66/288, http://www.un.org/ga/search/view_doc.asp?symbol=A/RES/66/288&Lang=E (accessed 20 April 2015).

4. Towards a sustainable climate and energy policy mix: insights from theory and the case of Japan*

Sven Rudolph, Takeshi Kawakatsu and Achim Lerch[1]

4.1 INTRODUCTION

The 2011 Fukushima nuclear disaster and rapid global warming emphasize the necessity of reorganizing our energy system; but how do we get there? Energy and climate policy are obviously interlinked, for example, via carbon dioxide (CO_2) emissions from fossil fuel burning in electricity generation. Policy targets are interdependent, sometimes even contradicting: The environmental soundness of current energy use has been seriously challenged by nuclear contamination and by greenhouse gas (GHG) emission reduction barriers from low coal prices, power grid insufficiencies, and oligopolistic market structures. Energy security has been threatened by military conflicts and volatile resource prices, while carbon pricing has made energy use more expensive.

In order to achieve the variety of climate and energy policy targets, a multitude of instruments has been implemented: market-based programs such as carbon cap-and-trade or energy taxes, command-and-control policies such as energy efficiency standards, support schemes such as feed-in tariffs. Obviously these policies directly affect each other: Climate policy cap-and-trade makes electricity generation from fossil fuels more expensive and increases electricity prices. Energy policy feed-in tariffs change the relative prices in power production and make carbon free technologies more attractive. Also, the low-cost provision of electricity has been heavily debated in the face of trade-offs between policy induced power price increases and the call for a fair distribution of energy transformation burdens.

But although interdependencies between climate and energy targets, instruments, and impacts on the economy, environment, and society are manifold, the theory on these issues is relatively new, in many parts incomplete, and practical experiences are few. While against this background some economists claim that using multiple policies only causes inefficiencies, others are strongly in favor. So is a mix of multiple policies really necessary? How can sustainability criteria be applied to such a policy mix? And what are the political chances and barriers of a sustainable climate and energy policy mix? This is the first set of questions we are going to discuss in this chapter.

In practice, Japan continues to be a key global player in climate and energy policy: It is still the third biggest economy in the world, the seventh biggest GHG emitter, and keeps more than 50 nuclear power plants ready for use. Energy and climate policy targets are yet not finalized, market-based instruments are sparsely used, but efficiency standards and the recent feed-in tariff are quite advanced. Hence, a case study makes an interesting trial case for evaluating some of the preliminary theoretical insights of this chapter. So does Japan follow a comprehensive climate and energy policy strategy? To what extent can the policy mix be considered sustainable? And what have been the political challenges? This represents the second set of questions dealt with in this chapter.

In order to answer the questions, we aim at merely mapping in-depth future research by reviewing selected literature on an energy–climate policy mix, discussing sustainability criteria, and adding a political economy perspective. We mainly argue that a policy mix is necessary, that sustainability criteria are indispensable but still hard to define, and that the political feasibility of such an approach is critical but still higher than for carbon pricing alone. Hence, we call for a stronger research emphasis on social justice and political feasibility questions of a climate and energy policy mix.

4.2   INSIGHTS FROM THEORY

4.2.1   The Necessity of a Policy Mix

Because the aims of providing both a stable global climate and a sustainable energy supply are faced with many aspects of market failure such as the public good character of the global climate, monopolies in the energy market, and external costs of electricity use, government action is inevitable. In terms of the ultimate goal, we will later argue that only a nuclear-free de-carbonization by the end of this century can be considered a sustainable strategy. In terms of concrete targets, Germany has exemplified what this means (BMU 2011):

- the phase-out of nuclear energy by 2022;
- a share of renewable energy in power consumption of 35 percent by 2020 and 80 percent by 2050;
- a reduction of primary energy consumption by 20 percent in 2020 and 50 percent in 2050 (base 2008); and
- a reduction of GHG emission by 40 percent by 2020 and 80–95 percent by 2050 (base 1990).

Following the Tinbergen Rule (Tinbergen 1952), already this gigantic task with its multiple objectives calls for multiple instruments. But some scholars already lament an 'instrument invasion' (Hansjürgens 2012: 7). While the influx of a multitude of policy instruments certainly cannot be denied, the question remains, if we are faced with a necessary and well-planned policy mix or with a more or less chaotic and ineffective policy mess. So is a mix of policies actually necessary? Here, for simplicity reasons, we focus our discussion on combining the EU Emissions Trading Scheme (EU ETS) with the German-style feed-in tariff (FIT).

Critics of a policy mix mainly claim, that in view of a fixed climate target, an efficient cap-and-trade scheme should be the one and only policy, because any added instrument would only increase overall compliance cost without producing additional environmental benefits (Sinn 2008; Weimann 2008).

Proponents of a policy mix (Diekmann and Kemfert 2005; Fischedick and Samadi 2010; Lehmann and Gawel 2011; SRU 2011; Weber and Hey 2012), on the other hand, first and foremost, argue on the basis of welfare economics. According to this, in energy and climate policy multiple externalities exist and they cannot be internalized by an isolated carbon market. Besides climate change, additional externalities of energy conversion processes arise for example, from sulfur dioxide (SO_2) or nitrogen oxides (NO_X) emissions, from possible nuclear contamination, and from impacts of digging for energy resources. In addition to negative externalities, positive externalities arise from an energy transformation such as a greater independence from undemocratic oil and gas producing regimes as well as knowledge spill-overs from innovation in renewable energy and energy efficiency technologies. In order to internalize externalities, proponents of a policy mix consider complementary instruments to carbon pricing such as efficiency standards or feed-in tariffs justified.

Second, applying evolutionary economics, path dependencies matter (Kosinowsky and Groth 2011). Investments in the energy sector are highly asset specific: They are only designated for this specific purpose and, once made, are irreversible. But current investment decisions are made based on a cost structure that distorts competition in many ways, for example, due to substantial subsidies for fossil fuels and nuclear energy versus the externalization of respective negative environmental and health effects in the past. In this artificial situation, distortions lead to investments in a long-term sub-optimal electricity generation path and prevent investments in fundamentally new technologies. A carbon pricing scheme such as the EU ETS alone cannot provide a sufficient remedy for this 'carbon [and nuclear] lock-in' (Fischedick and Samadi 2010: 24). Instead, as long-term oriented investments are needed, a renewable energy support system such as the German FIT provides planning reliability and helps overcoming established structures.

Third, according to political economy reasoning (Gawel et al. 2014), it is very likely that decisions on crucial design features of carbon pricing schemes such as the ETS cap size are rather based on the political accepta-bility than on environmental necessities or overall abatement costs. Hence, real-world cap-and-trade schemes will probably never be cost efficient or sufficiently effective. But instead of utterly condemning the instrument, complementing a politically weakened ETS with additional measures could be a more reasonable alternative.

Fourth, political consulting has to take into consideration real-life political and institutional constraints instead of asking the world to adapt to economic models (Hansjürgens 2012: 11). Besides the above-mentioned barriers to perfect carbon markets, institutional constraints have to be taken into account. In politics, these involve policymaking styles, institutional arrangements, and multi-level governance structures. In the latter case, modern literature on environmental federalisms suggests that supranational carbon markets should be complemented by national or even regional poli-cies in order to cope with specific local circumstances (Morotomi 2014).

And fifth, the energy transformation towards a nuclear-free low carbon society calls for profound changes in the socio-technological system (Hansjürgens 2012: 11). Carbon price signals alone might not be enough to trigger the changes necessary, spanning from technological infrastructure issues such as the power grid structure to socio-economic questions on the sustainability of modern lifestyles.

Weighing the arguments, we are convinced that in order to realize a nuclear-free de-carbonization by the end of this century we need to rely on a well-balanced policy mix. But if so, what could be the criteria for the design of such a policy mix?

4.2.2   The Sustainability of a Policy Mix

Sustainability was established as an important guiding principle for public policy at the Rio Summit in 1992 (Lerch and Nutzinger 2002). Ever since, besides intra- and intergenerational justice, three pillars—environment, society, economy—and five notions of stringency—from very weak to very strong—have been emphasized. In the latter case, even the rather unpretentious concept of critical sustainability calls for boundaries, safe minimum standards or environmental guardrails.

Applying these basic ideas to energy and climate policy, environmental effectiveness, economic efficiency and social justice should be guiding principles (Rudolph et al. 2012). Concerning the environment, issues such as climate protection, air pollution control, responsible resource and land use or nuclear safety have to be considered. Exemplifying for the first and the last, fairly clear criteria can be identified. In climate protection, the Intergovernmental Panel on Climate Change (IPCC 2007) scientifically founded—and the global community even publically acknowledged at the Copenhagen Summit—the 2°C target as a safe minimum standard, which calls for emission reductions of 80–90 percent in industrialized countries by 2050. This de-carbonization of energy supply calls for a fuel switch from fossil fuels to renewable energy. Nuclear energy, although carbon-free, cannot be considered sustainable, because of the high risk related to nuclear accidents and the still unsolved questions around nuclear waste treatment. Thus, any climate and energy policy mix has to be evaluated against the guardrail of a nuclear-free de-carbonization. While the operationalization of such a guardrail is certainly still quite a challenge, some evaluation criteria such as a policy's accuracy in reaching pre-given targets, its suitability for target adjustment in the case of new knowledge, its capability to set long-term innovation incentives, its ability to deal with carbon leakage, and its fitness to prevent rebound effects have already been developed and applied to carbon cap-and-trade (Rudolph et al. 2012). For policy interaction Oikonomou and Jepma (2008) developed a framework and additionally pointed to the importance of energy effectiveness, which refers solely to specific energy targets such as security of supply.

In the case of economic criteria, the definition of an optimal level of pollution and a complete internalization of externalities remains impossible, leaving cost efficiency as the guiding principle (Baumol and Oates 1971). Market-based approaches such as energy taxes or carbon cap-and-trade are considered cost-efficient and have reduced compliance cost by up to 50 percent compared with command-and-control in various cases in practice (Ellerman et al. 2000). But as outlined above, even many economic arguments support the call for complementing measures in order to cope with multiple externalities, lock-ins, and politics-induced problems. Again, nuclear energy must be excluded, simply because of actual costs being higher than those of many alternative energy resources (Oshima 2014). Thus, a nuclear-free de-carbonization needs well-designed market-based approaches, combined with other instruments in such a way that the combination does not set perverse incentives jeopardizing carbon pricing's cost efficiency. In addition to overall cost-efficiency and company-level flexibility, the minimization of administrative and transaction costs, the prevention of (further) competitive distortions, and the definition of clear property rights are important criteria (Rudolph et al. 2012). For policy interaction, Oikonomou and Jepma (2008) also point to the importance of preventing double regulation—a situation, in which one target group is affected by more than one policy instrument that achieve the same objectives—and double counting—which occurs when the targets for the same emissions are assigned to different obligated parties. Double counting can be further differentiated into double coverage, double crediting, and double slippage. Double coverage occurs when the same emission allowance is required twice in order to address the same target quantity in for example, two interlinked carbon cap-and-trade schemes; double crediting happens when two allowances are generated from one reduction action; and double slippage occurs when an emission is neither covered by one nor the other scheme. Also, a climate–energy policy mix can be evaluated against its ability to foster an energy market liberalization.

The main line of discussion on social justice aspects of the energy transformation in Germany has so far focused on the criteria of electricity price effects (Heindl et al. 2014). At least two arguments support the notion that the financial burden resulting from the energy transformation is significantly higher for poor households than for rich households. First, energy prices are regressive in so far as the relative burden for poor households is bigger than for rich households. Second, poor households are less capable of short-run reactions to higher energy prices such as buying more efficient appliances or replacing heating systems. In addition, due to the trend of a widening income spread, the share of households threatened by poverty has increased in many industrialized countries. Thus, poor households appear to shoulder a bigger part of the energy transformation than rich households, a steadily increasing share of low-income households have to spend a steadily increasing part of their income on energy, and altogether the energy transformation so far can be considered unfair—a specifically obvious example being poor people living in small apartments subsidizing solar panels of house owners by paying the feed-in tariff apportionment. This notion is also underlined by a multi-level governance perspective, because for example, in the case of renewable support schemes not all European power producers are treated equally, some German Länder subsidize other Länder, and German energy intensive industries are at least partly exempted from the apportionment. Hence, energy price effects have to be a major criteria for judging the sustainability of a climate and energy policy mix. In addition, for policy interaction, Oikonomou and Jepma (2008) also mention employment, business opportunities, and government revenues as relevant criteria.

However, it should not be forgotten that the energy transformation also fosters social justice, because a nuclear-free, decarbonized energy supply would significantly lower the ecological rucksack passed on from the current to future generations. In addition, several other aspects of social justice such as procedural versus result-based justice, have to be taken into consideration when evaluating the fairness of a climate and energy policy mix (Lerch 2011). In an attempt to solve related issues, Rawls (1971) groundbreaking contribution calls for equality in terms of rights and freedom as well as chances and opportunities, and only accepts inequalities in income and capital, if they provide the highest benefit to the poorest compared with a situation of equality where the poorest benefit less. However, operationalizing this idea for policy mix design still remains a big challenge.

Altogether, we think it critically important to unequivocally define and apply sustainability criteria for a climate and energy policy mix. And as research as well as policy discussion on economic efficiency and environmental effectiveness are far more advanced than debates on social justice, we consider it necessary to put a stronger focus on the latter issue.

4.2.3 The Feasibility of a Policy Mix

Public Choice wisdom has it that market-based environmental policies such as tradable emission permits or environmental taxes are difficult to implement (Kirchgässner and Schneider 2003). As a consequence, it seems very unlikely that carbon pricing schemes ambitious enough to incentivize a nuclear-free de-carbonization by the end of this century are politically feasible (Weber and Hey 2012); a fact also clearly supported by several empirical studies on cap-and-trade in the US (Ellerman et al. 2000), the EU (Rudolph 2009) and Japan (Rudolph and Schneider 2012). In line with these arguments, some economists claim that for example, combining the EU ETS with other instruments such as the German feed-in tariff raises overall compliance costs and thus further increases covered industries' resistance to ambitious carbon pricing (Weimann 2008).

However, several arguments support the view that an ambitious policy mix might be easier to implement than a single adequate carbon pricing scheme (Gawel et al. 2014). First, if industries' would really care about total climate protection costs, they should support a least cost instrument such as carbon cap-and-trade or taxation; but in reality they do not. Public Choice already tells us that overall cost-efficiency features characteristics of a public good and that, instead, the attribution of costs to sectors or even individual economic units is the key factor for mobilizing opposition. Therefore, in many countries industry resistance to carbon pricing has been one of the major obstacles of cost-efficient climate policy (Rudolph 2009; Rudolph and Schneider 2012).

Second, if opposition against carbon pricing is mobilized by sectoral abatement costs borne by well-organized interest groups rather than by overall climate protection costs, and if abatement cost in the regulated sectors are lower the smaller their share of total climate protection costs is, shifting burdens from well-organized industry groups to less organized groups such as households could increase the political feasibility of more ambitious carbon pricing schemes. Subsidizing renewable energies by a feed-in tariff mainly paid by households, although highly questionable from the fairness perspective, lowers sectoral abatement costs for industry covered by a carbon pricing scheme. Thus, it might even weaken industries' opposition to more ambitious carbon pricing scheme designs compared with the case of a sole economic instrument.

Third, technology support programs such as the German feed-in tariff, by overcoming path dependencies and carbon-nuclear lock-ins, could provide clean technologies on a large scale in time, which in turn might prevent sudden carbon price hikes and reduce cost uncertainty for industry.

Forth, supporting renewable energy and thus fostering the renewable energy industry creates a new potent political player in the energy policy discourse and weakens the relative influence of traditional fossil-fuel based utilities. And as providers of renewable energy greatly benefit from carbon pricing that burdens fossil-fuel based power production, they are possible proponents of ambitious carbon pricing schemes, providing the necessary stakeholder support.

And fifth, the necessary de-carbonization by a sole carbon pricing instrument would cause prohibitively high political costs. A carbon price capable of completely de-carbonizating energy supply would have to be between 70 (production costs of wind onshore) and 300 euros per ton of CO_2 (production costs of photovoltaic). Compared with current price levels, the financial burden of an average German entity covered by the EU ETS would increase by at least 30 million Euros. This is because in the case of decarbonizing by a single pricing instrument, the energy transformation is organized by financially punishing established technologies and devaluing productive capital of politically influential industries. Instead, partially de-carbonizing by financially supporting renewable energies might be politically less costly.

Altogether, while a policy mix still faces a lot of political barriers, there are reasons to believe that the political barriers of an energy transformation based on a single sufficiently stringent market-based instrument are higher than complementing insufficient carbon pricing with other policies such as renewable energy support schemes. However, the real political costs, related interests, and the actual power balance in the climate and energy policy realm still have to be analyzed in more detail.

4.3 CLIMATE AND ENERGY POLICY IN JAPAN

4.3.1 Policy Programs and Targets

In order to achieve a nuclear-free low-carbon society in Japan, energy-related CO_2 emission control measure have to be strengthened and the use of renewable energy has to be enhanced. Today, CO_2 emissions account for around 90 percent of Japanese GHG emissions and are still increasing (+2.8 percent in 2012 from the previous year). And despite of the one year anniversary of Japanese electricity supply without nuclear power on September 15, 2014, a phase-out strategy is not yet available.

In Japan, climate and energy policy issues used to be—and are partly still—discussed separately. Even before the Fukushima nuclear disaster on March 11, 2011, the former Japanese government led by the Democratic Party of Japan (DPJ) proposed the 'Basic Act on Climate Change Countermeasure' on May 12, 2010. The Act outlined mid- and long-term GHG reduction targets:

- −25 percent by 2020 (base 1990).
- −80 percent by 2050 (base 1990).

In addition, the Act included the renewable energy goal of a 10 percent share in total primary energy supply by 2020. A target for nuclear energy, however, was not set, because Japan's climate protection strategy at the time very much relied on the continuation of nuclear power use. Anyway, while the Act had passed the Lower House on May 18, 2010, it later failed in the Upper House.

After 3/11 significant doubt in the Japanese energy system led to DPJ's 'Innovative Strategy for Energy and the Environment' (EECJ 2012) on September 14, 2012; a major step towards interlinking energy and climate policy. The green energy revolution was considered the main linkage, as the promotion of energy efficiency and renewable energy would both lower CO_2 emissions and the dependence on nuclear energy, while at the same time securing a stable and inexpensive power supply. The Innovative

Strategy referred to the 2010 Climate Act's GHG targets, and concretized energy policy targets:

- phase-out by of nuclear energy by the 2030s;
- 30 percent share of renewable energies in electricity production in 2030; and
- 20 percent reduction of total final energy consumption by 2030 (base 2010).

In order to achieve these aims, besides the feed-in tariff and the carbon tax, first and foremost, the government intended to liberalize the electricity market by eliminating regional monopolies, decentralizing power supply, and decoupling generation and distribution. The nuclear phase-out was to be advanced by a strict limitation of the operating permits for nuclear power plants to 40 years, the limited re-start of plants considered safe by the newly established independent Nuclear Regulation Authority, and the abandonment of any plans to construct new plants.

Major policy changes arrived with the currently ruling Liberal Democratic Party (LDP) in 2012. On February 28, 2013, Prime Minister Abe announced a revision of the Innovative Strategy from scratch in order not to interfere with economic recovery. As a consequence, on November 15, 2013, the GHG reduction commitment was reduced to 3.8 percent by 2020 (base 2005), an actual emission increase by 3.1 percent compared with 1990 levels. While holding onto the renewable energy target, a decision on the future of nuclear energy has still not been made.

Altogether, while the eventually unsuccessful Innovative Strategy for the first time interlinked climate and energy policy and set rather ambitious targets, current goals are not the least in line with the necessities of limiting global warming to the 2°C target and phasing out nuclear energy. The continuing failure has been mainly due to the strong resistance from the well-known Iron Triangle of energy intensive industries and utilities, the Ministry of Economy, Trade and Industry (METI), and the now ruling Liberal Democratic Party (LDP) (Rudolph and Schneider 2012).

4.3.2   Policy Instruments

Already the unsuccessful 2010 Climate Act proposed three specific policies to achieve its targets:

- domestic emissions trading scheme (ETS);
- carbon tax; and
- feed-in tariff (FIT).

ETS was tested in Japan between 2005 and 2012 (MoE 2012). The Japan Voluntary Emissions Trading Scheme (JVETS), a baseline-and-credit scheme without a fixed overall emission cap, was administered by Japan's Ministry of the Environment. Participants received subsidies for achieving self-set absolute volume CO_2 reduction targets and were rewarded with free tradable credits for over-compliance. In 2008, however, JVETS was merged with the Integrated Domestic Market of Emissions Trading (IDMET), administered by both the Ministry of the Environment (MoE) and METI. In order to increase voluntary participation, IDMET, other than JVETS, allowed credit borrowing, extensive offset use, and specific emission intensity targets but did not offer subsidies. Experiences with the trading programs were ambivalent: While IDMET never took off, JVETS' participants achieved their voluntary targets, but overall emission reductions, participation, and trading activities remained very limited to the end.

Following the 2009 change in government, preparations for the Domestic Emissions Trading Scheme intensified. A government committee report proposed several design options for a mandatory scheme starting from 2013 and aiming at emission reductions in line with Japan's former 25 percent reduction target for 2020. However, crucial design issues such as the overall cap size, the possibility of intensity targets, and the initial allocation scheme were not solved. Anyway, in December 2010 the DPJ government called off the implementation of the Domestic ETS; the major reason again being the Iron Triangle's opposition (Rudolph and Schneider 2012). Instead of an ETS, the DPJ went for a carbon tax and a feed-in tariff, mainly in order to overcome this opposition while at the same time at least partly fulfilling its former commitment to GHG and nuclear power dependency reduction.

With the aim of controlling energy-related CO_2 emissions, the Tax for Climate Change Mitigation was introduced in 2012. The tax is imposed on the consumption of fossil fuels such as petroleum, natural gas and coal. Specifically, by using the CO_2 emissions factor of each fuel, the tax rate per quantity unit is set in a way that each tax burden equals 289 yen per ton of CO_2. Hence, carbon tax rates vary between fuels. The carbon tax is added onto the pre-existing petroleum and coal tax, the tax base of which is all fossil fuels (760 yen/kl crude oil and petroleum products, 780 yen/t for gaseous hydrocarbons, 670 yen/t for coal). To mitigate the burden, carbon tax rates are only to be raised gradually in the future (Table 4.1) and exemptions and refunds are provided for certain fields such as imported and domestic volatile oil for petrochemical production.

Tax revenues are to be used for various measures of energy-related CO_2 emission control, such as energy-saving measures, the promotion of

Environmental pricing

Table 4.1   Carbon tax rates in 2012

Object of taxation	Petroleum and Coal Tax	Carbon Tax		
		Oct, 2012	April, 2014	April, 2016
Crude Petroleum and Petroleum Products (per kilo liter)	2,040 yen	250 yen (2,290 yen)	500 yen (2,540 yen)	760 yen (2,800 yen)
Gaseous Hydrocarbon (per ton)	1,080 yen	260 yen (1,340 yen)	520 yen (1,600 yen)	780 yen (1,860 yen)
Coal (per ton)	700 yen	220 yen (920 yen)	440 yen (1,440 yen)	670 yen (1370 yen)

Source: MoE (2010).

renewable energy, and the clean and efficient use of fossil fuels. Thus, in terms of emission reductions, a revenue effect will add to the price effect.

As the carbon tax only started its operation on October 1, 2012, empirical results are limited. However, revenues are estimated to be 39.1 billion yen for 2012 and 262.3 billion yen for each year after 2016. Thus, MoE (2010) estimates the sum of the revenue and the price effect to be a CO_2 reduction of 0.5 percent to 2.2 percent by 2020 compared with 1990 levels. Lee et al. (2012) modeled the potential economic and environmental effects and confirmed a 1–3 percent emission reduction but found no significant impact on the gross domestic product (GDP) and employment.

The Japanese feed-in tariff (FIT) for renewable energy was launched on July 1, 2012. It obliges utilities to purchase electricity generated from photovoltaic, wind power, hydraulic power (below 30 MW), geothermal, and biomass based on a fixed-period fixed-price contract. Purchase rate and contract period are determined corresponding to the type and the form of installation as well as the scale of renewable energy resources (Table 4.2). The rates and periods are announced by METI, based on considerations by an independent committee and the ministries concerned. For the benefit of renewable energy electricity suppliers, special consideration is given in decisions on FIT rates for three years from the FIT-introduction.

In order to cover additional costs of renewable energy, utilities may request customers to pay the Surcharge for Renewable Energy on top of the electricity price in proportion to electricity usage. However,

Table 4.2 FIT tariffs and durations in 2014

Energy source	Solar PV		Wind power			Geothermal power		Small- and medium-scale hydraulic power			Small- and medium-scale hydraulic power (utilizing installed water-introducing passage)		
Procurement category	10kW or more	Less than 10kW	20kW or more	Less than 20kW	Floating wind turbine	15MW or more	Less than 15MW	1MW or more but less than 3MW	200kw or more but less than 1MW	Less than 200kW	1MW or more but less than 3MW	200kW or more but less than 1MW	Less than 200kW
Tariff(per/kWh)[a]	32 yen[b]	37 yen[c]	22 yen	55 yen	36 yen	26 yen	40 yen	24 yen	29 yen	34 yen	14 yen	21 yen	25 yen
Duration(years)	20	10	20			15		20			20		

Energy source			Biomass		
Biomass type	Biogas	Wood fired power plant (Timber from forest thinning)	Wood fired power plant (Other woody materials)	Waste (excluding woody wastes)	Wood fired power plant (Recycled wood)
Tariff (per/kWh)	JPY 39	JPY 32	JPY 24	JPY 13	JPY 17
Duration (years)	20				

Notes:
a. Tax-exclusive price.
b. 40 Yen in 2012, 36 Yen in 2013.
c. 42 Yen in 2012, 38 Yen in 2013.

Source: http://www.enecho.meti.go.jp/category/saving_and_new/saiene/kaitori/kakaku.html.

customers affected by the 2011 earthquake and energy-intensive industries are exempted from the surcharge.

In terms of effects, while there have only been few studies, the Japan Renewable Energy Foundation presented early ex-post study results (JREF 2014a, 2014b). According to these studies, the share of renewable energy, mainly photovoltaic, in power generation has rapidly increased up to 2.5 percent in 2013 and 4.2 percent in the period April to May 2014. This is remarkable, because this share increased by only 0.7 percent between 2002 and 2011. This increase has reduced fossil fuel costs by 325.7 billion yen and CO_2 emissions by 12.3 million tons or around 1 percent compared with 1990 levels in 2013. In terms of the burden on electricity consumers, the share of the renewable energy surcharge in the total electricity rate is very low. Between 2010 and 2013 the final electricity rate has increased by 4.31 yen per kilowatt hour for households, but the share of the surcharge is only 8 percent of the electricity rate (0.35 yen/kWh). Instead, the main factor for an increase in power prices is the increase of fossil fuel market prices.

In sum, at the policy level, while an ambitious ETS failed due to the opposition of the Iron Triangle, the Japanese government implemented a low-level carbon tax and combined it with a rather ambitious FIT. While it is yet too early to judge the results, ex ante estimations show a very small emissions reduction effect by the carbon tax, which is mainly caused by the use of revenues for climate protection; the FIT, however, is more promising in terms of environmental effects. But it is most certain that the emission reduction contribution even of the two instruments together is insufficient considering the challenges of climate protection. In terms of economic efficiency, carbon pricing continues to play only a minor role, so that market forces can only partially play their role in (re)directing resources to the most efficient use. In terms of social justice, major parts of the climate and energy policy costs are now born by Japanese households, while industry is protected from extra burdens in many ways. However, it should not go without mentioning that, despite of the failure of a domestic ETS, combining a carbon tax with a feed-in tariff may have significantly increased their political feasibility after almost two decades of intense, but politically fruitless discussion on carbon pricing.

4.4   CONCLUSIONS

In search of guidance on the pathway to a sustainable climate and energy policy future with the sufficiently plausible target of a nuclear-free de-carbonization by the end of the century, we have found the theoretical arguments on the necessity of a policy mix convincing. The main reasons are the existence of multiple externalities, carbon and nuclear lock-ins, and the insufficiency of the political process to provide sufficiently ambitious carbon pricing schemes.

However, defining sustainability criteria for a policy mix remains a great challenge. While environmental economics has provided economic and environmental criteria for single climate policy instruments such as accuracy in meeting the target, innovation incentives, and cost efficiency, already defining criteria for a policy mix poses new questions. Still, as an interim result, we argue that market-based approaches are preferable to support and regulation approaches and that, due to its environmental advantages, cap-and-trade is the most promising carbon pricing option. In addition, double regulation has to be avoided as well as setting contradicting incentives. For social justice issues, the challenges appear to be bigger. Already for single climate policy instruments justice criteria are not well defined, let alone for the use of multiple energy and climate policies. Still, as preliminary insights, we think that regressive effects of carbon pricing should be avoided as much as possible. But at carbon price levels sufficient to stimulate a nuclear-free de-carbonization, revenues of taxes or auctions most certainly have to be used for compensating poor communities or households. However, it also has to be kept in mind that a rapid nuclear-free de-carbonization even at currently high costs contribute to intergenerational justice, because it may prevent more serious climate and energy consequences in the future. Considering politics, we have found convincing arguments that the feasibility of a policy mix is higher than that of an equally ambitious sole carbon pricing. Major reasons for this belief are that a policy mix mobilizes new actors groups, spread compliance costs more widely, and provides early low-cost green technology alternatives.

In our case study on Japan, we have shown Japan has neither targets ambitious enough to organize a nuclear-free de-carbonization by the end of this century nor an integrated energy and climate policy strategy in place. In addition, Japan still does not use efficient, effective, and possibly even socially just market-based approaches as the main pillars of its climate and energy policy. Hope however persists, as the year 2012 saw the introduction of a low-level carbon tax and an ambitious feed-in tariff. But still, emission reductions are expected to be insufficient, efficient market allocation of scarce resources will be limited, and current generation households as well as future generations will continue to carry heavy burdens in terms of possible negative impacts of global warming and continuing nuclear energy use. However, while strong opposition to a nuclear-free de-carbonization persists in Japan, the debate around the 2010–2012 climate and energy proposals showed that the combination of instruments might actually increase the feasibility of a sustainable climate and energy policy mix.

But without doubt fairness and feasibility questions will dominate future discussions on a nuclear-free de-carbonization. Hence, we think that research efforts should reflect this focus more convincingly.

NOTES

* This research was partially supported by the Ministry of Education, Culture, Sports, Science and Technology in Japan, Grant-in-Aid for Scientific Research (A), 2012–2014 (80303064, Toru Morotomi).
1. Dr Sven Rudolph, Associate Professor, Graduate School of Economics, Kyoto University, Japan; Takeshi Kawakatsu, PhD, Associate Professor, Faculty of Public Policy, Kyoto Prefectural University, Japan; Dr Achim Lerch, Professor, Hessian University of Cooperative Education (Hessische Berufsakademie). Contact: rudolph@econ.kyoto-u.ac.jp.

REFERENCES

Baumol, W.J. and Oates, W.E. (1971), The Use of Standards and Prices for Protection of the Environment, *Swedish Journal of Economics*, **73**, 42–54.

Diekmann, J. and Kemfert, C. (2005), Erneuerbare Energien—Weitere Förderung aus Klimaschuztgründen unverzichtbar, *DIW-Wochenbericht*, **29**, 439–451.

Ellerman, A.D. et al. (2000), *Markets for Clean Air*, Cambridge: Cambridge University Press.

Energy and Environment Council of Japan (EECJ) (2012): Options for Energy and the Environment, Tokyo.

Federal Ministry for the Environment, Nature Conservancy, and Nuclear Safety (BMU) (2011), *The Energy Concept and its Accelerated Implementation*, Berlin.

Fischedick, M. and Samadi, S. (2010), Die grundsätzliche wirtschaftstheoretische Kritik am EEG greift zu kurz, *Solarzeitalter*, **22**, 18–25.

Gawel, E. et al. (2014), A public choice view on the climate and energy policy mix in the EU—How do the emissions trading scheme and support for renewable energies interact? *Energy Policy*, 64, 175–182.

Hansjürgens, B. (2012), Instrumentenmix der Klima- und Energiepolitik—Welche Herausforderungen stellen sich? *Wirtschaftsdienst*, **92**, Sonderausgabe 2012, 5–11.

Heindl, P. et al. (2014): Ist die Energiewende sozial gerecht? *Wirtschaftsdienst*, **94** (7), 508–514.

Intergovernmental Panel on Climate Change (IPCC) (2007), *Climate Change 2007 Synthesis Report*, Geneva.

Japan Renewable Energy Foundation (JREF) (2014a), *Evaluation of Feed-in Tariff for One Year and Propositions on its Design*, Tokyo.

Japan Renewable Energy Foundation (JREF) (2014b), *Effects of Feed-in Tariff after Two Years and Challenges of Renewable Energy Policy*, Tokyo.

Kirchgässner, G. and Schneider, F. (2003), On the political economy of environmental policy, *Public Choice*, **115** (3), 369–396.

Kosinowski, H. and Groth, M. (2011), *Die deutsche Förderung erneuerbarer Energien*, Marburg: Metropolis.

Lee, S., Hector, P. and Ueta, K. (2012), An assessment of Japanese carbon tax reform using the E3MG econometric model, *The Scientific World Journal*, **2012**.

Lehmann, P. and Gawel, E. (2011), Why should support schemes for renewable electricity complement the EU Emissions Trading Scheme? *Energy Policy*, **52**, 597–607.

Lerch, A. (2011), CO_2-Emissionshandel—effizient oder gerecht? *Zeitschrift für Sozialökonomie*, **48**, 39–47.

Lerch, A. and Nutzinger, H.G. (2002), Sustainability—economic approaches and ethical implications, *Journal of Economic and Social Policy*, **6** (2), 1–20.

Ministry of the Environment (MoE) (2010), *Details on the Carbon Tax (Tax for Climate Change Mitigation)*, Tokyo.

Ministry of the Environment (MoE) (2012), *Consideration of Emissions Trading Scheme in Japan*, Tokyo.

Morotomi, T. (2014), 'Climate change policy from the bottom up—Tokyo's cap-and-trade scheme and multilevel governance', in Niizawa, H. and Morotomi, T. (eds), *Governing Low-carbon Development and the Economy*, Tokyo: United Nations University Press, pp. 117–131.

Oikonomou, V. and Jepma, C.J. (2008), A framework on interactions of climate and energy policy instruments, *Mitigation and Adaptation Strategies for Global Change*, **13**, 131–156.

Oshima, K. (2014), 'On the economy of nuclear power—Calculating the actual cost of power production', in Niizawa, H. and Morotomi, T. (eds), *Governing Low-carbon Development and the Economy*, Tokyo: United Nations University Press, pp. 235–249.

Rawls, J. (1971), *A Theory of Justice*, Cambridge: Harvard University Press.

Rudolph, S. (2009), 'How the German Patient Followed the Doctor's Orders—Political Economy Lessons from Implementing Market-Based Instruments in Germany', in Lye, L.H. et al. (eds), *Critical Issues in Environmental Taxation vol. VII*, Oxford: Oxford University Press, pp. 587–606.

Rudolph, S. et al. (2012), 'Towards Sustainable Carbon Markets—Requirements for Ecologically Effective, Economically Efficient, and Socially Just Emissions Trading Schemes', in Kreiser, L. et al. (eds), *Carbon Pricing, Growth and the Environment—Critical Issues in Environmental Taxation vol. XI*, Cheltenham, UK and Northampton, MA: Edward Elgar Publishing, pp. 167–183.

Rudolph, S. and Schneider, F. (2012), Political barriers of implementing carbon markets in Japan—A Public Choice analysis and the empirical evidence before and after the Fukushima nuclear disaster, *Environmental Economics and Policy Studies*, **15** (2), 211–235.

Sachverständigenrat für Umweltfragen (SRU) (2011), *Wege zur 100% erneuerbaren Stromversorgung*, Berlin: SRU-Sondergutachten.

Sinn, H.-W. (2008), *Das grüne Paradoxon*, Berlin: Econ.

Tinbergen, J. (1952), *On the Theory of Economic Policy*, Amsterdam: North-Holland.

Weber, M. and Hey, C. (2012), Effektive und effiziente Klimapolitik—Instrumentenmix, EEG und Subsidarität, *Wirtschaftsdienst*, **92**, Sonderausgabe 2012, 43–51.

Weimann, J. (2008), *Die Klimapolitik Katastrophe*, Marburg: Metropolis.

5. European renewable energy market governance and economic crisis: a taxation makeover with Greece as a case study

Ioanna Mersinia[1]

5.1 INTRODUCTION

With the background of climate change urgently calling for a shift to green energy, it is up to strategic planning to be adapted to allow alternative energy sources to pave the way for a new industrial revolution based on sustainability. The increased regulatory activity for the establishment of an internal European energy market may contribute to the implementation of a coherent energy strategy. However, the measures adopted by Member States on a national level have often been proved inadequate when responding to the common challenges set by EU energy policy, indicating the need for an interpretation of public policies and adjustment to the energy status quo of each Member State. The focus of this chapter is set on the renewable energy sources (RES) regulatory measures enacted at year end 2012 and regularly amended within the last two years in Greece, at times of a profound economic crisis, as well as within the context of putting effort into reaching the aftermath of recession. The main objective of this study is the assessment of the day ahead after the implementation of a framework including retroactive taxation measures, suspension of new photovoltaic projects, a so-called 'special solidarity levy' as an emergency tax imposed on the turnover of RES producers, a drastic reduction of feed-in tariffs (FIT), as well as a unilateral non-negotiated change of the contractual terms for operational RES projects. The Greek case study concentrates on the oxymoron arising from the wide challenges set by climate change and the contradiction between the measures adopted by the Greek government imposing severe retroactive taxation measures on RES, instead of promoting alternative energy sources via investment incentivization. This case study concludes with an evaluation of the legal procedures launched during the last two years causing significant instability in the taxation framework for RES in an effort to detect potential incompatibility issues with the European Law and Energy Policy, which incentivize RES and oppose any obstacles set to the large scale penetration of RES into the energy mix of each country.

5.2   THE IMPACT OF THE ECONOMIC CRISIS ON EU ENERGY POLICY AND THE FEED IN TARIFF REGIME

The outcome of the increased regulatory activity in order to build and safeguard a stable, competitive internal market, where the 2020 targets have potential to be achieved, is substantially judged by the effectiveness of the European energy policy. European energy policy plays an important role in providing Member States with the guidelines and setting targets; it is however up to each member country to develop a National Renewable Energy Action Plan for the deployment of RES technologies.

After the global renewable energy sector growth had been continually breaking its own record year after year since 2004, in late 2008 the impact of the financial crisis began to show through, particularly in the flow of debt from banks to renewable energy project developers. The investment surge of recent years was just starting to ease the supply chain bottlenecks when the credit crunch arrived and cut demand. The result has been a dramatic and permanent change to the dynamics of the industry. On the supply side prices are falling towards marginal costs, and several players will consolidate. On the demand side renewable energy targets will still drive utilities to build projects, but fewer developers and independent power producers will be involved, while the main impetus for investment in renewable energy will have to come from national government policies.[2]

Although there is a differentiation on the influential level for each country, the economic crisis undoubtedly exerts a substantial impact on energy governance and especially on the future of RES. There are however several interpretations of the impact of the crisis on energy governance. From one perspective, the lack of liquidity and availability of investments for RES infrastructure and deployment of new technologies may lead to a slowdown of the development of RES and a persistence to use fossil fuels. On the other hand, green growth ranks high on the agenda of international organizations and many individual countries and is seen by some as a panacea for coming out of the global financial and economic crisis (for example, OECD, 2011).[3] In the aftermath of a global economic crisis the challenge is to achieve growth in conventional national income without large and irreversible negative impacts on the environment. By redirecting the economy from dirty sectors to clean sectors one can achieve green growth without shrinking the size of the economy. Structural change and technological efficiency improvements are necessary but not sufficient when there is a lack of political support.[4]

As Butler and Neuhoff (2004)[5] explained, the stability of the FIT policy is considered as the main driver of its success. Until recently, there seemed to be no threat to the success and the stability of FITs. However, the financial crisis has forced the governments of several countries which apply FITs (in other words, Germany, Greece, Spain and Italy) to cut their subsidies (Radowitz et al. 2010[6]) since the costs of these policies have become too large and government deficits have become too high. In Spain, the subsidy cuts were found to be large and abrupt. In January 2011, the Spanish Parliament approved a law that retroactively cut FITs for photovoltaics by 30 percent (Johnson, 2011[7]). These subsidy cuts in combination with the financial crisis might have changed the preferences of investors regarding renewable energy and climate policies. Not only the decrease in the level of FITs might have reduced their popularity, but the decline in the stability of FIT policies might have led to the reduction of their popularity as well.[8]

In order to reduce the emission of greenhouse gases and to secure future energy supplies, governments around the world are working on the stimulation of the deployment of RES. Due to the recent subsidy cuts as a result of the financial crisis, it can be argued that FITs are no longer the best renewable energy and climate policy to increase private equity investments in renewable energy. However, FITs remain the most popular renewable energy and climate policy among cleantech venture capital and private equity investors, as they provide the most stable incentives for investors. Europe's renewable energy sector is searching for answers amid the sovereign debt crisis. As government subsidies have been cut, utilities and independent energy producers have mothballed projects and refocused on countries that still offer guaranteed—though reduced—returns for clean energy investment.

The drop in investment comes despite legally binding commitments by the European Union to produce 20 percent of its energy from renewable sources by the end of the decade. Countries like Greece and Spain attracted multi-billion dollar investments from developers looking for guaranteed profits. Yet as local governments are forced to cut domestic budgets in search of cost savings, clean energy subsidies have been among the first targets. Spain has already stopped new funding for renewables because of the debt problems. The Italian government has also reduced support, limiting new subsidies to €500 million for 2013, while the figure for 2012 was about €6 billion. Greece has reduced FITs by more than

50 percent and has suspended the authorization of new PV projects for two years. Other governments, including Germany's, have reduced FITs, though they continue to provide financial support to small-scale renewable projects which allow local factories and businesses to produce their own green energy. However, what also needs to be taken into consideration is that the reduction in subsidies has gone hand in hand with a fall in the cost of renewable technology, like wind turbines and solar panels, but also with the fall of coal and natural gas prices, leading the renewable industry to face mounting competition from fossil fuels.

5.3 GREECE AS A CASE STUDY: THE POTENTIAL FOR THE DEVELOPMENT OF RES, THE CRISIS AND THE MEASURES ENACTED

5.3.1 The 2020 Commitments for Greece and the Potential of RES Development

Following the adoption of the Third Energy Package and in view of designing the way forward so that Greece achieves the targets set by Directives 2009/28/EC and 2009/29/EC, the Greek government enacted Law 3851/2010 (Government's Gazette A' 85), which has set the National targets for 2020 regarding the share of RES in final energy consumption, electricity generation and contribution in heating, cooling and transport, as follows: (a) contribution of the energy produced from RES to the gross final energy consumption with a share of 20 percent; (b) contribution of the electrical energy produced by RES to the gross electrical energy consumption with a share of at least 40 percent; (c) contribution of the energy produced by RES to the final energy consumption for heating and cooling with a share of at least 20 percent and (d) contribution of the electrical energy produced by RES to the gross electricity energy consumption in transportation with a share of at least 10 percent (YPEKA, 2010).[9,10] Meeting the above targets set by 2020 calls for the elaboration of policies and measures, which aim at the simultaneous fulfillment of the above '20–20–20' obligations and the acceleration of the Greek economy through green development and enhanced competitiveness of the private sector.

As far as the country's potential for the deployment of RES is concerned, substantial proof thereof is the Mediterranean climate itself, with more than 2,700 hours of sunshine annually in most of the country, mild temperatures, limited rainfall and different kinds of seasonal winds. Undoubtedly, the country's potential for renewable energy sources such as solar energy or wind power is very high and it is therefore crucial to develop a comprehensive strategy for growth and investment in infrastructure for the expansion of the RES network. The wind energy remains in Greece the dominant form of renewable energy, but also photovoltaics attract special interest and solar energy was until recently heralded as the economic savior of Greece presenting a higher growth rhythm. Indicatively, in 2011 transactions and procurement for photovoltaics reached 2 GW, marking a 300 percent increase in comparison with 2010.[11]

Renewable energy can be viewed as a long-term solution to fiscal austerity, international dependency and European energy security. Although Greece has experienced consecutive years of economic turmoil and fiscal austerity, renewables can be viewed as a potential solution to both energy and economic problems. Solar energy is at the fore of the political desire for sustainable economic growth and the creation of much needed employment. A green paradigm however, based on energy thriftiness, solar and renewables generally, remains inapplicable without the indispensable policy coherence, and what's more, in a case like the Greek one, where the government fails to design the RES market efficiently on an incentive based model due to subsequent amendments of the applicable RES taxation framework.

5.3.2   The Economic Recession and the Measures Adopted by the Greek Government for RES

In the context of a challenging economic environment, the Greek economy is going through a volatile transition period. The ongoing crisis and the recession make it imperative to look for new opportunities and development potential across all sectors of the economy. The energy sector is no exception, and it is expected to play a key role in the recovery of the economy. As stated in the Greek energy roadmap to 2050:[12] 'the energy sector constitutes a cornerstone for economic development and has either direct or indirect impact on every sector of the economy'. Therefore it becomes obvious that energy planning is an important tool in the implementation of a country's development policy, with a tremendous impact not only on the economic activity, but on the national activity as a whole. Facing this major crisis and trying to encounter a huge debt and deficit, the Greek government took action in November 2012 by voting the 'Approval of the Medium-Term Fiscal Strategy Framework 2013–2016 Urgent Application Measures' (Law 4093/2012 Government's Gazette A' 222). The specific regulatory framework had an immense impact on the RES sector, as the Greek government in an effort to balance the pressures stemming from public finances, the lack of liquidity of private investors and the reduced incomes of households, led to the sequence of measures analyzed below that changed the scenery of the Greek RES market.

5.4   SUSPENSION OF NEW PV PROJECTS AND DRASTIC REDUCTION OF FITS

In August 2012, two Ministerial Decisions by the Ministry of Environment, Energy and Climate Change (MD/2300/16932 and MD/2301/16933, Government Gazette B' 2317), included the following two measures: first, upon publication of these decisions, the licensing procedure for new photovoltaic power stations was suspended as well as the offers for connection to the grid, and second, the rates of the FITs drastically dropped. Both changes have been brought on by the Greek Ministry of Environment, Energy and Climate Change (YPEKA) in what it described as a bid to restore liquidity in the electricity market and limit the burden on consumers.

In more detail, no new applications for producer licenses and connection requests would be accepted by the National Regulatory Authority (RAE). Only projects already licensed but not yet accomplished were allowed to proceed. This decision was not applicable for the residential sector's PVs (<10 kW) and for fast-track projects. The approval process for projects which already have a producer license or which are exempted from having to obtain one and have binding connection requests, would reportedly proceed as normal. With the continuation of these PV projects, the Ministry argued that the energy objectives for 2020 are more than covered.

As far as the reduction of FITs is concerned, the government has decided to slash the most generous regime in Europe by more than 50 percent. This significant reduction has taken place in three stages, initiated in August 2012, further amended and increased in June 2013 and completed in April 2014, when via the enactment of the so-called 'New Deal' framework, it reached an average of over 50 percent compared with the FITs of 2010. As indicated in the next section where the currently applicable framework is analyzed, the last reduction in FITs has been designed based on a gradient approach depending on the characteristics of each operating project, namely on the time of the connection of the park to the grid and on whether the electricity producer has received a grant from the State for the construction of the PV park.

5.5   RETROACTIVE TAXATION

The Greek Parliament enacted in November 2012 Law 4093/2012 on the 'Approval of the Medium-Term Fiscal Strategy Framework 2013–2016 Urgent Application Measures' which includes, among other hard austerity measures, a framework according to which a retroactive taxation is imposed on operational or shortly-to-be operational renewable energy projects. The reactions have been very strong and the argumentation against this 'emergency' tax refers not only to the damage the RES sector will have, as this tax could work as an incentive against investing in RES, but also to the fact that the special solidarity levy will be calculated on the turnover of companies active in the renewable energy business and not based on profits at all. The duration of this taxation mechanism had been set for two years, with an extension possibility of one more year, namely until 2015. This however has not been forwarded as new measures were adopted in 2014 with the implementation of the so-called 'New Deal'.

More specifically in Law 4093/2012 a 25 percent, 27 percent and 30 percent tax on the turnover of photovoltaic electricity producers was foreseen, while another 10 percent was imposed on the turnover of all other RES and combined heat and power (CPH) stations. The differentiation of the percentages is related to the concluded FITs accordingly, depending on the respective time frame of the connection of the solar park to the grid. The higher the FIT a solar park had secured upon agreement with the system operator for the next 20 years for the energy produced and supplied to the network, the higher the percentage of the special solidarity levy. Furthermore, Law 4093/2012, apart from the crucial percentages mentioned above, included drastic measures in order to accelerate the completion of projects already licensed but not yet constructed and connected to the grid.

Moreover, following the significant changes introduced by Law 4093/2012, in May 2013 the Greek Parliament adopted Law 4152/2013 (Government's Gazette A' 107), according to which the percentages of the special solidarity levy were further increased reaching up to 42 percent of the turnover of businesses active in the production of energy from photovoltaics on top of VAT. The scale of the taxation as a result was readjusted from 25 percent, 27 percent and 30 percent to 34 percent, 37 percent, 40 percent and 42 percent of the revenues exhausting in this way PV producers, making their business inexpedient and unsustainable.

The rationale behind the backdated taxation was to address the €370 million deficit of the Market Operator caused by the now defunct but back then most generous in Europe FiT regime. It is however already recognized from government cycles and it is proven by the introduction of further measures—such as the suspension of new PV projects up to yearend 2013 and the above-mentioned increase of the taxation percentages—that the special solidarity levy as a measure was not able to address the deficit problem and had no dynamic nor substantiated legal basis to be implemented on a permanent basis. Not only that, the de facto retroactive character of this measure collides with a basic principle of any good RES governance: the need for predictability and legal safety of the investment environment. Additionally, it is of paramount importance to note when exploring the rationale of this backdated taxation, that the deficit is not attributed solely to FIT subsidies, but also to the method the operator used for calculating an artificially low wholesale price of electricity for all generators.

5.6   THE 'NEW DEAL' ON RES

The special solidarity levy measure was followed by the highly debated 'New Deal' on RES which was voted for by the Greek Parliament in March 2014. This new framework has been designed with the target of achieving the complete elimination of the RES Special Account, namely the elimination of the deficit with which the Electricity Market Operator (LAGIE) is confronted. The Greek RES market has been redesigned via the significant changes introduced via Law 4254/2014 (Government's Gazette A' 85). More specifically the new measures adopted by the Greek government involved:

1. New reductions in FITs for all operating RES projects: As far as PV installations are concerned, an average 30 percent reduction compared with the initial tariffs is applied. In more detail, an average 30 percent reduction compared with the initial tariffs is implemented with the justification argumentation for the calculation of the reduction taking into consideration a number of factors, among which, the technology used, the time frame when the development took place, the cost of the installation, the location, as well as whether the project has received a grant from the State. In cases of projects which have received such aids, the cuts in the FITs are even sharper. A smoother FIT reduction is applicable for smaller PV projects up to 20 kW (those not installed on buildings) and for projects owned by farmers under the condition that they not exceed 100 kW each. Lastly, wind and hydro projects have been treated in the 'New Deal' more generously and have been subject to a much smaller FIT reduction of 5–6 percent on average.

2. A 20–37.5 percent contribution of the energy producers' income as a discount towards the Electricity Market Operator (LAGIE), depending on the date of electrification of the respective projects. To this point, it is important to highlight that RES producers were obliged to comply with this measure within two months after the enactment of the new Law, otherwise LAGIE was allowed to suspend the power purchase agreements.
3. A seven year extension of the duration of the power purchase agreements (PPAs): Upon completion of the contract duration of current PPAs with LAGIE, these are extended for another seven years in order to counterbalance the significant reduction of the FIT. In particular, after the expiration of the current PPAs, all RES plants that in January 2014 had been operating for less than 12 years were given two options; either to sell the generated power pursuant to a methodology that will be determined by a decision of the Ministry of Environment, Energy and Climate Change and according to the current market rules, or to sell at a fixed price of 90 €/MWh for energy, which does not exceed an annual limit calculated on the basis of the following formula: installed capacity multiplied by the performance energy ratio (as determined for each type of RES technology).
4. Removal of the suspension of the licensing procedure for new photovoltaic power stations as imposed via Ministerial Decisions. However, an upper limit for RES capacity to be installed per year under the FIT system is set. For PV projects particularly, this limit is at 200 MW per year until 2020. In that respect, it is noted that the new parks to be connected yearly can be selected through a tender procedure.

The enactment of the 'New Deal' has been one more effort to address the immense deficit of the Market Operator, this time via more drastic measures. The prognosis is that the above referred to measures included in the currently applicable framework are the ones to lead to the complete elimination of the deficit by the end of 2014. What is of particular interest however, relates to the timing at which the New Deal has been adopted. As analyzed in the next section, the previous RES legal framework in Greece included the special solidarity levy, a retroactive taxation measure with a two-year duration. The latter has been brought before the Greek Supreme Court by RES producers arguing that this levy is a retroactive taxation measure not compatible with both European legislation and the Greek Constitution. Though the Supreme Court rejected the argumentation of the RES producers, interestingly enough this decision followed the release of the New Deal, via which the special levy has been abolished, while the special levy for 2013 was forecasted to be recalculated on the basis of the income resulting following the above-mentioned discount.

5.7 LEGITIMACY OF THE 'SPECIAL SOLIDARITY LEVY' AND ITS IMPACT ON RES INVESTMENTS: THE RULING OF THE SUPREME COURT

The controversial Law 4093/2012 bundled many unpopular measures within the context of austerity aiming at the reduction of the deficit. Among these measures is the renewables legislation, which penalizes solar much more heavily than other forms of renewable energy. An initial assessment of this Law—which imposes taxes on revenue, rather than profits, of up to 30 percent on all solar installations since July 2012 and 10 percent on all renewable energy businesses and combined heat and power (CPH) stations—raised according to the RES electricity producers' advocates issues of legitimacy and compatibility not only with EU Law but also with the Greek Constitution. The special solidarity levy was argued to infringe the philosophy of the recent quasi-binding EU communication against the retroactive modification of the framework under which renewable providers produce energy. According to this EU Communication the aim needs to be the improvement of the support schemes for the deployment of RES and more precisely:

> Complicated authorization procedures, the lack of one-stop-shops, the creation of registration procedures, planning processes that may take months or years and fear of retroactive changes to support schemes, increase project risk. Such high risks, particularly, in countries with stressed capital markets, result in a very high cost of capital, raising the cost of renewable energy projects and undermining their competitiveness.[13]

Additionally, it has also been argued that the specific regulation could be considered a selective tax, that is, a tax adopted to solve a particular deficit problem. Selective taxes are prohibited by EU law, but can be implemented if the EU is notified and gives its approval. It could therefore be supported that the specific tax measure constitutes state aid within the meaning of Article 107 (1) TFEU.[14] Coming to a possible violation of the Greek constitution, this claim refers first to the infringement of the right to property (Article 17). Investors in RES could not have known that they would be taxed on revenue rather than profit. Whether one accepts the government's argument about the role played by subsidies in the deficit or not, investors can argue that this is a problem related to poor planning by the government rather than something they should be held responsible for, especially since they are already charged with a 40 percent tax on profit (solar parks). Second, in order for this measure to comply with the principle of proportionality (Article 25, para. 1), it is required that the State proves with justified figures and data analysis that this was the only possible remedy to the problem.

In late 2013, a group of companies owning photovoltaic parks in Greece brought the special solidarity levy case before the Greek Supreme Court under the 'pilot trial' procedure provided for in Law 4055/2012 (Government's Gazette A' 51) questioning the legitimacy of the enacted measure and raising compatibility issues with both national and European Law. Law 3900/2010 introducing the pilot trial mechanism allows for a case normally brought before the Administrative Courts to be sent to the Supreme Court, because there is no previous case law and the decision of the Supreme Court will be considered as guidance for the Administrative Courts. This was exactly the special solidarity levy case, as hundreds of RES producers had lodged to the Administrative Courts their complaints about the legitimacy of the measure and requested the full payment for the electricity produced prior to the imposition of the levy. The Supreme Court released its decision (No. 2406/2014) in June 2014, with Law 4254/2014 (New Deal) already introduced and changing the contractual terms for the operation photovoltaic parks.

Coming to the substance of the ruling of the Supreme Court, it rejected the incompatibility argument, arguing in favor of the measure as a tax measure compatible with the Greek Constitution and European Law with the following justification:

1. The levy is an emergency tax measure, within the concept of taxation policy enacted at times of austerity and justified by national interest, which is considered to be in this case the protection of the final energy consumer, who would be burdened with extra charges imposed in order to face the deficit.
2. The specific tax measure can burden a specific category of electricity producers as taxpayers, since this is justified if the taxable asset allows the burden of this particular cycle taxpayers.
3. The special solidarity levy has the character of a tax imposed on transactions, since it is imposed on the amount resulting from the transaction, in other words, on pre-tax price of electricity sales as injected from the electricity production system or grid.

Further on, the Supreme Court argued that having Power Purchase Agreements (PPAs) concluding the sale of electricity at the price fixed by law does not mean it is tax-free and it cannot be held that the provisions of Law 4093/2012 are in breach with Article 5 para. 1 of the Constitution, while not violating the constitutional principle of legitimate expectations of the citizen to the state. Moreover, the reasoning arguing an infringement of the provisions of Articles 15, 16 and 17 of the Charter of Fundamental Rights of the European Union on freedom of occupation and the right to work, free enterprise and the right to property is rejected as having no legal ground. Lastly, the levy is traced back on electricity sales from July 1, 2012 and is not contrary to paragraph 2 of Article 78 of the Constitution and constitutes an acceptable restriction on property within the meaning of Article 1 of the First Additional Protocol to the European Convention on Human Rights.

To this point and as a concluding part of this research it is very interesting to look into a recent ruling of the High Court in the UK on *Breyer Group Plc & Ors* v. *Department of Energy & Climate Change*. In this recent case 14 British solar and construction companies achieved victory against the government claiming damages due to unlawful policy changes to FIT regime introduced in 2011. These companies are seeking £132 million in compensation from the Department of Energy and Climate Change arising from the retrospectively introduced early cuts to the FITs, which had devastated the fledgling industry, led to chaotic trading conditions, shattered consumer confidence and caused thousands of redundancies. The £132 million claim reflects the extent of commercial damage inflicted by the government's policy mismanagement in 2011, while the exact damages awarded will be decided according to the value of contracts lost as a result of the government's illegal actions. To conclude, the *Breyer Group Plc & Ors* v. *Department of Energy & Climate Change* case has been a novel case for the solar industry for two main reasons: first, human rights violations were introduced in relation to compensation for commercial losses suffered by solar firms and second, contracts for solar projects relying on FITs qualified as 'possessions'. The signed or concluded contracts represented an element of the marketable goodwill in the claimants' businesses and therefore are 'possessions' for the purposes of Article 1 Protocol 1 of the European Convention on Human Rights. The Court found that the measures applying retrospective changes to FITs in 2011 amounted to an 'unlawful interference' with these possessions that was not justified. Therefore, the photovoltaic companies are in principle entitled to just satisfaction for damages suffered as a result of this interference.

5.8   CONCLUSION

The European Union considers itself as a forerunner in climate protection and indeed, the EU is so far the only geopolitical region that has adopted a binding unilateral greenhouse gas emission reduction target for 2020.[15] The energy sector constitutes a cornerstone for economic development with tremendous impact not only on a national but also a Union level and it is therefore an indispensable need for it to be viewed as such in the Greek case too. The economic turmoil is not a national issue, but has a European dimension which makes the role of the policies to be adopted even more crucial, being the prerequisites for the fulfillment of the objectives set by the EU for 2020 and beyond.

Renewable energy sources can play an important role in boosting Greece's economy taking into consideration the country's high RES potential.[16] It is estimated that one-third of Greece's energy requirements could be met with solar energy while experts believe that the market will grow impressively and have a value of more than 4 billion Euros in just few years.[17] Via the measures enacted, solar got the biggest hit, however, up to 2012 it enjoyed the most favorable FIT regime in Europe, overcompensating RES electricity producers and leading therefore to the creation of an immense deficit of the electricity market operator.

The financial crisis is a major turbulence with a variety of aspects influencing among other sectors energy too. With respect to the case of Greece, the impact of the recession is unfortunately assessed on a background of an unstable political environment and governance characterized by chronic systemic problems of corruption, bureaucracy, anti-reform mentality and lack of central planning. Today's economic hardship however leaves no margin for any more mistakes. Greece has no other choice but to work hard to correct the inefficiencies of the past and grow. The recent belated measures adopted by the Greek Parliament within the austerity context so as to reduce the deficit, are considered to be the last resort of the State in an effort to strike a balance between the detected ineffectiveness of the previous framework and the loopholes of the RES market design.

To conclude, the aim of this study was to present the significance of a consistent energy policy and taxation framework at times of recession, as a condition which guarantees green progress and the effective implementation of the EU targets for 2020 and beyond. The example of Greece and the recent developments concerning RES governance was chosen as an indicative case study of a country being at the center of attention not only due to its high potential for the deployment of RES but mainly because of the impact of the economic crisis on the RES market and the experience gained by the sequence of the measures enacted at times of austerity.

NOTES

1. PhD Candidate, University of Eastern Finland. Attorney at Law, LL.M. (Competition Law and Economics—European Regulation of Network Industries, University of Bonn) at the Regulatory Authority for Energy (RAE) in Greece (International Affairs & Energy Planning Department).
2. The global financial crisis and its impact on renewable energy finance. April 2009. UNEP, SEFI, new energy finance, Frankfurt School of Finance and Management—Bankakademie HfB.
3. OECD (2011). Towards Green Growth. OECD, Paris.
4. van der Ploeg, R. and Withagen, C. (2012). Green Growth, Green Paradox and the Global Economic Crisis. *Environmental Innovation and Societal Transitions*, **12**, 14–30.
5. Butler, L. and Neuhoff, K. (2004). Comparison of feed-in tariff, quota and auction mechanisms to support wind power development. Working Paper 70, CMI, 2004.
6. Radowitz, B., Hromako, J. and Moloney, L. (2010). Renewable investors fear withdrawal of subsidies, retrieved from http://online.wsj.com/article/SB10001424052748703 649004575437131517120738.html (accessed August 19, 2010).
7. Johnson, S. (2011). Investors may walk after Spain's solar cut, retrieved from http://www.ft.com/intl/cms/s/0/a2982e50-1a95-11e0-b100-00144feab49a (accessed January 9, 2011).
8. Hofman Daan, M. and Huisman, R. (2012). Did the financial crisis lead to changes in private equity investor preferences regarding renewable energy and climate policies?, retrieved from http://fsinsight.org/docs/download/hofman-huisman-renewable-energy.pdf (accessed April 11, 2012.
9. YPEKA (2010). Law 3851/2010 Accelerating the Development of Renewable Energy Sources to Deal with Climate Change and Other Regulations Addressing Issues Under the Authority of the Ministry of Environment, Energy and Climate Change. Official translation of Law 3851/2010 in English, retrieved from http://www.ypeka.gr/LinkClick.aspx?fileticket=qtiW90JJLYs%3D&tabid=37 (accessed April 21, 2015).
10. Especially for Greece, the target for the non-emission-trading green- house gas emissions is a 4 percent reduction compared with 2005 levels and 18 percent penetration of renewables in gross final consumption.
11. Greek Energy (2012). Special Edition for the Greek Energy Market and the involving enterprises. Energy Press 2012, retrieved from http://issuu.com/citroniogr/docs/greekenergy2012_mockup/1?e=3814280/11494158 (in Greek).
12. The Greek Energy Roadmap to 2050 (2012), retrieved from http://www.energia.gr/article_en.asp?art_id=25871 (accessed April 3, 2012).
13. COM (2012) 271. Communication from the Commission to the European Parliament, the Council, the European Economic and Social Committee and the Committee of the Regions. Renewable Energy: a major player in the European energy market. Brussels, June 6, 2012.
14. Xeniti, E.A. and Mersinia, I.D. (2013). News from the Member States: Greece, 'Special Solidarity Levy' Imposed on RES Producers: A Selective State Aid? European State Aid Law Quarterly, Issue 3/2013.
15. At the Spring Summit in March 2007, the European Council agreed upon an ambitious climate policy with unilateral greenhouse gas emissions reductions in 2020 by at least 20 percent compared with 1990 levels. This target was put into legal force in December 2008 upon mutual agreement between the European Council, the European Parliament, and the European Commission.
16. Schubert, T. (2011). Could solar help avert Greek tragedy? *Renewable Energy Focus*, September/October 2011 (pp. 16–18).
17. Souladaki, V. (2012). Energy as an Opportunity for Tackling the Greek Economic Crisis. *Journal of Energy Security*, retrieved from http://www.ensec.org/index.php?option=com_content&view=article&id=388:energy-as-an-opportunity-for-tackling-the-Greek-economic-crisis&catid=130:issue-content&Itemid=405 (accessed November 21, 2010).

PART II

The challenges of subsidies

6. Reforming fossil fuel subsidies: will it make a difference?

Malgorzata Kicia and Manfred Rosenstock[1]

6.1 INTRODUCTION AND BACKGROUND

Environmentally harmful subsidies (EHS) occur across different sectors and take different forms. The most obvious ones are direct budgetary grants and tax reductions or exemptions, but there also exist more indirect ones, such as: concessionary loans at reduced interest rates; state guarantees below costs; lack of full cost pricing; indirect support by for example financing infrastructure; or reducing liability for environmental disasters. They lead to a double damage: environmental and economic. They induce inefficient production and consumption choices resulting in higher levels of waste, emissions, resource extraction, or negative impacts on biodiversity.

Economic theory states that providing a subsidy to any product on the market will have a distorting effect, unless it is introduced to correct an externality. Beneficiaries of the subsidy will increase their demand for the product, other sectors of the economy will face a lower demand and the overall efficiency will fall. With producer subsidies, costs of production are lowered, production is increased or sustained for those who produce 'on the margin' and the companies have fewer incentives to innovate. An additional distortion will occur through the government's need to finance the subsidy, which it can do by increasing taxes or social security contributions. The former will reduce households' purchasing power or the ability of companies to invest, the latter will result in lower incentive to work or to hire labour.[2] From a budgetary point of view, many such subsidies also lead to inefficient use of scarce public resources, especially in the fields where the subsidies original rationale is no longer applicable.

EHS also undermine EU energy, climate and environmental policies, lock us into inefficient technologies and business structures, and hinder investment in green technologies. Therefore, they delay the transition towards a more resource-efficient low-carbon economy. User subsidies benefiting specific sectors or social groups are often inefficient from a social policy perspective. As they are often provided in a form of lower tax rates, rebates or exemptions with respect to VAT and excise taxes, poor households for example benefit less from tax rebates on energy than rich ones. The International Monetary Fund (IMF) estimated that 80 per cent of subsidies to petrol in 2009 went to 40 per cent of the richest households.[3]

There are however various social, political or strategic reasons behind particular subsidies which will be addressed below. For example access to heating is crucial and therefore subsidising low income families by making energy affordable to them can be justified. Furthermore, local, regional or national employment concerns are raised to justify support to energy intensive industries. Support to certain groups (farmers, fishermen) often serves to gain political support.

After a short analysis of how the reform of environmentally harmful subsidies is addressed in various strategic documents at EU level, we will present conclusions from recent research projects led by the Commission and their implications for policy development. The projects were looking at the impact of removing fossil fuel subsidies on carbon emissions, employment and budgetary revenues. The chapter will also discuss different methodological approaches towards definitions of a subsidy and will show how they influence data collection and final figures.

Furthermore, it will discuss how the revised rules on state aid in the European Union address the issue of fossil-fuel subsidies and environmentally harmful subsidies in general.

6.2   EHS REFORM IN POLITICAL STRATEGIES

The reform of environmentally harmful subsidies has figured high on the political agenda for a number of years, both in the EU and internationally.

6.2.1   Europe 2020

At the EU level, the Europe 2020 Strategy[4] adopted in 2010 and its flagship initiative *A resource efficient Europe* from 2011 were conceived as a means to exit from the financial crisis and prepare the EU economy for the challenges of the next decade, in particular the transformation towards a sustainable and competitive economy. They list phasing out of environmentally harmful subsidies and limiting them to people with social needs as one of the measures the Member State should undertake. The 'Roadmap to a resource efficient Europe'[5] adopted within the flagship initiative sets the milestone that 'by 2020 EHS will be phased out, with due regard to the impact on people in need'. To do so, Member States were called upon to identify the most significant EHS, prepare plans and timetables to phase out EHS and report on these as part of their National Reform Programmes (NRPs).

Some Member States have undertaken such measures: Finland in its 2014 NRP, announces that it will remove and re-allocate environmentally harmful subsidies. The German 2014 NRP[6] mentions that in the context of the tax subsidies report, the federal government will review more strictly whether measures are sustainable. Lithuania published a study that gives an overview of types and amounts of EHS in 2014 and includes recommendations for reform.[7]

The Commission has been following up on this via the annual European Semester.[8] The Annual Growth Surveys have regularly listed the phasing out of environmentally harmful subsidies as one of the priorities and a tool for a growth friendly fiscal consolidation.[9] In 2014, for the first time, Member States: France,[10] Belgium[11] and Italy[12] were given a Country-Specific Recommendation (CSR) by the European Council in this respect. The Commission follows up the implementation of these CSRs and reports on them.

6.2.2 'Sectoral' Policy Documents and the EU Budget

While Europe 2020 is the EU's overall economic reform strategy, EHS reform also figures in the more specific policy strategies.

The EU 7th Environmental Action Programme[13] which will guide EU policy action on environment and climate policy for the next seven years calls for establishing the right conditions to ensure that environmental externalities are adequately addressed. This involves applying the polluter-pays principle more systematically, in particular through phasing out environmentally harmful subsidies at Union and Member State level. Member States are also requested to report on their actions in their NRPs.

The avoidance of environmentally harmful subsidies also figures in the EU's medium-term financial framework, inter alia the reforms of the Common Agricultural and Fisheries Policies and in the new Cohesion Policy instruments.

6.2.3 State Aid Rules

On the basis of Articles 107–109 of the EU Treaty, the Commission assesses Member States projects for granting State aid. To operationalize these provisions, it has adopted a number of guidelines with specific rules for different types of aid. The Commission's State Aid Modernization (SAM) exercise calls for a phasing out of subsidies that are environmentally harmful or leading to inefficient resource use. This general principle has been translated into more concrete provisions, in particular the revised Guidelines on State aid for environmental protection and energy,[14] which entered into force in July 2014.

While, like the previous environmental aid guidelines, they focus on rules for environmentally beneficial subsidies, such as those for investments going beyond EU environmental standards or for the promotion of renewable energy sources, they also contain a number of provisions that might, at first sight, be considered to condone environmentally harmful subsidies.

In its introduction, these Guidelines recall the political commitments given in the EU strategies by emphasizing the need to consider negative impacts of environmentally harmful subsidies, while taking into account the need to address trade-offs between different areas and policies as recognized by the flagship initiative for *A resource efficient Europe*. Aid for the extraction of fossil fuels is not included in these Guidelines.

More concretely, this concerns, for example, reductions of environmental taxes for energy-intensive industries which are permitted when the application of the full rate would seriously affect their competitiveness. However, either the minimum tax level fixed by the Energy Products Taxation Directive must be respected or the derogation must be linked to the conclusion of agreements between the government and the companies, which makes the state aid conditional on the companies reaching specific energy or environmental targets within a fixed time schedule. In this case, regular monitoring and penalty arrangements must also be fixed in the agreement. The guidelines specify that the targets of the agreement must have the same effect in terms of environmental or energy-efficiency benefit as the application of the minimum tax rates under EU legislation would have.

The logic of such aid is that without the application of such special rules there is a risk that the industries that would be most affected by the full tax would relocate outside the EU. Furthermore, such derogations will allow the application of higher general tax rates, thus ensuring overall environmental benefits.

While usually such aid has been granted in the past by reducing applicable tax rates for the beneficiaries, the revised guidelines specifically point to the possibility of grant fixed levels of annual compensation. This option would have the advantage of maintaining the marginal incentive to reduce pollution or emissions in its entirety and thus be more effective, both from an economic and environmental perspective.

Another case in point is State aid for so-called capacity mechanisms, in other words, for electricity generation capacity that can back up renewables with fluctuating output, such as wind or solar. This might involve aid for fossil fuels, but it also increases the attractiveness of expanding renewable sources. Furthermore, the guidelines stress that preference should be given to demand-side management and interconnectors instead of such aid.

There are also other guidelines, such as those for aid to projects of common European interest (IPCEI) that contain provisions against EHS, while the Council decision on State aid to coal mines phases out these long-standing aids to cover the current operating losses of coal production until 2018, limited to coal production units which are part of a closure plan.[15] References also figure in the guidelines for aid for research and development.

6.2.4 The International Dimension

On the international scene, pledges on subsidy reform have also been made at high-level events such as the G20 meeting in Pittsburgh in September 2009, the 10th Conference of Parties to the Convention on Biodiversity in Nagoya, October 2010 and the Rio+20 conference in June 2012.[16]

6.3 WAYS TO TACKLE SUBSIDIES

Despite repeated and long-lasting calls to phase out EHS, action at the national level is still unsatisfactory. There are a number of reasons for this. Limited transparency of information on their magnitude and scope reduces the basis for concrete debates. Many of the subsidies are not visible in budgetary bills, such as tax exemptions, not reported (for example local charges) or not even recognized. Additionally, a number of those tax exemptions are foreseen by the EU legislation and some Member States do not report on them. Finally, Member States might want to maintain such subsidies, as they have been introduced because of social, strategic or competitiveness reasons (see above).

There are claims that the lack of a widely agreed definition of EHS makes the phase out impossible. However, in the absence of a perfect definition, a pragmatic approach consists in using a workable definition and then focusing on concrete measures. Among several attempts to define EHS, one proposed by the OECD and broadened by Withana et al.[17] serves the purpose well:

> [A] result of a government action or non-action[18] that confers an advantage on consumers or producers, in order to supplement their income or lower their costs, but in doing so, discriminates against sound environmental practices.

Taking a selective approach towards subsidies and narrowing the scope of analysis and action to one sector can be a promising solution. The OECD has successfully followed this approach and focused the research on sub-sidies in the energy sector, and fossil-fuel subsidies (FFS) in particular, basing itself on the G-20 commitment mentioned above. They are easier to identify and quantify and this is the area where contradictions with climate and resource-efficiency objectives are most evident. The OECD also employed a more restrictive definition of subsidies and only collected data on 'both direct budgetary expenditures and tax expenditures that in some way provide a benefit or preference for fossil fuel production or con-sumption relative to alternatives'.[19]

FFS are of a significant scale – the IMF estimates that on a post-tax basis, they were worth USD 1.9 trillion worldwide in 2011 (2.5 per cent of global GDP or 8 per cent of total government revenues). For the EU 27 Member States, budgetary support and tax expenditures to fossil fuel, reached €25.2 billion in 2011, as the OECD and the Institute for Environmental Studies (IVM, 2013)[20] research demonstrates and this figure reflects the OECD's above-mentioned restrictive approach. These calculations are based, however, on Member State assessments of what constitutes a fossil-fuel subsidy, and so coverage varies between Member States: IVM (2014)[21] using a harmonized methodology estimated public support to fossil fuels as €35.8 billion in the 28 Member States of the EU in 2011.

It's important to note here that the bulk of FFS in the EU is granted in a form of tax exemptions and rebates to energy users (both industry and households) whereas producer subsidies dominate outside the EU, in par-ticular in developing countries. This is not surprising given that extraction of hydrocarbons is limited to a few Member States. State-aid to coal mines in the EU, while accounting for more than half of OECD-wide support to coal production, seems more of a temporary issue now as it will need to be phased out by the end of 2018 on the basis of the relevant state aid regulation (see above).

However, we might see some increase in the share of producer subsidies with the development of onshore shale gas activities. In 2014, for example, Poland offered six-year tax breaks to the shale gas industry to speed up exploration work and reduce the country's reliance on Russian gas.[22] In the 2013 Autumn Statement, the UK confirmed tax breaks to all onshore oil and gas explorers (not just those looking for shale gas) to attract 'billions of pounds of investment'[23] and create jobs. Security of supply and job creation concerns prevail in the argumentation defending support to pro-ducers, others being high costs, long project timelines and capital intensity.

In case of industrial sectors, agriculture or fisheries, reduced energy taxes are often claimed to be a precondition to stay on the market. In the EU, where the energy market is liberalized and price stabilization schemes are not applied, tax reductions are the easiest way to reduce the cost of energy.[24]

6.4   RECENT RESEARCH ON FOSSIL FUEL SUBSIDIES

6.4.1   Data Collection/Inventory

So far the most comprehensive collection of fossil-fuel subsidies has been published by the OECD in 2012 (updated in 2013) and was complemented in 2013 by the Commission to cover those six Member States that are not OECD Member Countries and Croatia which joined the EU in 2013. The inventory is limited to two forms of subsidies only – budgetary support and tax expenditures.

Nevertheless, it sheds a light on the mechanisms and scale of support, most of which is support to consumers (both private and business): in 2011 the EU Member States spent 0.01 to 0.58 per cent of their GDP on fossil fuel subsidies which makes €25.2 billion in the region (or 0.2 per cent of the EU GDP). Data in Table 6.1 compares budgetary spending on fossil fuels with revenues from environmental taxation. In some Member States more than a quarter of revenues generated by environmental taxes 'finance' subsidies potentially harmful to environment. This demonstrates policy inconsistency. Energy and other environmental taxes (75 per cent of which in revenue terms are taxes on energy) provide incentives to reduce emissions over time to meet the agreed EU environmental and energy objectives, while fossil-fuel subsidies give the opposite incentive.

The OECD and the Commission data served as an input to modelling[25] where the objective was to analyse the macroeconomic effects of phasing out fossil fuel subsidies in the EU as a whole and in Member States: impact on GDP, employment, energy consumption and CO_2 emissions.

Figure 6.1 presents results[26] at the European level and shows where the changes in GDP come from. Phased out subsidies are injected back into the national economies in the form of reductions in the standard rate of income tax – the subsidy removal and revenue recycling balance out and the extra benefits come from removing inefficient subsidies given to producers and from reducing fossil fuel imports. Once the secondary multiplier effects are taken into account, a net yearly increase in GDP of €9.3 billion (in 2005 prices) is realized for 2014 (€49 billion by 2020). The reform would bring about benefits without any additional financing needs.

A more detailed analysis at the Member State level demonstrates in nearly all cases that removing subsidies to fossil fuels has a small, rarely

*Table 6.1   Fossil fuel subsidies per Member State in relation to GDP and
environmental taxes*

	FFS	%GDP	Env taxes	% ENV taxes
Austria	392.4	0.13%	7,324.0	5.36%
Belgium	2,138.8	0.58%	8,342.4	25.64%
Bulgaria	35.9	0.09%	1,051.2	3.41%
Cyprus	20.0	0.11%	506.0	3.95%
Czech Rep	161.6	0.10%	3,571.0	4.53%
Denmark	982.2	0.41%	9,445.9	10.40%
Estonia	75.1	0.46%	426.0	17.62%
Finland	106.9	0.06%	4,975.0	2.15%
France	2,753.9	0.14%	35,919.0	7.67%
Germany	5,095.2	0.20%	54,669.0	9.32%
Greece	208.0	0.10%	5,488.0	3.79%
Hungary	332.2	0.34%	2,545.3	13.05%
Ireland	78.2	0.05%	3,689.9	2.12%
Italy	2,124.0	0.13%	40,424.6	5.25%
Latvia	106.2	0.53%	432.8	24.54%
Lithuania	50.8	0.16%	512.2	9.92%
Luxembourg	3.7	0.01%	958.0	0.38%
The Netherlands	339.3	0.06%	23,536.0	1.44%
Poland	783.9	0.21%	9,157.9	8.56%
Portugal	143.3	0.08%	4,306.4	3.33%
Romania	153.7	0.12%	2,502.8	6.14%
Slovakia	164.9	0.24%	1,230.1	13.41%
Slovenia	140.5	0.39%	1,290.7	10.88%
Spain	1,865.3	0.18%	17,333.0	10.76%
Sweden	2,111.930	0.55%	9,551.0	22.09%
United Kingdom	4,804.9	0.27%	44,608.6	10.77%
EU-26	25,172.9	0.20%	292,786,30	

Note: Data for 2011 in millions of euros, conversion rate for national currencies into EUR
is the average 2011 ECB exchange rate, no data for Malta are available, Croatia not yet a
Member State in 2011.

Sources: OECD, Eurostat, own calculations.

higher than 0.1 per cent, positive impact on national GDP. In almost all
cases, final energy consumption falls, by as much as 2 per cent of the
national level. Consequently the potential reduction in energy-related CO_2
emissions is of a similar magnitude.

In terms of environmental impacts, the exact size of reductions in
CO_2 emissions depends on the behavioural responses; CO_2 emissions are

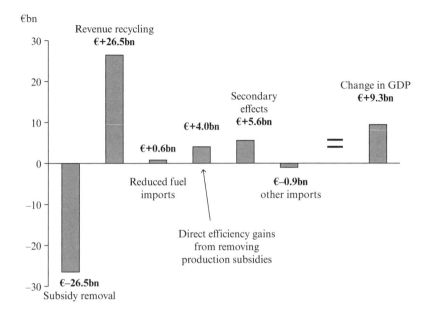

Figure 6.1   EU GDP changes as a result of the phasing out of FFS

estimated to fall by 0.5 per cent by 2020. Reduction in primary energy consumption is expected to be of a similar scale in the region.

Similarly, in most individual cases, a small increase in overall employment is observed, however the aggregate results indicate that there could be an adverse impact on vulnerable groups, such as the low-skilled workers which might require additional flanking measures under social policy.

6.4.2   Overcoming Limitations of the OECD Methodology

The OECD measured relative support within the context of the country's tax system, which made a comparison across countries impossible. For example, a country that applies high rates of taxation to fossil-fuel end products and wants to limit their impact on industrial competitiveness by differentiating tax rates, may have higher measured support to fossil fuels[27] than a country with lower but uniform excise-tax rates.

Beyond this issue, the OECD study also revealed that the coverage of certain types of subsidies differs significantly between Member States: some of them do not perceive certain measures as subsidies, for example, tax exemptions imposed by the Energy Tax Directive or international agreements, while others report on them. This reduces the information value of the data in the inventory. Table 6.2 shows categories of

Table 6.2   Categories of energy support identified in the OECD (2013) and IVM (2013) reports

Member State	Specific sectors							Specific fuels		Households	
	Commercial aviation (domestic)	Commercial shipping (domestic)	Public transport; railways; taxis	Large energy users; energy intensive industry	Agriculture (incl. horticulture)	CHP and district heating	Other sectors	Difference between diesel and petrol	Exemption or reduction for e.g., LPG, LNG	Energy and excise taxes	Value Added Tax (VAT)
Austria	X	X	€	€	€	€	—	—	—	—	—
Belgium	—	X	€/X	€/X	€	—	€	—	—	€	X
Bulgaria	—	—	—	—	€	—	—	—	—	€	—
Croatia	—	—	—	—	—	—	—	—	—	—	—
Cyprus	X	X	X	—	€	X	X	—	—	X	—
Czech Republic	X	X	X	—	X	€	—	—	€	€	—
Denmark	X	—	—	X	€	€	€/X	€	—	—	X
Estonia	X	€	—	€	€/X	€	€/X	—	—	€	X
Finland	€	€	€	€	€	€	€/X	€	X	€	—
France	€	X	€	€	€	€	€	€	€	€	€/X
Germany	€	€	—	€	€	X	€	—	€	X	—
Greece	—	—	€	—	€	—	—	—	—	X	X
Hungary	—	—	€	—	€	—	—	—	—	—	€

Ireland	–!	–!	–	–	–	–	–	–	–!	–	–	–	–	X
Italy	–!	€	€	€	–	€	X	€	–!	€	€	X	X	X
Latvia	€	€	–	–	–	€	X	€	–!	€	€	X	X	€
Lithuania	X	–	X	–	–	X	€	–	–!	X	X	€	X	X
Luxembourg	–	–	–	–	–	€	–	–	–!	–	–	€	€	X
Malta	X	X	–	–!	–	–	X	–	–!	–	–	–	X	X
Netherlands	X	–!	X	X	X	X	X	X	–!	€	€	€	X	–
Poland	X	X	X	X	€	€	X	X	X	X	X	X	X	X
Portugal	–!	€	€	€/X	€	€	€	€	–!	X	€	€	€	–
Romania	X	X	€	–	€	€	€	–	–!	–	–	X	X	X
Slovakia	–!	€	X	X	€	€	–	–	–!	€	€	€	€	–
Slovenia	€	€	X	–	€	€	€	–	–!	€	€	–	–	–
Spain	€	€	X	–	€	€	€	–	–!	€	€	€	–	–
Sweden	€	€	€	€	€	€	€	€	€	€	€	€	€	€
United Kingdom	–	–	–	–	X	–	–	–	–	–	–	–	–	€

Note: (X = reported: € = reported and quantified; – = not reported; –! = not reported, but known to exist).

Source: Oosterhuis et al. (IVM, 2014).

energy support identified in the OECD (2013) and IVM (2013) and their status.

To overcome those limitations and to allow meaningful comparisons between Member States a study undertaken for the Commission by IVM[28] proposes a harmonized methodology to reporting on fossil fuel subsidies across EU Member States. For this purpose, the study reports on certain types of tax expenditures and budgetary expenditures in all Member States, regardless of whether they are defined as subsidies in those Member States or not. It also expands coverage of the database by indirect subsidies to fossil fuels such as for example financing infrastructure for fossil fuels (pipelines, storage facilities).

To determine direct public support, budgetary reports and other statistical information were used. To get insight on the scale of tax rebates, and to make a reasonable comparison between Member States, a benchmark was applied. IVM discusses two options and for the purpose of this chapter we will take the more pragmatic one:[29] for taxes on energy use, the proposed rates in the Commission's 2011 proposal for amending the Energy Taxation Directive[30] and for VAT the standard VAT rate as applicable in the respective Member State.

Under such a harmonized approach, levels of subsidies to fossil fuels are in total significantly higher than in the OECD (2013) inventory: fossil fuel subsidies reach €35.8 billion in EU-28 as compared to 25.2 billion reported by the OECD/Commission. The higher figures for 20 Member States come mainly from the fact discussed above, that many Member States do not report on certain measures like for example tax differential between petrol and diesel. For a few Member States[31] we observe lower levels of subsidies granted to fossil fuels, they are mainly those countries whose energy tax design matches the logic of the Commission proposal to revise the Energy Tax Directive from 2011: tax rates reflect the energy content and the CO_2 factor of the fuel. This is one of the benchmarks proposed by IVM.[32]

6.5   CONCLUSIONS

Subsidy reform has been integrated within a number of EU strategy documents which demonstrates the importance the Commission, Council and the EP attach to the problem. Recent research demonstrates that there is a very good economic reason to phase out fossil fuel subsidies. Small, but positive effects on employment levels and energy consumption are observed within Member States contributing to the energy efficiency target[33] and climate policy objectives. The research also shows that EHS reform alone will not ensure reaching these objectives, hence other policies, remain necessary.

The impact on Member State economies is also positive through reductions in both inefficient production subsidies and fossil fuel imports. The reform could also address the issue of fairness, since those subsidies are financed by someone, most often by households and small and medium-sized enterprises. This aspect is not addressed in this chapter but merits further discussion.

Increased transparency of the existing subsidies, their impacts and the distribution of benefits and costs can help to increase social acceptance and weaken the pressure from sectoral lobbies. A number of Member States have made efforts to catalogue their subsidies and make them more transparent: for example, Sweden, Finland and Germany do so on a regular basis, while France and Belgium (Flanders) have started. In the project for a new environmental law, the Italian government plans to establish a catalogue of environmentally harmful subsidies and intends to apply a wide definition of subsidies.[34]

There is no doubt that the OECD inventory triggered a broader discussion on FFS reform among the decision-makers. The current economic context provides a great opportunity for pushing it forward: many Member States need to reduce government spending to balance their budgets. Phasing out tax rebates to fossil fuels could be a solution and this fact is picked up by some Country Specific Recommendations under the European Semester process.

However, transparency alone will not ensure the phasing out of all subsidies. Taking into account the aspect of political feasibility requires the introduction of accompanying policies that facilitate the transition for those that had benefited from the subsidies. Some of the rules of the new environment and energy state aid guidelines demonstrate this approach. Reform also needs to consider the social implications of such action; this fact is reflected in the Commission calls for a reform in the resource-efficiency roadmap. Support must reach only those in need and should not encourage consumption through lower energy prices, but should be granted by means of lump sum payments or allowances linked to the family income, not to energy consumption. Alternative measures to meet societal objectives may deliver more cost-effective and efficient solutions to achieving policy goals; these could include measures to increase energy efficiency.

NOTES

1. The authors wish to thank their colleague Timo Lehtomaki for helpful comments on the state aid related elements of the chapter.
2. European Commission (2011a).
3. IEA, OECD, World Bank joint report (November 2010).
4. European Commission (2010).
5. European Commission (2011a).
6. German Federal Ministry for Economic Affairs and Energy (2014).
7. Smart Continent Research and Consulting Alliance (2014).
8. The European Semester is a yearly cycle of economic policy coordination where the Commission undertakes a detailed analysis of EU Member States' programmes of economic and structural reforms and proposes recommendations for the next 12–18 months, which the Council then adopts.
9. European Commission (2013).
10. Council of the European Union (2014a).
11. Council of the European Union (2014b).
12. Council of the European Union (2014c).
13. See http://eur-lex.europa.eu/legal-content/EN/TXT/PDF/?uri=CELEX:32013D1386& from=EN (accessed 21 April 2015).
14. European Commission (2014).
15. European Commission (2010).
16. UN (2012).
17. Withana et al. (2012).
18. Non-action can be relieving a sector, certain group or business operators from certain obligations: for example, not applying road pricing to cover costs of roads, not covering risk of accidents (for example, by nuclear operators). As a result social costs are not fully covered.
19. OECD (2013).
20. Oosterhuis F. et al. (2013).
21. Oosterhuis F. et al. (2014).
22. See http://online.wsj.com/articles/SB10001424052702304020104579432993095714468 (accessed 17 November 2014).
23. See http://www.telegraph.co.uk/finance/budget/10498330/Autumn-Statement-Shale-gas-tax-breaks-to-attract-billions-of-pounds-of-investment.html (accessed 5 September 2014).
24. See discussion on state aid above.
25. Cambridge Econometrics (2013).
26. The difference in totals (25.2bn vs. 26.6bn) comes from including reduced VAT rate on electricity in the UK, coal support in Finland and updating data for NL.
27. Sweden can be such an example.
28. IVM (2014).
29. The second choice was the highest tax rate per unit of energy consumption in a given category.
30. European Commission (2011b).
31. Austria, Belgium, Denmark, Germany, Hungary, Sweden and the UK.
32. See Appendix for details.
33. The Commission proposed a new energy efficiency target of 30 per cent for 2030 in its Energy Efficiency Communication, released on 23 July 2014. The Communication assesses the EU's progress towards its 20 per cent energy efficiency goal for 2020 and analyses how energy efficiency can drive competitiveness and strengthen security of supply in the European Union in the future.
34. See http://www.leggioggi.it/allegati/testo-del-ddl-collegato-alla-legge-di-stabilita-2014-ambiente-e-risorse-naturali/ (accessed 15 January 2015).

REFERENCES

Cambridge Econometrics (2013), *Modelling of Milestones for achieving Resource Efficiency: Phasing out Environmentally Harmful Subsidies*, a Report for the European Commission – DG Environment.

Council of the European Union (2010), 2010/787/EU, *Council Decision of 10 December 2010 on State aid to facilitate the closure of uncompetitive coal mines*.

Council of the European Union (2014a), 2014/C 247/09, *Council Recommendation of 8 July 2014 on the National Reform Programme 2014 of France and delivering a Council opinion on the Stability Programme of France*.

Council of the European Union (2014b), (2014/C 247/01), *Council Recommendation of 8 July 2014 on the National Reform Programme 2014 of Belgium and delivering a Council opinion on the Stability Programme of Belgium*.

Council of the European Union (2014c), (2014/C 247/11), *Council Recommendation of 8 July 2014 on the National Reform Programme 2014 of Italy and delivering a Council opinion on the Stability Programme of Italy*.

European Commission (2010), *Europe 2020 A strategy for smart, sustainable and inclusive growth*, COM(2010)2020 final.

European Commission (2011a), *Roadmap for a Resource Efficient Europe*, COM(2011)571 final.

European Commission (2011b), *Proposal for a Council Directive amending Directive 2003/96/EC restructuring the Community framework for the taxation of energy products and electricity*, COM(2011)169 final.

European Commission (2013), *Communication from the Commission. Annual Growth Survey 2014*, COM(2013)800 final.

European Commission (2014), *Guidelines on State aid for environmental protection and energy 2014–2020*, OJ C 200/1 of 28 June 2014.

Federal Ministry for Economic Affairs and Energy (2014), *National Reform Programme 2014*, http://ec.europa.eu/europe2020/pdf/csr2014/nrp2014_germany_en.pdf (accessed 15 January 2015).

http://www.leggioggi.it/allegati/testo-del-ddl-collegato-alla-legge-di-stabilita-2014-ambiente-e-risorse-naturali/ (accessed 15 January 2015): Disposizioni in materia ambientale per promuovere misure di green economy e per il contenimento dell'uso eccessivo di risorse naturali (Environmental provisions to promote green economy and measures to contain the excessive use of natural resources), C/2093.

http://www.telegraph.co.uk/finance/budget/10498330/Autumn-Statement-Shale-gas-tax-breaks-to-attract-billions-of-pounds-of-investment.html (accessed 5 September 2014).

IEA, OECD, World Bank joint report (November 2010), *The scope of fossil-fuel subsidies in 2009 and a roadmap for phasing out fossil-fuel subsidies*.

OECD (2013), *Inventory of Estimated Budgetary Support and Tax Expenditures for Fossil Fuels 2013*, Paris: OECD.

Oosterhuis F. et al. (IVM, 2013), *Budgetary support and tax expenditures for fossil fuels. An inventory for six non-OECD EU countries*, a Report for the European Commission – DG Environment.

Oosterhuis F. et al. (IVM, 2014), *Enhancing comparability of data on estimated budgetary support and tax expenditures for fossil fuels*, a Report for the European Commission – DG Environment, UN (2012), *Report of the United Nations*

Conference on Sustainable Development, Rio de Janeiro, Brazil 20–22 June 2012, http://www.uncsd2012.org/content/documents/814UNCSD%20REPORT%20 final%20revs.pdf (accessed 15 January 2015).

Smart Continent Research and Consulting Alliance (2014): *A study on the 'Naming of environmentally harmful subsidies, and determination of their common values in the tax system setting. Methodology for evaluation of environmentally harmful subsidies'*, Report for the Lithuanian Ministry of the Environment.

Withana, S., ten Brink, P., Mayeres, I., Franckx, L., Hirschnitz-Garbers, M., Porsch, L. and Oosterhuis, F. (2012), *Study supporting the phasing out of environmentally harmful subsidies*, a Report for the European Commission – DG Environment.

APPENDIX

Methodology used in Oosterhuis et al. (2013, IVM)

The following producer subsidies are reported by IVM:

1. **Direct support to primary producers**, mainly restricted to coal mining in a few Member States and being phased out by 2018, driven by EU State Aid rules.
2. **R&D subsidies to the fossil fuels industry**.
3. **Public investment in energy infrastructure**. State aid and **'dual use' subsidies** for infrastructure that could be used both by fossil fuels and for instance biofuels.
4. **Fiscal incentives for oil and gas exploration and exploitation**.

Consumer subsidies usually take the form of tax expenditures and their level is measured against a specified benchmark, for excise taxes and other specific taxes on energy use, the proposed rates in the Commission's 2011 proposal for amending the Energy Taxation Directive (COM(2011)169) were taken. This benchmark is the highest tax level (per unit of energy and per unit of CO_2 emissions) in the respective Member State in each of the three main categories: transport, process/heating, electricity. For tax expenditures in the Value Added Tax, the standard VAT rate was chosen.

7. Tax expenditures to promote environmentally responsible investment[1]

María Amparo Grau Ruiz

7.1 INTRODUCTION

There is a trend towards increased use of multi-targeted tax incentives. When drafting them to promote environmentally responsible investment, it is necessary to be aware of some possible problems and solutions. The following sections explain how tax incentives may be contemplated as tax expenditures, with their pros and cons, as compared with direct outlays. Nowadays, environmental tax expenditures may be affected by some blurred limits on gaps and artificially exploited mismatches, but there is also room for corporate social responsibility initiatives. The main efforts made by the public administrations to identify, measure and control the tax expenditures are assessed. Despite the lack of comparative legal studies in this field, some lessons can be learned from a review of the heterogeneous practices existing at different territorial levels. In addition, a particular comment is included on developing economies.

7.2 THE TREND TOWARDS INCREASED USE OF MULTI-TARGETED TAX INCENTIVES

7.2.1 Preliminary Remarks: Tax Incentives as Tax Expenditures

A policy objective may be achieved by way of subsidies, other direct outlays or tax incentives. Economists have long recognized the equivalence of direct subsidies (which appear as expenditures in the public budget) and implicit subsidies offered as tax breaks of various sorts (which are not itemized in the budget). Both entail costs to the government: direct subsidies in the form of costs to general revenue, and implicit subsidies in the form of forgone general revenues.[2]

As regards nomenclature, the term tax expenditures is often used interchangeably with tax concessions or tax incentives. These instruments are usually implemented in the form of deductions, exemptions, rebates, changes to the timing of income recognition or deductions taken, as well as reduced tax rates.[3] The specific reference to tax expenditures emphasizes the revenue cost to government of granting certain tax concessions (or tax preferences) such as credits, exemptions or deductions that are generally designed to favour a particular industry, activity or class of taxpayer.[4]

Environmental incentives may be granted to taxpayers investing in assets designed to prevent or abate pollution, or to protect the environment (through accelerated depreciation, higher deductions, tax-exempt investment premiums or research and development tax concessions).[5] All these subsidies are seen as rewards.[6] They can stimulate innovation by shifting decision-making to the private sector, and they are used extensively because they are more politically acceptable than taxes.[7]

Genuine environmental taxes still generate distrust because they deviate from traditional tax principles. On the contrary, when public expenditures pursue economic and social principles, including environmental protection, they can be readily justified in terms of economy and efficiency. In fact the role of tax expenditures may differ depending on the tax affected. Whereas a 'partly' environmental tax (which mainly pursues a fiscal goal) must adhere more strictly to the ability-to-pay principle in collection, a 'fully' environmental tax does not.[8] In addition, 'partly or fully' environmental tax expenditures may affect such taxes in various ways.

A normal tax base set according to taxation standards protects against arbitrary taxation by setting reasonable limits for the tax base, as well as serving to identify when the tax system has been used for non-revenue purposes.[9] The advantageous treatment that a tax measure entails may be seen as derogation from a previously identified reference system. The rules that make up the reference system are those implementing the fundamental guiding principle of the system (which may be either the 'ability to pay' principle or another specific principle like 'environmental protection').[10] The derogation may be justified by the nature or general scheme of the system if there is an inner logic to that derogation in a broader, comprehensive system.[11] Alternatively, the system may contain an alien element which cannot be explained by the fiscal goal of the tax measure (for example tax base distinctions based on environmental facts).[12] Some measures may form part of a subsystem governed by a specific principle (for example protection of the environment) existing parallel to the general tax system. In examining whether the scope of the general system or a subsystem is appropriately defined, it is important to consider the system's objective.[13]

Direct spending comes under parliamentary and public scrutiny through the normal process of budgetary approval, and so publishing an annual tax expenditure report enables comparable levels of scrutiny when using special measures in the tax system.[14] A tax expenditure budget could contribute to efficient and effective public decisions by quantifying the division in the tax structure between provisions that represent revenue policy and others that represent budget policy. When properly designed, it permits open comparison between support for individuals and businesses through direct spending or through tax preferences.[15]

7.3   TAX EXPENDITURE OR DIRECT OUTLAY: AN EVOLVING PATH

Preferences, whether for tax expenditures or direct outlays, change over time. Tax expenditures are extraordinarily low-salience[16] policy instruments, which explains why parliaments have made extensive use of them.[17] Their main drawback is that tax expenditures may augment fiscal illusion, which in turn drives poor policy.[18] Thus, the abandonment of negative taxation is sometimes seen as a success.[19]

When tax benefits are no longer the preferred measure for the national legislator, tax expenditure budgets are alleviated, and direct expenditure may grow accordingly. Caution should be exercised in removing or adjusting fiscal provisions that have an effect on the environment, as there is sometimes a 'hidden welfare State'.[20] Some subsidies are provided to support certain social objectives and sectors of the economy, and their sudden removal could lead to social disruption unless transitional measures are put in place through social support programs.[21] Direct expenditure can help reinforce control, since it is more easily adapted to the budgetary situation in the country and requires annual supervision when approving the General Budget. Converting tax expenditures into direct spending programs is seen as an unalloyed good because the institutions that design and administer those programs possess subject matter expertise. However, when back door subsidies move to the front door, more permeable limits may appear, because those specialized institutions are also more subject to capture.[22]

7.4   MULTI-TARGETED TAX INCENTIVES

At the Organisation for Economic Co-operation and Development in 2014, 36 countries agreed to step up efforts to achieve the economic transformation necessary to deliver sustainable growth, including through 'incentivising private investment' in low-carbon infrastructure and climate-resilient infrastructure. The alignment of different policies (tax, investment, climate and development cooperation) could provide a basis for an effective partnership among governments and the private sector.[23] For instance, when private-sector input is sought, the objectives are often pursued through tax measures, in the form of tax benefits or tax increases or decreases.[24] Incentives are provided to industries in the forefront of developing some technologies and to consumers who embrace them.[25]

Clear regulation with adequate information about investment opportunities is needed to eliminate the risk of conflicts in interpretation by the environmental administration, and of non-approval once investments have been made. A reference to the environmental relevance of an asset may serve to justify an investment if it is non-functional (that is, of environmental value but not integrated in the economic activity or not necessary for its pursuit).[26] Simplified administrative procedures (for small to medium-sized enterprises (SMEs)) may be useful[27] in avoiding long terms and cumulative requirements (for example, participation in a program or agreement with the administration, and additionally obtaining certification of the investment made). Some control mechanisms may be added: obligation to submit the investment plan and to include the relevant information in the annual accounts (under a specific regime in case of non-compliance).[28] Where the whole investment cannot be covered by one incentive, an additional one may be available if the incompatibility is financial rather than physical.

Within the European Union, similar objectives[29] could be achieved more speedily through Corporate Social Responsibility (CSR) strategies. The European Commission defines CSR as the responsibility of enterprises for their impacts on society,[30] in accordance with internationally recognized principles and guidelines. CSR is multidimensional and encompasses environmental issues (such as biodiversity, climate change, resource efficiency, life cycle assessment and pollution prevention). Regulatory measures may create an environment more conducive to the voluntary exercise of social responsibility by enterprises. An 'environmentally responsible investment'[31] requirement should be included when designing tax incentives.

Policies need to be coherent with one another. However, the inclusion of too many goals in a given tax expenditure may complicate management and control. This is particularly true where there are conflicting interests. Multi-targeted tax incentives pose similar problems to those of multi-purpose taxation (which objectives are to be achieved simultaneously or alternatively, which are primary or secondary goals).[32] Some margin is then allowed for CSR in compliance with the rules, as CSR entails actions by companies over and above their legal obligations towards society and the environment. Alternatively, groups of interdependent tax expenditures may be adopted.

7.5 CURRENT BLURRED LIMITS AFFECT ENVIRONMENTAL TAX EXPENDITURES

Corporate income tax in international taxation is suitable for both cooperation and aggression. The international community's interests are best served by cooperation, which is now pursued through the OECD project on Base Erosion and Profit Shifting (BEPS). BEPS refers to tax planning strategies that exploit gaps and mismatches in tax rules to artificially shift profits to low or no-tax locations where there is little or no economic activity, resulting in little or no overall corporate tax being paid.[33] This debate calls for a clear distinction between a desired (environmental) incentive and a gap or mismatch; and their exploitation with or without artificiality.

Some taxes are not collected (in full or in part) where the country's constitution allows the legislator to deviate from the ability-to-pay principle, for environmental purposes. Likewise, certain types of incentives are enacted because there are perceived legitimate reasons for their use (for example, incentives for the installation and operation of renewable energy systems).[34]

Tax expenditures generally represent revenue forgone by governments, but manipulation of these measures by taxpayers under the guise of implementing environmental policy further contributes to the erosion of the revenue base.[35] Tax expenditures may be a useful way to account for erosion of the tax base caused by special provisions. These are reductions in revenue resulting from deliberate policy decisions made by Parliament, and it is appropriate to re-examine those policy decisions in tax reform efforts. But tax reductions resulting from the ability of creative tax lawyers and others to take advantage of features of the 'normal' income tax also should be part of the debate.[36]

Tax avoidance transactions are not reflected in tax expenditure estimates unless the avoidance involves manipulation of a provision that is itself a tax expenditure (for example, tax avoidance techniques that result in overstatement of a research credit would be reflected in the cost estimate for the credit because it is a tax expenditure). Therefore, a provision is not per se either desirable or undesirable just because it is classified as a tax expenditure.[37]

7.6 IDENTIFICATION OF TAX EXPENDITURES FOR ENVIRONMENTAL PROTECTION

A frame of reference is required to assess whether or not tax expenditures are consistent with the promotion of environmental protection. Some criteria may be agreed at a national, global or at least regional level. Any benchmark tax system is a matter of government policy.

Given the foreseeable lack of agreement on what constitutes an optimal tax system, a benchmark should be defined as broadly as possible, and based on transparent and understandable principles.[38] The evolving state of the art of International Environmental Law may be helpful in this task.[39] However, the method whereby the structural elements of a tax system are taken as a benchmark within that system has its limits.[40] The meaning of tax expenditure in each country may vary depending on what is considered structural or not, and may also change throughout the years.[41]

How can one identify the sources of forgone revenue that constitute tax expenditures to inform the Parliament and the public about the revenue costs of pursuing environmental policy objectives? Dividing a tax structure between its benchmark or normal structure and deviation or preference components lies at the heart of the tax expenditure budget. This classification splits the structure between revenue policy and expenditure policy. If most of the tax system is classified as part of the norm, the tax expenditure will be smaller. Conversely, if the benchmark is narrowly defined, many provisions in the law will become preferences and the tax expenditure budget will be larger. A review of US State practices shows three models: a conceptual baseline, a reference tax law, and a revenue reducer list.[42]

The OECD describes tax expenditure budgeting as a classification exercise: dividing the provisions of the tax system into a benchmark or norm and a series of deviations from that norm.[43] Each tax system combines both revenue and budgetary policies. The revenue policy part of the system (the benchmark or norm) raises revenue according to an agreed scheme for distributing governmental costs across the private economy and should be evaluated according to the traditional revenue policy principles (yield, equity, economic efficiency and collectability). The expenditure policy part of the system (deviations from the norm) provides preferences that favour certain economic activities or relieve personal hardships and ought accordingly to be evaluated by budget policy standards.[44]

Within the European Union, there are conceptual and methodological differences among the Member States, so the available information may generate confusion. Eurostat groups environmental taxation into four areas: energy, transportation, pollution and natural resources. Under environmental protection expenditure it includes the money devoted to activities that help prevent, reduce or eliminate pollution from the production or consumption of goods and services (investment and operational expenses to prevent and deal with pollution); and excludes the amounts devoted to activities that are environmentally friendly but respond to technical, health or security requirements.[45]

The Spanish experience regarding the tax expenditure budget is not easy to analyse since incentives are not connected to the environment in terms of the functional classification. We must therefore look at other partial sources of information.[46]

7.7   MEASUREMENT OF ENVIRONMENTAL PROTECTION EXPENDITURE

The procedure of isolating the cost of tax expenditures on a one-by-one basis using the existing tax system as the status quo (instead of starting from the position that no other tax expenditures are in place) gives a better idea than estimating the costs of groups of interdependent tax expenditures. Specific measurement problems arise when tax expenditures are interdependent, or when they involve the postponement of tax liabilities.[47] Comparison of tax expenditure estimates over time can yield some information about trends in tax expenditures, especially if there is no pronounced change in the composition of these expenditures.[48] Some European countries have made efforts to justify their tax expenditures,[49] and the OECD has recently undertaken an exercise to inform the international dialogue on fossil-fuel subsidy reform.[50]

It is important to explain how tax expenditures are calculated, to describe the objectives of specific tax expenditures, and to detail changes in tax expenditure provisions since the publication of the previous year's accounts. Tax expenditures may be presented by functional category and provide an exhaustive listing within each category. The document may include a mix of tax expenditures for which cost estimates are presented, those whose costs are considered too small to be reported, and those for which estimates are not possible because of data limitations (as in Canada, for instance[51]). Evaluations may include a description of the provision, its cost, impact and rationale, together with a summary assessment of the arguments for and against the provision (for example, the US Budget groups tax expenditures by budget category[52]).

7.8   HOW TO IMPROVE THE CONTROL OF TAX EXPENDITURES IN ORDER TO PROMOTE ENVIRONMENTALLY RESPONSIBLE INVESTMENT

Writers of tax legislation and administrative agencies which enforce tax law can also be captured by groups seeking favourable treatment. However, it is more difficult for any particular interest to capture tax writing committees and tax collectors than it is to capture specialized committees and administrative agencies with narrow jurisdictions. In the setting of taxes, any particular interest competes for control against more and more diverse rivals.[53] But this notwithstanding, tax expenditures should not just be reviewed by tax writers and tax administrators, but also by specialized legislative committees and agencies with jurisdiction in particular subject matters (for example those concerned with the environment).[54] It may be possible to fashion a legislative rule where new tax expenditures require the approval of both tax writing and specialized committees, while the legislature's tax writers can abolish tax expenditures on their own.[55]

Large tax expenditure estimates have sometimes created unrealistic expectations concerning potential revenue gains.[56] Many observers propose framework legislation for tax expenditures to apply some sort of cap or trigger to the cost of existing tax subsidies. Too much has always been expected of tax expenditure analysis.[57] Some tax expenditures may be a fragile instrument for implementing environmental policy due both to their inherent structural features and to external developments.[58] A paradox has been pointed out in this connection: the tax expenditure movement has succeeded procedurally but failed substantively. Tax expenditure budgets, pursued as devices to control and limit tax expenditures, have been counterproductive in that they encourage organized interests to seek tax expenditures by highlighting the benefits obtained by others through the tax system. The net unintended effect has been to legitimate and expand tax expenditures.[59]

Attempts to measure and control tax expenditures are much newer than comparable systems for direct expenditure, and not all governments believe tax expenditure budgets to be worth the effort.[60] As Justice Clarence Thomas wrote, it makes no difference 'whether the benefit is provided at the front or back end of the taxation process'.[61] But from the standpoint of transparency the issue goes beyond equivalence: tax expenditures 'allow politicians to appear to be reducing the size of government (reducing taxes) while actually increasing it (increasing spending)'.[62]

Tax measures may be an important factor in the fight against climate change, but tight supervision is necessary since their cost-effectiveness is not always clear.[63] The cost of tax expenditures to revenue neither measures the extent of their economic benefit nor identifies their ultimate beneficiary. Complex rules are therefore required to ensure that tax concessions are correctly applied and that they actually influence the behaviour that the policy targets.[64] Periodically evaluating the size and effectiveness of tax expenditures is a necessary (although not sufficient) requirement for good government.[65] In addition, transversal policies and the co-existence of different vertical territorially competent authorities can pose a problem of duplicated public funding for the same environmental investment or activity.[66]

Tax expenditures could be brought more directly into the budget-setting process by developing different framework rules that could even impose a modest procedural presumption against new tax subsidies.[67] Also, there is room for improvement regarding the performance of tax expenditures in meeting their stated objectives, and neutral rules addressing the externalities induced by the current fiscal illusion that tax expenditures are costless.[68] Some sort of automatic pilot device would be worth considering.[69]

Control of tax incentives needs to be improved both in the home and host countries and within regional groupings. Do the tax incentives legally established to internationalize economic activity take account of possible environmental impacts abroad? Is this a matter of Corporate Social Responsibility? Policy frameworks at the national level should facilitate and mobilize investment in low-carbon, climate-resilient infrastructure.[70] Each State can implement improvements in the design of domestic environmental tax incentives to afford a measure of stability,[71] and also some cooperative compliance schemes depending on the strength of the control mechanisms.

7.9   THE COMPLEX SITUATION IN DEVELOPING ECONOMIES

Sovereignty gives developing countries the right not only to make decisions about the general features of their tax systems, but also to devise special measures that will make it attractive for companies to carry on business activities within that country's territory. Such measures may take the form of allowances, exemptions, rate relief, tax deferral or credits. Some are aimed at stimulating a particular activity, whereas others seek to attract foreign capital in general.[72] Developing economies should identify and overcome barriers to private investment in clean energy infrastructure, using the available tools and considering some Clean Energy Investment Policy Reviews in other countries.[73]

Transparency may also be achieved through a tax expenditure budget, and there are many options as regards preparation, contents and periodicity.[74] The tax expenditure budget may be prepared either by legislative or executive agencies and, if executive, by the revenue department, the budget agency or some other fiscal agency. Tax expenditure budgets do not always include all taxes that the State levies. They may encompass only State taxes, or include regional or local tax expenditures. Quite often States that do include smaller taxes frequently limit coverage to taxes with yields that exceed some revenue limit (for instance environmental taxation). Tax expenditure budgets are prepared and transmitted on a regular cycle, typically annually or biennially. Separation of expenditure and tax expenditure budgets reduces the chance that the tax expenditures will be evaluated as alternatives to direct expenditure.

As regards the debate surrounding tax for development or dependence on official development aid, tax should replace aid in the long run. Nowadays, developing countries receive official development aid directly – and indirectly receive some environmental benefits from investments as good governance conditions are usually imposed on aid. If aid were withdrawn, this would pose a serious risk to the maintenance of environmental protection financed through the investors. One answer might be 'no tax' for aid, through environmental tax expenditures suitable for sustainable development. Given the environmental responsibility toward, within and from the European Union,[75] some revenue losses could be accepted by the home State if they result in benefits for certain stakeholders in the host State.

7.10   CONCLUSION

Tax expenditures to promote environmentally responsible investment are technically feasible, and politically, the current socio-economic climate is favourable. However, some precautions are needed to control their efficiency. A regional or international agreement on minimum criteria for an environmental tax expenditure budget and more transparency would be desirable. Detailed implementation would of course depend on the specific circumstances of each country or regional grouping.

NOTES

1.   María Amparo Grau Ruiz, PI DER2012-36510, Universidad Complutense de Madrid, grauruiz@ucm.es.

2. Boadway, R. (2007), 'The Annual Tax Expenditure Accounts-A Critique', *Canadian Tax Journal*, **55** (1), 107.
3. Ashiabor, H. (2002), 'Critical Appraisal of Tax Expenditures and the Implementation of Environmental Policy in Australia', *Bulletin for International Taxation*, **56** (5), 204–205.
4. The US Budget Act definition is limited to special provisions in the income tax. Explicit subsidies like ethanol benefits are not treated as tax expenditures, because they are delivered through an excise tax benefit, not an income tax benefit. Buckley, J.L. (2011), 'Tax Expenditure Reform: Some Common Misconceptions', *Tax Notes, Special Report*, **132** (18 July 2011), 257.
5. Rogers, J. (ed.) (2014), *International Tax Glossary*, Amsterdam: IBFD.
6. Kleinbard, E.D. (2010), 'Tax Expenditure Framework Legislation', *National Tax Journal*, **63** (2), 364.
7. Subsidies applied to green power products tend to be more effective than environmental taxes on conventional power products in encouraging consumers to choose the renewable energy option. Ashiabor, H. (2005), 'Fostering the Development of Renewable Energy through Green Taxes and Other Instruments', *Bulletin for International Taxation*, **59** (7), 300.
8. Chico de la Cámara, P., M.A. Grau Ruiz and P.M. Herrera Molina (2003), 'Incentivos a las energías alternativas como instrumento de desarrollo sostenible (Incentives for renewable energies as an instrument for promoting sustainable development)', *Quincena Fiscal (Spanish Fortnightly Tax Review)*, (2), 10.
9. Mikesell, J.L. (2002), 'Tax Expenditure Budgets, Budget Policy and Tax Policy: Confusion in the States', *Public Budgeting & Finance*, **22** (4), 49.
10. Some perspectives on State Aids within the European Union may serve us. Szudoczky, R. (2013), 'Chapter 8: Selectivity, Derogation, Comparison: How To Put Together the Pieces of the Puzzle in the State Aid Review of National Tax Measures?', in *EU Income Tax Law: Issues for the Years Ahead*, Amsterdam: IBFD, p. 20.
11. Rossi-Maccanico, P. (2009), 'Chapter 14: The Point on Selectivity in State Aid Review of Business Tax Measures', *Part Four – Direct Action: State Aids, Legal Remedies in European Tax Law*, Amsterdam: IBFD, p. 5.
12. Wattel, P.J. (2013), 'Interaction of State Aid, Free Movement, Policy Competition and Abuse Control in Direct Tax Matters', *World Tax Journal*, **5** (1), 134.
13. See Szudoczky, n 10, 15.
14. See Boadway n 2, 107.
15. See Mikesell n 9, 34.
16. Zelinsky, E.A. (2012), 'The Counterproductive Nature of Tax Expenditure Budgets', *Tax Notes, Special Report*, **137** (12) (17 December), 1322. Zelinsky, E.A. (1986), 'Efficiency and Income Taxes: The Rehabilitation of Tax Incentives', *Texas Law Review*, **64**, 973.
17. By excluding tax expenditures from the reach of most budget framework processes, Congress privileges tax expenditures over explicit spending. In doing so, Congress largely ignores the social costs of using tax subsidies to distort private sector allocations of goods and services, and the deadweight loss of higher taxes used to pay for these subsidies. See Kleinbard, n 6, 354–356.
18. Not just taxpayers but also many members of Congress underestimate the tax increases implicit even in revenue-neutral legislation, by virtue of the way the legislation is framed. One consequence of this predilection for tax expenditures is the obfuscation of the size and activities of our government. Shaviro, D. (2004), 'Rethinking Tax Expenditures and Fiscal Language', *Tax Law Review*, **57** (2), 187–231. Shaviro, D. (2006), *Taxes, Spending and the US Government's March Towards Bankruptcy*, Cambridge, MA: Cambridge University Press (cited by Kleinbard, n 6, 365).
19. Velarde Aramayo, M.S. (2012), 'Promoción de la energía renovable en la Unión Europea, subvenciones y gastos fiscales (Promoting renewable energy in the European Union, direct outlays and tax expenditures)', *Noticias de la Unión Europea (European Union News Spanish Review)*, (326), 4.

20. 'He [Eric Toder] documented a marked shift away from business tax expenditures – savings incentives, investment tax credits, accelerated depreciation, special provisions for favored industries, etc. – in favor of social tax expenditures – programs that look like federal assistance programs for individuals'. Burman, L.E. (2003), 'Is the Tax Expenditure Concept Still Relevant?', *National Tax Journal*, **56** (3), 626 (refers to Toder, Eric, *The Changing Composition of Tax Incentives 1980–99*, The Urban Institute. Washington, DC, 1999, and Howard, C., *The Hidden Welfare State: Tax Expenditures and Social Policy in the United States*, Princeton University Press, Princeton, 1997).
21. See Ashiabor, n 7, 303.
22. See Zelinsky n 16, 1320.
23. 2014 OECD Ministerial Statement on Climate Change, Meeting of the OECD Council at Ministerial Level, Paris, 6–7 May 2014.
24. See Velarde n 19, 4.
25. Tax expenditures are variations in the tax regime which are used to achieve certain policy objectives or to correct perceived market failures. They are a useful tool for dealing with the removal of barriers to industries in the renewable energy sector and for providing flexible incentives to accelerate the phasing-in of sustainable forms of energy generation. See Ashiabor, n 3, 205.
26. Déniz Mayor, J.J. and M.C. Verona Martel (2008), 'Incentivos fiscales y medio ambiente. Opinión de las empresas canarias del sector secundario (Tax incentives and the environment. Opinion given by secondary sector companies in the Canary Islands)', *Hacienda Canaria (Spanish Canaries Finance Review)*, **26** (1), 14.
27. Neither the Reserve for Investments in the Canary Islands in assets related to environmental improvement and protection or the Deduction for Environmental Investments were exploited by the companies. Ibid. 6, 29, 72–75.
28. Discrepancies may appear between accountancy and tax rules regarding the concept of environmental investment. Ibid. 14, 28–31.
29. Among the objectives to be reached by 2020: environmentally harmful subsidies are to be phased out and the share of environmental taxes in public revenues should increase substantially; market and policy incentives should be in place to reward business investments in efficiency. European Environmental Agency (2013), *Towards a green economy in Europe – EU environmental policy targets and objectives 2010-2050*, Report No.8, 25 July 2013.
30. 'The development of CSR should be led by enterprises themselves. Public authorities should play a supporting role through a smart mix of voluntary policy measures and, where necessary, complementary regulation, for example to promote transparency, create market incentives for responsible business conduct, and ensure corporate accountability'. A Renewed EU Strategy 2011–14 for Corporate Social Responsibility, Brussels, 25 October 2011, COM(2011)681 final. Previously, COM(2001)366 defined CSR as 'a concept whereby companies integrate social and environmental concerns in their business operations and in their interaction with their stakeholders on a voluntary basis'. The European Commission has developed the EU Eco-Management and Audit Scheme to evaluate, report and improve environmental performance.
31. Somehow this could connect with the United Nations-supported Principles for Responsible Investment Initiative, which acknowledges the relevance to the investor of environmental, social and governance factors. A Report from KPMG – A New Vision of Value: Connecting corporate and societal value creation (2014) – explores how corporations' social and environmental externalities are increasingly being internalized by new regulation.
32. See Velarde n 19, 5–8.
33. Sanz Gadea, E. (2014), 'Corporate Income Tax as of 2013 (III)', *RCyT CEF*, (375), 6. The purpose is to 'give countries the tools they need to ensure that profits are taxed where economic activities generating the profits are performed and where value is created, while at the same time give business greater certainty by reducing disputes over the application of international tax rules, and standardising requirements'. See http://www.oecd.org/tax/beps-about.htm (accessed 21 April 2015).

34. Bal, A. (2014), 'Tax Incentives: III – Advised Tax Policy or Growth Catalysts?', *European Taxation*, **54** (2–3), 64. China has provided incentives for the consumption of energy-efficient vehicles. Hong Kong has introduced tax incentives on the purchase by individuals of environment-friendly vehicles. Australia provides tax incentives to consume fossil fuels and has indulged the business usage of motor vehicles. Hu, B. and R.S. Simmons (2014), 'China and Australia' s Responses to Environmental Challenge: A Comparative Analysis – Environmental Tax Reforms', *Bulletin for International Taxation*, (6–7), 374–375.
35. Ashiabor, H. (2003), 'Australia's Experience in Tackling the Problems of Land Degradation through the Use of Fiscal Instruments – Challenges and Prospects', *Bulletin for International Taxation*, **57** (3), 309.
36. See Buckley n 4, 257.
37. Surrey, S.S. and P.R. McDaniel (1980), 'The Tax Expenditure Concept and the Legislative Process', in H.J. Aaron and M.J. Boskin (eds), *The Economics of Taxation*, Washington DC: The Brookings Institution, p. 124.
38. See Boadway n 2, 110.
39. 'It is not easy to develop a well-designed incentive system. There are numerous factors that must be taken into account (for example, administrative capacities, budgetary impact and the tax policy of neighbouring countries). As an incentive system is heavily influenced by its legal and institutional environment, these aspects must also be included in design considerations'. See Bal n 34, 67. Bodansky, D. (2010), *The Art and Craft of International Environmental Law*, Cambridge, MA: Harvard University Press. Bodansky, D., J. Brunnée, and E. Hey (eds) (2007), *The Oxford Handbook of International Environmental Law*, Oxford: Oxford University Press.
40. Schön mentions that this method works only with regard to rules defining the tax base but does not help to identify the 'normal' tax rate amongst a range of different tax rates. He cites the example where a state sets two differing rates under its car taxation system for polluting and non-polluting cars, in which case it is impossible to determine which rate expresses the underlying principle of the system and thus is the general rate. See Szudoczky, n 10, 15.
41. OECD (2010), *Tax expenditures in OECD countries*, Paris: OECD.
42. *Conceptual baseline.* Identifies a benchmark normal tax base driven by a logic of tax policy, somewhat akin to the 'normal income tax law' concept of the Joint Committee on Taxation that applies a broader concept of income than defined under current US tax law (for income taxation, Haig-Simon income; for retail sales taxation, total household consumption).
Reference law baseline. Estimates tax expenditures according to exemptions and exclusions identified by specific statutory provision. However, some tax provisions are considered part of the normal or baseline structure of the tax (they define the normal base).
Revenue reducer list. Treats each section of tax law, regulation or line of a tax return that reduces revenue below what would have been raised in its absence as a tax expenditure. See Mikesell n 9, 45–47.
43. OECD (1996), Tax Expenditures: Recent Experience, Paris: OECD, 9.
44. See Mikesell n 9, 35.
45. EUROSTAT: *Environmental Statistics and Accounts in Europe, Statistical books*, 2010, p. 299. EUROSTAT: *Energy, transport and environment indicators*, 2009, p. 161.
46. Carbajo Vasco, D. and L.A. Peragón Lorenzo (2010), 'Gastos fiscales de contenido medioambiental en el presupuesto de gastos fiscales para el año 2010 (Environment-related tax expenditures in the tax expenditure budget for 2010)', *Crónica Tributaria: Boletín de Actualidad (Spanish Tax Chronicle Review: Current Affairs Bulletin)*, (6), 13. They refer to the Report on Tax Expenditures (in Vol. II Economic-Financial Report, State General Budgets), a piece of research dealing with the period 1978–2010 (FUNCAS-Spanish Savings Banks Foundation), and Court of Auditors Report No.721 asking the Tax Agency to control and follow up tax incentives.
47. See Boadway n 2, 106–109.

48. See Burman n 20, 615.
49. In France the government must include an evaluation of the efficacy of each tax expenditure in the document annexed to the General Budget Act. In the UK the tax benefits granted are voluntarily included in the Tax Ready Reckoner.
50. OECD (2013), *Inventory of Estimated Budgetary Support and Tax Expenditures for Fossil Fuels*, Paris: OECD, http://www.oecd-ilibrary.org/environment/inventory-of-estimated-budgetary-support-and-tax-expenditures-for-fossil-fuels-2013_9789264187610-en (accessed 21 April 2015). Provides preliminary quantitative estimates of direct budgetary support and tax expenditures supporting the production or consumption of fossil fuels in selected OECD member countries.
51. Canada, Department of Finance, Tax Expenditures and Evaluations 2005, Department of Finance, Ottawa, 2005. Tax expenditure reports from 1995 onward at http://www.fin.gc.ca/purl/taxexp-e.html, Tax Expenditures: Notes to the Estimates/Projections (accessed 21 April 2015). See Boadway n 2, 127.
52. The Congressional Research Service of the Library of Congress conducts a systematic and comprehensive evaluation of tax expenditures every two years for the Senate Budget Committee. See Burman n 20, 624. 'Reviews of tax expenditures could be integrated with functionally related outlay programs, which could make the government's overall funding effort more efficient'. General Accounting Office, Tax Policy: Tax Expenditures Deserve More Scrutiny, GAO Report GAO/GGID/ AIMD–94–122, June 1994. Each year the Joint Committee Staff publishes a report on Tax Expenditures with a discussion of their concept, the identification of new tax expenditures enacted into law, and a general explanation on how the Staff measures tax expenditures, estimates and distributions of selected individual tax expenditures by income class. Joint Committee on Taxation: 'Estimates of Federal Tax Expenditures for Fiscal Years 2014–2018', JCX-97-14, Joint Committee on Taxation, Washington, DC, 8 August 2014, retrieved from https://www.jct.gov/publications.html?func=select&id=5 (accessed 21 April 2015).
53. Capture 'means that the groups and interests within the committees' and agencies' purview exercise effective political control over those institutions and their decision-making processes . . . Day-to-day contact among legislators, their staffs, administrators and industry lobbyists can foster mutually supportive relationships' . . . 'As a matter of transaction costs, the tax system is a pre-existing device by which the government can efficiently transmit its policies and programs to taxpayers as part of the annual and ongoing process of complying with the tax law?' See Zelinsky n 16, 1320.
54. Welcoming the involvement of the Department of Energy in a variety of tax-based energy programs, see Halperin, D. (2012), 'Tax Expenditures: Budget Control and the Nonprofit Sector', *Tax Notes*, **134** (23 January 2012), 447.
55. Likewise, it is more difficult for any group to capture the decision-making process. See Zelinsky n 16, 1323–1324.
56. See Buckley n 4, 256.
57. See Kleinbard, n 6, 378.
58. See Ashiabor n 3, 208. In Australia, problems encountered in implementing an environmental management system based on tax expenditures included: structural constraints imposed by a federal constitutional system, inherent limitations of tax expenditures, abuse of tax expenditures and the impact of technological developments. According to the OECD, tax expenditures inevitably involve picking winners and tax subsidies may indirectly increase pollution. OECD Environmental Taxation (2011), 'A Guide for Policy Makers', based on the OECD's book *Taxation, Innovation and the Environment*, Paris: OECD, 3. Tax preferences 'should be directed as closely as possible to the true externality. In order to minimise the hazards of trying to pick winners, eligibility should ideally be based on performance measures that are technology-neutral rather than use of particular inputs or technology. Eligibility criteria should represent behaviour that goes clearly beyond normal practice. In addition, regular review and tightening of thresholds are important as conditions change (for example, as new technologies develop), in order to limit windfall benefits to free-riders. To ensure fiscal accountability, transparent

and regular reporting of tax expenditures is required, as well as periodic evaluations'. Greene, J. and N.A. Braathen (2014), 'Tax Preferences for Environmental Goals: Use, Limitations and Preferred Practices', *Environment Working Paper*, **71** (7 October 2014), 37.

59.   Tax expenditure budgets thereby legitimate tax expenditures and, in a classic case of unintended and counterproductive consequences, reinforce a scramble for parity in the form of comparable tax benefits. See Zelinsky n 16, 1317.

60.   See Mikesell n 9, 36.

61.   Concurring opinion in *Rosenberger* v. *University of Virginia*, 515 US 819 (1995).

62.   Steuerle, C.E. (2000), 'Summers on Social Tax Expenditures: Where He's Wrong . . . or at Least Incomplete', *Tax Notes*, **89** (18 December 2000), 1639.

63.   IMF (2008), *The fiscal implications of climate change*, Washington DC: IMF, 27. Spanish environmental policy has depended too much on subsidies, without considering efficiency or self-financing. OECD (2010), Environmental Performance Reviews (2001–2009), Set of the Conclusions and Recommendations approved by the OECD Working Party on Environmental Performance Review, Paris: OECD, 333.

64.   See Ashiabor, n 3, 210.

65.   See Burman n 20, 621.

66.   See Wattel n 12, 130.

67.   See Kleinbard, n 6, 353–382.

68.   Ibid. 367.

69.   A multi-year constraint on tax subsidies as a percentage of GDP, enforced through automatic tax surcharges if those subsidies were projected to pierce the target ceiling. The prospect of scheduled tax surcharges that Congress could have avoided, but did not, would wonderfully concentrate the minds of its Members. Ibid. 378–379.

70.   OECD Report 'Towards a Green Investment Policy Framework: The Case of Low-Carbon, Climate-Resilient Infrastructure' (2012) and case studies (for example, on sustainable transport). Another case study (2014) with CDC Climate considers the role of public financial institutions in scaling up private investment in low-carbon infrastructure.

71.   The non-assurance of tax stability from the government has particular damaging effects on miners' capital investment decisions. Australia's reform is in danger of creating similar investment problems for oil and gas extractors due to its fluctuating tax incentives. See Hu and Simmons, n 34, 374–375.

72.   See Bal n 34, 63.

73.   The OECD 'Policy guidance for investment in clean energy infrastructure' (2013) comprises investment policy, investment promotion and facilitation, competition, financial market and public governance policies.

74.   See Mikesell n 9, 37, 41–44.

75.   Cerioni, L. (2014), 'International Tax Planning and Corporate Social Responsibility (CSR): Crucial Issues and a Proposed "Assessment" in the European Union Case', *European Business Law Review*, **25** (6), 845. More information on this subject available at https://www.ucm.es/proyecto-desafio/ (accessed 21 April 2015).

8. Do you get what you pay for with United States climate change tax provisions?

Hans Sprohge and Larry Kreiser

8.1 INTRODUCTION

Production tax credits for the development of non-fossil fuel sources of energy are pointless and lead to harm to the environment. Fossil fuel sources of energy are deemed to be inimical to the environment because they emit greenhouse gasses, such as, carbon dioxide (CO_2), into the atmosphere resulting in global warming. Global warming is undesirable because it harms the environment. Ostensibly, non-fossil fuels such as, wind, biomass, and solar, are not harmful to the environment because they do not emit CO_2 into the atmosphere. The cost of energy from non-fossil fuels is higher than from fossil fuels. The rationale for production tax credits is to provide economic support for alternatives to fossil fuel sources of energy until such time as when these alternatives become cost competitive with fossil fuels.

The production tax credits for alternative sources of energy are pointless—like tilting at windmills. Taxpayers do not get what they pay for. The combined effect on greenhouse gas emissions of current United States (US) federal tax provisions is less than 1 percent of total US emissions. Furthermore, the Earth is cooling despite increased levels of CO_2 in the atmosphere. One study shows that global warming is caused by chlorofluorocarbons, not by CO_2. Another study shows that even if CO_2 causes global warming, CO_2 is not suppressed by renewable energy.

Given the intent to prevent environmental damage from global warming, then at the very least, the alternative sources of energy benefiting from production tax credits should do no harm to the environment—*primum non nocere*. This is not the case. Just because alternative sources of energy do not emit CO_2 into the atmosphere does not mean that they are not harmful to the environment. Wind energy contaminates groundwater and kills birds. Biomass emits pollutants into the air which are hazardous to health and leads to deforestation. Solar energy destroys habitat, burns birds in mid-air, and has the potential for noxious chemicals leaching into the soil or released into the atmosphere.

8.2   DO YOU GET WHAT YOU PAY FOR?

In 2008, the US Congress directed the US Department of the Treasury to work with the National Academy of Sciences (NAS) to undertake 'a comprehensive review of the Internal Revenue Code of 1986 to identify the types of and specific tax provisions that have the largest effects on carbon and other greenhouse gas emissions and to estimate the magnitude of those effects.'[1] The NAS is a private, non-profit society of scientists established by an Act of Congress and signed by President Abraham Lincoln in 1863. The NAS is charged with providing independent, objective advice to the nation on matters pertaining to science and technology.[2] Scholars with outstanding contributions to research are elected to membership in the NAS by their peers. Nearly 500 members of the NAS have won Nobel Prizes. In 2011, Congress appropriated funds so the study of how tax code provisions impact carbon dioxide and other greenhouse gas emissions could commence.[3] The National Research Council (NRC), the principal operating arm of the NAS, established the *ad hoc* Committee on the Effects of Provisions in the Internal Revenue Code on Greenhouse Gas Emissions to conduct the review.[4] The committee consisted of experts in tax policy, energy and environmental modeling, economics, environmental law, climate science, and related areas.

The NRC released a report of its findings entitled *Effects of US Tax Policy on Greenhouse Gas Emissions* on Thursday, June 20, 2013 which can be found, in its entirety, on the website of the National Academies Press. The greenhouse gas taxes and incentives that the NRC assessed include various renewable energy production tax credits, credits relating to capital depreciation and investment, and even health care and homeownership. The report states that the combined effect on greenhouse gas emissions of current US federal tax provisions is minimal.[5] Their combined impact is less than 1 percent of total US emissions and could be either positive or negative.[6] Some specific tax provisions contribute to, reduce, or have no effect on greenhouse gas emissions. Ethanol subsidies added to greenhouse gas emissions. Production and investment tax credits slightly (0.3 percent) reduce US greenhouse gas emissions.[7] Depletion allowances have no impact on emissions. The Department of the Treasury estimates that the cost, for virtually no environmental benefits, to US taxpayers of the combined energy-sector tax subsidies in 2011 and 2012 totaled $48 billion.[8]

8.3   TILTING AT WINDMILLS?

The Earth has not warmed significantly for the past 15 years despite an 8 percent increase in atmospheric CO_2.[9] According to most climate models, global temperatures should have risen by around 0.45°F over the past 10 years.[10] Instead, the increase over the last 15 years was just 0.11°F—a value very close to zero.[11] Even proponents of the global warming view, such as Nate Cohn[12] and Brad Plumer,[13] acknowledge that global warming has ceased in the last 15 years. Various explanations are proffered for the warming hiatus. These explanations include the following: (1) The Earth is warming but the heat is going somewhere other than the atmosphere, such as, the oceans. (2) Stratospheric water vapor and aerosols and other pollutants reflect solar energy back into space. (3) Reduced levels of solar radiation account for the hiatus.

In a study published by Qing-Bin Lu, Professor of Physics and Astronomy, Biology and Chemistry in the University of Waterloo Faculty of Science, Professor Lu argues that the failure of global warming despite increased atmospheric CO_2 is due to a decline in atmospheric chlorofluor-ocarbons (CFCs) and cosmic rays. Professor Lu observed data going back to the Industrial Revolution. This data shows that CO_2 levels increased significantly as a result of the Industrial Revolution, but the global temperature, excluding the solar effect, kept nearly constant. Professor Lu's paper shows that CFCs and cosmic rays cause both the polar ozone hole and global warming. According to Lu, the reason there is currently no global warming is because of a decline in CFCs in the atmosphere. Whether global warming is dogma or science will be settled in five years. A 20-year pause in global warming does not occur in any climate model.[14] So, if the pause in global cooling continues for another five years, the climate models are wrong and Professor Lu is probably right.

The ostensible rationale for replacing fossil fuels with renewable energy is that CO_2 emissions will be reduced. As applied to solar energy, the argument goes something like this: Compared with the current national energy landscape in the US replacing 1,000 kWh with solar power would reduce the emissions of sulfur dioxide by 8 pounds, nitrogen oxides by 5 pounds, and carbon dioxide by more than 1,400 pounds. In 2012, the average American home used 10,837 kWh. That is a reduction of 7.6 tons of carbon dioxide being released into the atmosphere per American home by switching to solar energy.

In a study published in *Nature Climate Change*, Richard York shows that the assumption that the expansion of renewable energy will suppress fossil-fuel energy production in equal proportion is clearly wrong. Renewable energy from hydropower, nuclear, geothermal, solar, wind, tidal and wave energy, combustible renewables and waste do replace energy from fossil fuels such as, coal, oil, and gas, but only modestly so. The average pattern across most nations of the world over the past fifty years is one in which each unit of total national energy use from renewable energy displaced less than one-quarter of a unit of fossil-fuel energy use. Focusing specifically on electricity, each unit of electricity generated by renewable energy sources displaced less than one-tenth of a unit of fossil-fuel-generated electricity.

8.4   *PRIMUM NON NOCERE* (FIRST DO NO HARM): WIND ENERGY

Not only do tax incentives for green energy fail to significantly reduce CO_2 emissions but—contrary to the presumed rationale for tax subsidies—they result in wreaking havoc on the environment. Every wind turbine has a magnet made of a metal called neodymium. There are 2,500 Kg of it in each wind turbine. China controls 98 percent of current production. The mining and refining of neodymium uses toxic chemicals, acids, sulfates, and ammonia. The environmental problems include air emissions of fluorine and sulfur, and wastewater that contains acid and radioactive thorium. This has resulted in unusable groundwater in parts of Mongolia.

Additionally, the production tax credit for wind energy facilities results in the death of many species of birds and the destruction of their habitats. According to an estimate published in the *Wildlife Society Bulletin* in March 2013, wind energy facilities have killed about 651,000–888,000 bats, nearly 83,000 raptors, and about 573,000 birds of all types.[15] Furthermore, wind turbines destroy and fragment avian habitat.[16] Included in the annual slaughter is the bald eagle—the very symbol of America—and other birds protected by the Migratory Bird Treaty Act and/or the Bald and Gold Eagle Protection Act. Between 1997 and 2012, wind energy facilities have killed at least 85 golden and bald eagles and avian fatalities may be even higher.[17]

The federal government has prosecuted and fined oil companies for bird deaths. From 2009 to April 2013, the Justice Department has handled more than 200 cases under the Migratory Bird Treaty Act and more than 100 cases under the Bald and Golden Eagle Protection Act and the National Wildlife Refuge Act.[18] BP was fined $100 million for harming migratory birds during the 2010 Gulf spill and PacifiCorp paid $10 million in 2009 for electrocuting eagles along power lines and at its substations.[19] Despite numerous violations of the Migratory Bird Treaty Act and the Bald and Golden Eagle Protection Act, the Obama administration—like the Bush administration before it—has never prosecuted or penalized a single wind turbine company.[20] In January 2014, the US Congress passed and President Obama signed a one year extension of the Wind Energy Production Tax Credit.[21]

8.5   ENERGY FROM BIOMASS

Biomass is any non-fossil organic matter. Material is organic if it contains carbon. Anything that is alive or was alive contains carbon. Fossil organic matter is not biomass because it was formed over a period spanning millions of years. Biomass includes wood and wood waste, arable crops and grasses, animal manure, food processing wastes, animal carcass residues, and gardening wastes.

8.5.1   Open Loop versus Closed Loop Biomass

Bioenergy is energy produced from organic matter of recent origin. Bioenergy is derived through three basic conversion technologies: direct combustion, gasification and pyrolysis. Combustion is the most common technology used by biomass power plants. Closed loop biomass refers to energy crops grown specifically for conversion to bioenergy. Energy crops are closed loop when the CO_2 released during combustion roughly equals the CO_2 absorbed from the air through photosynthesis by the replacement growth of the same energy crops. For this reason closed loop biomass is considered to be a clean source of energy, in other words, carbon neutral. Open loop biomass refers to all other types of biomass. Bioenergy from open loop biomass releases CO_2 that was previously 'sequestered'. Most open loop biomasses will release CO_2 anyway, although slowly. For example, decaying forest residues will release CO_2 over a few years. Therefore, most open loop biomasses are 'closed' over a relatively short period of time; say 10 years—unlike fossil fuels, where the timescale is millions of years.

8.5.2   Air Pollution from Biomass

Biomass is not a source of 'clean' energy regardless of whether it is open loop or closed loop. Biomass power plants are major air polluters. The level of air pollutant from burning biomass depends on the feedstock, combustion technology, and type of pollution controls. Burning organic matter emits particulate matter, nitrogen oxides carbon monoxide, sulfur dioxide, lead, mercury, and other hazardous air pollutants (HAPs).

The greatest quantities of HAPs emitted by burning biomass are the organic HAPs styrene, acrolein, and formaldehyde, and the acid gases hydrofluoric acid and hydrochloric acid. Biomass power plants commonly emit ten tons or more of the acid gases and from one to five tons of the organic HAPs each year. Most of the biomass used for energy today is wood.[22] Even cutting and burning trees in power plants emits these chemicals and more CO_2 than burning coal or natural gas.[23] Carbon dioxide emissions from trees per unit of energy generated are about 1.5 times higher than from coal and three to four times higher than from natural gas.[24] Wood from construction and demolition debris increases emissions of arsenic, chromium, copper, lead, and mercury, as well as dioxins/furans and pentachlorophenol. Even very small amounts (1 or 2 percent) of contaminated wood can lead to significant emissions of metals when burned. The EPA recognizes that burning wood results in air pollution. It has set standards for the emission pollutants for biomass under the 'boiler rule', which is part of the Clean Air Act.

Using trees as a source of energy not only is not carbon neutral but leads to increased CO_2, and destruction of habitat. Forest biomass combustion increases atmospheric CO_2 because of a timing difference between the release of CO_2 and subsequent re-sequestration from new growth. Replacing trees that have been cut for biomass power plants feedstock take decades to replace. It is intuitively clear that saplings cannot absorb as much CO_2 as is released from burning mature trees. The result is twofold: On the one hand, atmospheric CO_2 increases from smokestack emissions. On the other hand, re-sequestration is reduced from deforestation. The use of genetically engineered trees may shorten the time for regrowth. However, genetically engineered trees may introduce a completely invasive species into the native ecosystem that may cause irreparable damage. Deforestation destroys habitat. Also, removal of dead wood in forests managed for forest products destroys habitat. Dead wood is habitat for at least 40 species.[25]

8.5.3   Impact of Biomass Air Pollution on Health

Particulate matter has been linked to:[26]

- premature death in people with heart or lung disease;
- nonfatal heart attacks;
- irregular heartbeat;
- aggravated asthma;
- decreased lung function; and

● increased respiratory symptoms, such as irritation of the airways, coughing or difficulty breathing.

The Environmental Protection Agency recognizes two size classes of biomass air pollution: PM_{10} and $PM_{2.5}$, with the numeric value referring to the particle size in microns (a micron is one millionth of a meter).[27] There is no current health standard for PM_{10}. $PM_{2.5}$ poses the greatest health threat. It can get deep into lungs. It can even get into the bloodstream. EPA's 24-hour and annual exposure standards for $PM_{2.5}$ are 35 micrograms per cubic meter ($\mu g/m^3$) and 15 $\mu g/m^3$.

Nitrous oxide emissions causes ground-level ozone, or smog, which can burn lung tissue and can make people more susceptible to asthma, bronchitis, and other chronic respiratory diseases.[28] Exposure to sulfur dioxide causes breathing difficulty for people with asthma. Carbon monoxide interferes with oxygen absorption in the blood. Hazardous air pollutants (HAPs) and arsenic are carcinogenic. Dioxin/furans affect hormone levels and functions, fetal development, the immune system, and reproduction. The Energy Justice Network lists many professional health associations opposed to energy from biomass because of the deleterious health effects.[29] This list includes (among many others): American Academy of Family Physicians, American Heart Association, American Lung Association, and Physicians for Social Responsibility.

8.6   SOLAR ENERGY

The sun converts hydrogen to helium in its core by nuclear fusion. Nuclear fusion is the combining of light elements into heavier ones. In its core, the sun's extreme high pressure and hot temperature cause hydrogen atoms to be stripped of their electrons and their nuclei to fuse. Four hydrogen nuclei fuse to become one helium atom. In the process, energy is released in the form of gamma rays. Each second the sun produces energy that is roughly the equivalent to the energy of 100 billion tons of dynamite exploding. Gamma rays are a form of electromagnetic radiation with short wavelengths and high energy. All forms of radiation have properties of both waves and particles. The particles are tiny packets of energy called photons. The sun's core is thousands upon thousands of miles below its surface. It takes millions of years for the energy in the sun's core to make its way to the solar surface. On their way towards the surface, the photons lose their energy and increase their wavelength. By the time they reach the surface, the photons convert into visible, ultra violet, infra-red and radio photons, as well as high energy ones, producing a thermal spectrum.

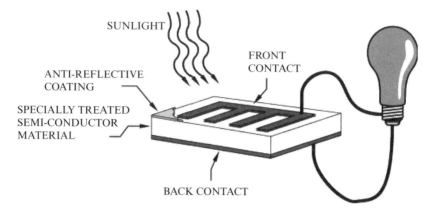

Source: http://science.nasa.gov/science-news/science-at-nasa/2002/solarcells/

Figure 8.1   Operation of a photovoltaic cell

Because of distance from the sun to the Earth, only a tiny amount of the energy radiated by the sun into space strikes the earth—one part in two billion. Yet this amount of energy is enormous. In just 20 days of sunshine, the amount of solar energy that falls on the earth's surface is equivalent to all the energy stored in Earth's reserves of coal, oil, and natural gas.[30] Bjorn Lomborg claims that 'we could produce the entire energy consumption of the world with present-day solar cell technology placed on just 2.6 percent of the Sahara Desert'.[31]

8.6.1   Harnessing Solar Energy

Energy from the sun is converted into electricity through a photovoltaic (PV) cell, also called a solar cell.[32] Figure 8.1 illustrates the operation of a basic PV cell:

PV cells are made of semiconductor materials, such as silicon. The semi-conductor material is specially treated to form an electric field, positive on one side and negative on the other. When photons strike the PV cell, a certain portion is absorbed within the semiconductor material. The energy of the absorbed photons is transferred to the semiconductor. The energy knocks electrons loose from the atoms in the semiconductor material, allowing them to flow freely. If electrical conductors are attached to the positive and negative sides, forming an electrical circuit, the electrons can be captured in the form of an electric current—that is, electricity.

8.6.2   Environmental Impact of Solar Energy Panels

Construction and operation of utility-scale solar energy plants requires the clearing of large tracts of land. Such power plants require around 5 to 10 acres of land per megawatt of power production.[33] Western states like California have deserts with abundant space and sunshine. The California desert, however, is home to thousands of species of plants and animals. Many are rare or endangered, including the desert tortoise and the desert bighorn sheep.[34] Such species may be killed even if relocated away from a solar energy plant site. Radio-tagged desert tortoises, classified as a 'threatened species', did not survive when left at the Kramer Junction Luz thermal solar site or soon after they were relocated away from the site.[35] The impact that solar energy sites have on individual species can send ripples throughout entire ecosystems.[36] For example, animals like the burrowing owls, reptiles, and kangaroo rats in California's Mojave Desert rely on burrows dug by desert tortoises for shelter.[37]

The National Fish and Wildlife Forensics Laboratory reports on bird deaths at three solar power plants in Southern California, including the Ivanpah Solar Electric Generating System.[38] Ivanpah attracts and kills birds. Insects are attracted to the bright light of the Ivanpah solar power plant's reflecting mirrors. Small birds such as finches, swallows and warblers feed on the insects. Bigger birds such as hawks and falcons feed on the insect eaters. Birds that enter the focal field of the mirrors, called the 'solar flux', are injured or killed in a few seconds. The reflected light from the mirrors is 800 to 1,000°F. Either the birds are incinerated in flight; their feathers are singed, causing them to fall to their deaths; or they are too injured to fly and are killed on the ground by predators. The report states that birds burn in mid-air every two minutes.

The report goes on to document the carnage at other California power stations that rely on solar panels, rather than mirrors and heating towers, to collect energy from the sun. Birds including water birds such as grebes, herons, ducks, and even pelicans do not die from the heat but from blunt force trauma from flying into the panels. The birds either die instantly or lie helpless for land-based predators. These birds mistake the panels for water.

8.6.3   Kicking the Can down the Road

The Silicon Valley Toxics Coalition warns of a potential danger to public health and the environment if toxic materials contained in solar panels are not disposed of properly when they reach the end of their useful lives.[39] Components of solar panels contain hexavalent chromium, lead, copper, nickel, silver, aluminum, zinc, molybdenum, antimony, brominated flame retardants, polybrominated biphenyls, and polybrominated diphenylethers.[40] If solar panels end up in landfills, the toxic materials they contain can leach into groundwater. If solar panels end up in incinerators, the heavy metals will gasify and a fraction of those will be released in the atmosphere.[41] If the incinerators are equipped with electrostatic precipitators the amount released can be as small as 0.5 percent with the balance of the heavy metals remaining in the ash.[42] The ash itself will have to be disposed of in landfills.[43] These materials pose environmental and health problems. The Agency for Toxic Substances and Disease Registry ranks arsenic, lead, cadmium, and hexavalent chromium among the top 18 of 275 priority hazardous substances.[44] As photovoltaic production grows, the potential for environmental damage and danger to health increases.

8.6.4   Inadequate Government Safeguards

Solar panels contain many of the same chemicals found in electronic waste (e-waste).[45] Federal and state hazardous waste laws provide inadequate environmental safeguards from the disposal of e-waste. According to EPA estimates, in 2008 more than 3.1 million tons of e-waste was generated in the United States.[46] Only 14 percent of that was collected for recycling. The remainder went to landfills and incinerators. Not included in these numbers are millions of stockpiled computers, monitors and TVs that are stored in basements, garages, offices, closets and homes awaiting disposal. The Silicon Valley Toxics Coalition argues that steps must be taken now to prevent similar lack of environmental safeguards from disposal of solar panels as the industry grows.

8.7   CONCLUSION

Although the goal of production tax credits is to save the environment, they have the effect of killing the planet a little bit at a time. Wind energy contaminates groundwater and kills birds. Biomass emits pollutants hazardous to health into the air and leads to deforestation. Solar energy destroys habitat, burns birds in mid-air, and has the potential for noxious chemicals leaching into the soil or being released into the atmosphere. Production tax credits create an illusion of responsibility and divert attention away from the real environmental problem: saving Earth's environment while meeting the energy needs of humanity. One way to achieve this goal is to eliminate the economic incentives to kill the planet one step at a time by repealing production tax credits for alternative sources of energy or allowing them to expire and replacing them with research and development (R&D) tax credits. R&D tax credits should be granted for investigating how any source of energy—both fossil and non-fossil—can be produced without environmental harm. For example, research could be conducted into the replacement of toxic materials in the manufacture of solar panels or how to economically recycle toxic materials in solar panels. By doing so, the pointlessness of the production tax credits for the development of non-fossil fuel sources of energy and the environmental harm to which they lead can be avoided.

NOTES

1. National Research Council, Effects of US Tax Policy on Greenhouse Gas Emissions, ix (2013).
2. National Academy of Sciences, *Mission* (visited November 27, 2013) http://www.nason line.org/about-nas/mission.
3. National Academy of Sciences, *Mission* (visited November 27, 2013) http://www.nason line.org/about-nas/mission.
4. National Research Council, *supra* note 1, at ix.
5. National Research Council, *supra* note 1, at 152.
6. National Research Council, *supra* note 1, at 152.
7. National Research Council, *supra* note 1, at 3.
8. National Research Council, *supra* note 1, at 152.
9. Craig D. Idso, Robert M. Carter, S. Fred Singer, Climate Change Reconsidered II: Physical Science Summary for Policy Makers 4 (2013) (visited April 21, 2015) http://heartland.org/media-library/pdfs/CCR-II/Summary-for-Policymakers.pdf.
10. Olaf Stampf and Gerald Traufetter, *Climate Expert von Storch: Why Is Global Warming Stagnating?*, Spiegel Online International (visited November 15, 2013) http://www.spiegel.de/international/world/interview-hans-von-storch-on-problems-with-climate-change-models-a-906721.html.
11. Olaf Stampf and Gerald Traufetter, *Climate Expert von Storch: Why Is Global Warming Stagnating?*, Spiegel Online International (visited November 15, 2013) http://www.spiegel.de/international/world/interview-hans-von-storch-on-problems-with-climate-change-models-a-906721.html.
12. Nate Cohn, *Explaining the Global Warming Hiatus: Grappling with climate-change nuance in a toxic political environment*, New Republic (visited November 16, 2013) http://www.newrepublic.com/article/113533/global-warming-hiatus-where-did-heat-go.
13. Brad Plumer, *Global warming appears to have slowed lately. That's no reason to celebrate*, The Washington Post (visited November 20, 2013) http://www.washingtonpost.com/blogs/wonkblog/wp/2013/06/14/global-warming-appears-to-have-slowed-lately-thats-no-reason-to-celebrate.
14. Olaf Stampf and Gerald Traufetter, *Climate Expert von Storch: Why Is Global Warming Stagnating?*, Spiegel Online International (visited November 15, 20013) http://www.spiegel.de/international/world/interview-hans-von-storch-on-problems-with-climate-change-models-a-906721.html.
15. H.S. Smallwood, *Comparing Bird and Bat Fatality-Rate Estimates Among North American Wind-Energy Projects*, 37 *Wildlife Society Bulletin* 8 (2013).
16. Technical Review Committee on Wind Energy Facilities and Wildlife, *Impacts of Wind Energy Facilities on Wildlife and Wildlife Habitat*, Technical Review 07-2, The Wildlife Society, 21–26 (2007).

17. Joel E. Pagel et al., *Bald Eagle and Golden Eagle Mortalities at Wind Energy Facilities in the Contiguous United States*, 47 *Journal of Raptor Research* 312 (2013).
18. Michael Bastasch, *Obama admin. not prosecuting wind farms for bird deaths* (visited November 5, 2013) http://dailycaller.com/2013/11/18/obama-admin-not-prosecuting-wind-farms-for-bird-deaths/#ixzz2m596fFXz.
19. James Conca, *Wind Energy Gets Away with Murder*, Forbes (visited October 28, 2013) http://www.forbes.com/sites/jamesconca/2013/09/22/wind-energy-gets-away-with-murder.
20. Michael Bastasch, *Wind turbine collapses from too much wind* (visited November 11, 2013) http://dailycaller.com/2013/11/08/wind-turbine-collapses-from-too-much-wind/#ixzz2lzor3nzZ.
21. Housely Carr, *Extended US Tax Credit Blows Fresh Air Into Wind Projects* (visited October 28, 2013) https://enr.construction.com/engineering/subscription/LoginSubscribe.aspx?cid=25108.
22. Partnership for Policy Integrity, *Biomass energy overview* (visited on June 12, 2014) http://www.pfpi.net/biomass-basics-2.
23. Partnership for Policy Integrity, *Air pollution from biomass energy* (visited June 12, 2014) http://www.pfpi.net/air-pollution-2.
24. Mary S. Booth and Richard Wiles, *Clearcut Disaster: Carbon Loophole Threatens US Forests* 18 (2010) (visited April 21, 2015) http://www.ewg.org/sites/default/files/report/EWG-clearcut-disaster.pdf.
25. Manomet Center for Conservation Sciences, Biomass Sustainability and Carbon Policy Study: Full Report 68 (2010) (visited April 21, 2015) https://www.manomet.org/publications?combine=biomass&=Search.
26. Environmental Protection Agency, *Particulate Matter* (visited May 17, 2014) http://www.epa.gov/oar/particlepollution/health.html.
27. Partnership for Policy Integrity, *Air pollution from biomass energy* (visited on June 12, 2014) http://www.pfpi.net/air-pollution-2.
28. Union of Concerned Scientists, *Environmental Impacts of Biomass for Electricity* (visited on June 12, 2014) http://www.ucsusa.org/clean_energy/our-energy-choices/renewable-energy/environmental-impacts-biomass-for-electricity.html.
29. Energy Justice Network, *Medical and Health Associations Opposed to Biomass* (visited May 22, 2014) http://www.energyjustice.net/biomass/health.
30. Union of Concerned Scientists, *How Solar Energy Works* (visited on June 12, 2014) http://www.ucsusa.org/clean_energy/our-energy-choices/renewable-energy/how-solar-energy-works.html.
31. Bjørn Lomborg, *The Skeptical Environmentalist: Measuring the Real State of the World*, 159 (2001).
32. National Aeronautics and Space Administration, *How do Photovoltaics Work?* (visited on June 17, 2014) http://science.nasa.gov/science-news/science-at-nasa/2002/solarcells/.
33. Robert L. Bradley Jr, *Renewable Energy: Not Cheap, Not 'Green'* (visited on July 10, 2014) http://www.cato.org/pubs/pas/pa-280.html.
34. Nicholas Lund, Solar Power Plants Are Literally Roasting Birds In-Flight (visited May 22, 2014) http://www.slate.com/blogs/wild_things/2014/07/08/solar_power_plants_burning_birds_usfws_report_on_california_facilities_and.html.
35. Robert L. Bradley Jr, *Renewable Energy: Not Cheap, Not 'Green'* (visited on July 10, 2014) http://www.cato.org/pubs/pas/pa-280.html.
36. David C. Laine, *Effects of Solar Power Farms on the Environment* (visited July 20, 2014) http://classroom.synonym.com/effects-solar-power-farms-environment-13547.html.
37. Southern California Public Radio, *Can Relocation Save the Endangered Mojave Desert Tortoise?* (visited July 23, 2014) http://www.scpr.org/programs/take-two/2013/08/09/33157/can-relocation-save-the-endangered-mojave-desert-t/.
38. Rebecca A. Kagan, Tabitha C. Viner, Pepper W. Trail and Edgard O. Espinoza, *Avian Mortality at Solar Energy Facilities in Southern California* (visited July 22, 2014) http://alternativeenergy.procon.org/sourcefiles/avian-mortality-solar-energy-ivanpah-apr-2014.pdf.

39. Silicon Valley Toxics Coalition, *Toward a More Just and Sustainable Solar Energy Industry* (visited July 20, 2014) http://svtc.org/wp-content/uploads/Silicon_Valley_Toxics_Coalition_-_Toward_a_Just_and_Sust.pdf.
40. Silicon Valley Toxics Coalition, *supra* note 40, at 20–23.
41. V.M. Fthenakis, *Overview of Potential Hazards*, in *Practical Handbook of Photovoltaics: Fundamentals and Applications*, 11–12 (T. Markvart and L. Castaner (eds) 2003) (visited April 21, 2015) www.bnl.gov/pv/files/pdf/art_170.pdf.
42. Fthenakis, *supra* note 41, at 11.
43. Fthenakis, *supra* note 41, at 11.
44. Agency for Toxic Substances & Disease Registry, 2007 Priority Hazardous Substances (visited April 21, 2015) www.atsdr.cdc.gov/cercla/07list.html.
45. Silicon Valley Toxics Coalition, *supra* note 40, at 9.
46. Electronics Take Back Coalition, *E-WASTE: The Exploding Global Electronic Waste Crisis* (visited June 24, 2014) http://www.electronicstakeback.com/wp-content/uploads/Ewaste-Briefing-Book.pdf.

9. Supporting emission reductions through a viable wind energy industry: lessons for Australia

Karen Bubna-Litic[1]

9.1 INTRODUCTION

Denmark has been the world's leader in wind energy for many years.[2] In 2011, Denmark produced 28.3 per cent of its electricity from wind power, the largest share of any country in the world.[3] Denmark has had a successful wind energy industry since the 1970s, supported by energy taxes for many years. In addition to these taxes, Denmark has initiated planning law reform and linked wind power development to industry development, heavily involving local communities. Over many years, these policies have helped provide certainty to the industry and allayed community concerns.

Australia, on the other hand, has been slowly developing a wind energy industry following the introduction of a mandatory renewable energy target (MRET) in 2001 and a carbon tax in July 2012. In 2013, Australia produced 4 per cent of its electricity from wind energy.[4] The recent repeal of the carbon tax and the review of the MRET has resulted in uncertainty for the wind energy industry and a consequent withdrawal of investment.

Australia and Denmark are different geographically and geopolitically. Australia is a large, sparsely populated land mass, with wind energy regulated by separate States. Energy security is not an issue. This is advantageous for Australia in that it enables Australia to have large buffer zones for wind turbines and the ability to capture wind at all times through wind turbines at different locations. Denmark is a small, densely populated land mass, whose wind industry has been necessary due to concerns over energy security. After 30 years of wind farm development, wind energy has been accepted as a standard form of energy in Denmark. But the dense population has meant that turbines are located quite close to buildings and this is now causing some concerns amongst Denmark's population.

The success of the wind energy industry in Denmark seems a good starting point to examine what lessons can be drawn and applied in the

Australian context. Although the share of wind energy in Australia is only 4 per cent, it has been suggested that Australia's strongest wind energy state, South Australia, has the potential to produce 100 per cent of its energy from renewables by 2030.[5] It currently provides around 30 per cent of its electricity from wind energy. This chapter will examine what makes the wind energy industry so resilient in Denmark and so fragile in Australia. Drawing from Denmark's experience, as well as the experience of South Australia, this chapter will examine the policies and laws that can best support a sustainable wind energy industry in Australia.

9.2   WIND INDUSTRY POLICIES

9.2.1   Denmark

Denmark has a long history in its development of a wind energy industry, spurred on by the oil crisis in 1973. From the late 1970s it embarked on four energy plans.[6] The first plan, in the mid-1970s supported a move to nuclear power, which attracted a lot of opposition. As a result, two alternative energy plans were published proposing wind power as one of the main alternatives to nuclear power.[7] These plans together with the anti-nuclear movement were significant drivers for the introduction of wind and other renewable energy sources.[8] Energy taxes were introduced in the mid-1970s and used to support R&D for renewables. The production of large wind turbines by Danish manufacturers led to the formation of local wind cooperatives, whereby people could invest jointly in shared wind turbines, enabling them to meet their own energy needs and to sell excess electricity into the grid.[9]

The second energy plan, in 1981, laid the foundation for home-grown energy production including oil and gas from the North Sea, nuclear power and renewables. This plan, through subsidies for wind turbines and taxes on oil and coal, increased the competitiveness of renewable energy plants and helped establish a strong home market for wind energy and an associated local industry.[10] This plan had an effect on innovation, niche market commercialization and mass production because of the context into which it was introduced. The Danish cooperative tradition allowed the demand-side subsidy to only be given to cooperatives or private wind turbine buyers. This tax incentive encouraged small-scale wind power development, and provided extra income for about a fifth of Denmark's population, which mobilized local wind power support.[11]

Another important development in the 1980s was the demand for Danish turbines driven by the large renewable energy market in California where tax rebates were given for wind turbine investments. This international niche market was essential for industry development because it allowed for mass production and allowed the Danes to focus on the logistics related to service and support. In 1985, the government agreed that the power companies should install 100 MW wind power between 1986 and 1990. This agreement supported the local wind industry's growth at a time when its overseas sales had fallen. The government provided capital grants of 30 per cent, which were later reduced to 10 per cent.[12] This support for large scale wind farms stirred up local objections and there were delays getting planning approval. This 100 MW target was not reached until 1992.

Installed capacity improved from 1994 with farmers investing heavily, due to various policy incentives. While reducing the capital subsidy, the government required utilities to interconnect and purchase wind power for a fair price. The planning process was streamlined to include restrictions on noise, resulting in less noisy and more visually appealing wind turbines and improving the conditions for mass production of these turbines, thus giving certainty to the industry. This was coupled with strong targets[13] with a change in rationale for wind power from energy security to stabilizing CO_2 emissions. The total installed wind power capacity increased to approximately 300 MW, mostly based on 100 kW wind turbines.

The third energy plan, from 1990, Energi 2000, excluded nuclear power and set a target providing 10 per cent of electricity from wind by 2005 with the fair price for wind power set at 85 per cent of the retail electricity rate.[14] National planning directives were put in place with the Minister for Environment and Energy ordering municipalities to find suitable sites for wind farms throughout the country and making provisions for public hearings before any applications for sitings were approved. This was a crucial step in gaining community acceptance.[15] A feed-in-tariff was introduced in 1993, decoupling the power purchase price from existing electricity rates and wind projects received a refund from the Danish carbon tax and a partial refund on the energy tax, doubling the payments to wind projects for the first five years of operation.[16]

Under the fourth energy plan in 1996, Energi 21, renewable energy was to provide 12–14 per cent of total energy consumption by 2005 and 35 per cent by 2030. A central national authority, the Danish Energy Agency, was created, charged with implementing renewable energy policies and supervising planning permissions.[17] By 1996, there were 2,100 cooperatives, forming the basis for continuing local support for wind farms and by 2001, wind farm cooperatives, including 100,000 families, had installed 86 per cent of all turbines in Denmark.[18]

In 1999, Denmark set a target for renewable sourced electricity consumption at 20 per cent by 2003. To be successful, Denmark's wind industry development needed certainty and trust. To maintain certainty and avoid direct government intervention by law, the power companies entered long-term agreements with the wind turbine owners granting them favourable feed-in-tariffs and guaranteeing grid connections.[19] A climate of trust was created by establishing the Riso Test Station in 2002 as an information centre and research and development (R&D) hub and this supported a bottom-up, incremental, trial and error based process of technical change. It facilitated long term loans for manufacturers and project developers.[20] However, due to limited political support during the period 2001–2008, the wind industry experienced stagnation.[21] The feed-in-tariff was abandoned in 2004. From 1993 to 2004, wind power grew from 500 MW to more than 3000 MW but from 2004 to 2008, there was only an additional 129 MW wind capacity installed.[22]

In 2008, the government committed to addressing climate change by increasing energy efficiency, increasing renewable energy and technological development.[23] It increased funding for R&D and demonstration of energy technology to 135m euro per year.[24] 2009 saw a significant rise in wind installation and this was mainly due to an environmental premium of 5 cents (US)/kWh for about 10 years of operation, in addition to the market price.[25] The combination of market price and premium ensured stable revenues for the producers and all subsidies were passed onto the consumers as an equal Public Service Obligation tariff on their total electricity consumption.[26]

The new government elected in 2011 declared that by 2050, all energy would be renewable. The greenhouse gas emission reduction target is 40 per cent from 1990 levels by 2020 and by 2020 half of the traditional electricity consumption will come from wind.[27] These were confirmed by Denmark's Climate Policy Plan,[28] released in August 2013. This document sees Denmark as a wealthy country with the ability to take a leadership role.[29] It recognizes that any action must not pose unreasonable burdens on Danish citizens and businesses, particular in the absence of international action. In the energy sector, the goal of the Danish government is that by 2035, 100 per cent of electricity and heating supply will be from renewable energy and by 2050 this will include energy consumption in the transport sector.[30] To help achieve this, oil for heating purposes and coal are to be phased out by 2030.[31] It has recognized that climate change issues need to be integrated into all other sector policies. This is to be achieved through vertical policy integration and long term green and structural transitions. In order for it to be a best practice model, the basis of its policy is to reconcile it with economic growth with a promise not to impose tax increases onto the business community.

9.2.2   Australia

The first commercial wind farm in Australia was the Salmon Beach wind farm,[32] established in 1987, which operated for 15 years before it was decommissioned due to urban encroachment. It was replaced in 1993 by the Ten Mile Lagoon wind farm, situated on a coastal ridge 16 kilometres west of Esperance in Western Australia, having a capacity of just over 2 MW.

Wind power has been slowly increasing in Australia since June 2006, though currently it only provides 4 per cent of Australia's energy mix. What policy has been driving this? Australia's renewable energy policy came into operation in 2001, with the Commonwealth Government's Mandatory Renewable Energy Target (MRET), which targeted the generation of 9,500 gwh of extra renewable electricity per year (a target of 2 per cent) by 2010. The MRET commenced on 1 April 2001 by means of the Renewable Energy (Electricity) Act 2000 (the Act) and the target was reached earlier than predicted in 2003–2004.[33] Analysis by the Australian Bureau of Agricultural and Resource Economics (ABARE) has found that without a mechanism like MRET, only about 3000 gwh of additional renewable electricity would have been generated each year.[34]

Despite the success of the MRET the target did not increase until there was a change of government in 2007. The first act of the new Australian government was to ratify the Kyoto Protocol.[35] It then proceeded to develop a price on carbon, which was described as a mechanism to encourage investment in renewable energy.[36] In 2009, the renewable energy target was increased to producing 46,000 gwh of renewable energy which, at the time, equated to a target of 20 per cent of renewable energy by 2020. Due to the current drop in electricity demand, it represents a target closer to 30 per cent.

Australia's wind energy industry has been encouraged through policies supporting renewable energy targets, both at the Federal level and at state level. The earlier MRET and the current RET encouraged investment in the lowest cost form of renewable energy that could be rolled out on a large scale. This has been wind energy. The federal RET has recently been reviewed by a well-known climate sceptic, Dick Warburton[37] and following this review, the government is proposing to cut the amount of renewable energy in the 2020 energy mix by 40 per cent arguing that the RET has been a major contributor to the increase in electricity prices. The data does not support this. According to the ABS, the carbon tax added 9 per cent to power bills and the RET added 4 per cent.[38] The carbon tax has now been abolished and the government review has called for the same fate for the renewable energy target. Politically, this may be more difficult to do.

The Clean Energy Council, in a 2013 report, has stated that Australians will pay a total of up to $1.4b (or $140 per household) extra each year after 2020 if the RET is removed.[39] This report shows how this policy has supported Australia's renewable energy industry and at the same time warns that a stable policy environment is crucial to encourage long term investment. The instability in the market can already be seen. From the time since the Abbott government announced the review of the RET, investment in renewables has slowed.[40] The policy settings supporting Australia's wind energy industry before the change of government in September 2013 included a carbon tax, the RET, the Australian Renewable Energy Agency (ARENA) funded renewable energy projects and a range of complementary programmes.[41]

Due to the current lack of political commitment at the Federal level in Australia, the remainder of this chapter will use South Australia as a case study and compare planning law and policy in Denmark and South Australia. South Australia makes a good comparison because similar to Denmark there is strong political will supporting wind energy and similar to Denmark, there have been recent days when 100 per cent of South Australia's energy needs have been met by renewable energy, predominantly wind. Unlike Denmark, there is some long term community opposition to wind farms.

9.3   PLANNING LAW AND POLICY

9.3.1   Denmark

Denmark has a vertically integrated planning scheme and the establishment of new wind farms is regulated within the legal framework of physical planning, which has a hierarchical structure, comprising national, regional and municipal authorities, each with their own physical plans.[42] Regional authorities are required to respect the national directives framework and municipal plans must comply with the regional planning guidelines.

It has been recognized[43] that where local authorities have substantial discretion in influencing planning processes, wind projects may be difficult to approve unless the local community can benefit from the investment. One way of doing this is for the investor and the government authority to provide compensation mechanisms and facilitate local ownership.[44] In Denmark, this is provided for at the national level by the Danish Energy Agency, the body that sets renewable energy policy and approves wind farm applications.

Denmark has recently introduced four specific legal measures into their

Promotion of Renewable Energy Act 2008 that are intended to enhance community acceptance of wind farms. These include the option to purchase shares, compensating the loss of property value, an incentive scheme for more local ownership through a guarantee fund to finance preliminary investigations and subsidizing initiatives to help promote local acceptance.

Any citizen with a minimum age of 18 and living within 4.5 km of new wind turbines has the option to buy shares in the local wind turbine.[45] The offer for sale can only be offered after the wind turbines have been approved under the Building Act and Rules and before the wind turbines are connected to the grid.[46] It applies to wind turbines greater than 25 m in height and the offer must be at least 20 per cent.[47] Any shares not taken up by citizens within 4.5 km of the turbines can then be offered to permanent residents within the municipality.[48] If the offer is oversubscribed, those with the preferential right under s15(4) will first receive 50 ownership shares.[49] There is an exemption for small wind turbines (those with an installed output of 25 kW or less) that are connected to their own consumption installation. Section 13(5) envisages that the wind turbine may be operated by an enterprise that can attract personal liability. In this case, the articles of association must state whether the enterprise may incur debt, in order to ensure that local citizens are aware that they may be liable for more than their investment, and to allow them to minimize their risk. If the operating entity is a limited company, then their articles of association must state that they are not marketable securities.[50] This is to keep ownership local. Recent amendments to this Act confirm the need to properly inform citizens of the offer and all relevant information.

If a property loses more than 1 per cent in value due to the erection of new wind turbines, the owner is ensured full compensation for the loss.[51] The amount of compensation is determined either through agreement between the parties or by the valuation authority.[52] This amendment was predicted to increase the cost of wind farms by 16 per cent but this has not eventuated. This compensation has been criticized on the basis that paying compensation implies that wind farms are a nuisance that need to be compensated for, which emphasizes the negative aspects rather than the positive emission reduction aspects. What has been lost in the debate around the compensation is that it is compensating for the loss of property value, rather than compensating for nuisance.[53]

The Guarantee Fund[54] provides for a maximum of $100,000 as support for preliminary investigations performed by local wind turbine owners or associations. It is intended to cover such things as preliminary investigations of sites, carrying out an environmental impact assessment or investigating the technical and financial aspects of a project.

The final initiative inserted into the Danish legislation is a green scheme protecting local scenic and recreational values.[55] Its stated purpose is to *'promote acceptance of the use of onshore wind farms in the municipality'*.[56] The basis of the scheme is that neighbours will be more accepting if they are compensated for the degradation of their surroundings. The downside of this initiative is that it can only be applied for by councils for new projects. This process makes it quite cumbersome. Examples include bicycle paths, nature restoration projects, renovation of sporting facilities, and instalment of renewables in public buildings (solar panels and geothermal energy).

9.3.2   South Australia (SA)

Unlike Denmark, Australia has no federal policy on wind energy. The carbon tax has been repealed, the Australian Renewable Energy Agency (ARENA) has been demolished, and the future of the RET hangs in the balance. The experience of South Australia (SA) offers a bright spot in a policy vacuum at the national level.

South Australia has political will supporting a viable wind energy industry. The Climate Change and Greenhouse Gas Emissions Reduction Act 2007 (SA) set a renewable energy target of 20 per cent by 2014,[57] which was reached in 2011. In 2009, the SA government committed to a target of 33 per cent renewables by 2020. At the end of 2013, it was producing around 30 per cent of its energy from renewables, with about 27 per cent coming from wind. In September 2014, the Premier of SA announced a new renewable energy target of 50 per cent by 2025.[58] In addition to these targets, in 2009, the SA government established RenewablesSA to promote and attract renewable energy investment to South Australia.

Under the planning process in SA, wind farms will be approved as long as they comply with the local development plan.[59] Unlike Denmark, renewable energy and planning policy are set and administered by different levels of government. Amendments in 2003 to planning schemes and zoning laws have resulted in council development plans generally supporting renewable energy projects.[60] They contain general principles for consideration of visual impact, and neighbour nuisance, including noise. There can be third party appeals depending on the scale of the project and the zoning of the site. On appeal, the court must be guided by the development plans, not the legislated renewable energy targets, in making its decision.

Recently, there have been two major cases objecting to wind farms on the basis of noise and visual amenity. *Quinn* v. *Goyder*[61] concerned an unsuccessful appeal on the grounds that the development complied with the provisions of the development plan. The appellants were local residents who objected to the wind farm proposal, consisting of 33 turbines, a substation and related infrastructure, on the basis of noise and visual amenity. On the issue of visual amenity, the court concluded 'In our assessment, the establishment of 33 turbines will add a new element to the landscape, but it will not deprive the landscape of its scenic quality. The character of the landscape will retain an open, rural character'.[62]

In *Paltridge* v. *District Council of Grant*,[63] the appellants were members of a local farming family (father, son and daughter-in-law) who owned and farmed dairy cattle on several parcels of land to the south and east of the proposed wind farm. They succeeded in stopping a $175m, 46 turbine wind farm on the basis of visual amenity, only. They were unsuccessful on the issues of noise, health, impact on flora and fauna and blade glint and shadow flicker. The Development Plan provided that wind energy facilities were to be sited in 'appropriate locations'.[64] The Court said that it was not its role to have regard to the Climate Change and Greenhouse Emission Reduction Act 2007 (SA), but instead to see if the development conformed to the Development Plan.[65] The court said, 'in our view, the height, scale, number, siting and overall appearance of 46 wind turbines will introduce into a generally flat, pleasant, rural landscape . . .. A foreign, prominent and discordant element.'[66] Winning on the grounds of visual amenity is somewhat surprising considering that in their traditional design, wind turbines are almost always visually intrusive. If approval is to be on a case-by-case basis, as provided for by the 2003 amendments, *Paltridge* will most likely lead to uncertainty and reliance on subjectivity of the court in determining the issue of visual amenity. Counsel for the developer argued, 'it is nearly impossible for a wind farm of any size to be anything but visually prominent in its locality'.[67] A more grounded approach was taken by the NSW Land and Environment Court in Taralga's case.[68] That case had to balance the need for renewable energy against the potential bird kill and objections based on visual amenity. The decision of the court was focused on the implications of climate change, concluding that the overall public benefit of the wind farm outweighed any visual impacts on the Taralga landowners.[69] The public benefit was referred to in *Paltridge*,[70] but the court specifically limited its role to whether the application complied with the Development Plan, stating that its role was not to consider the public aspect of renewable energy, which was covered by the Climate Change and Greenhouse Emissions Reduction Act 2007.[71]

The restrictions in the SA planning system resulting in the court's decision in *Paltridge* led the SA government to embark on an extensive consultation process to provide for certainty for wind farm development.[72] In October 2012, the Minister for Planning released the Statewide Wind Farm Development Plan Amendment (DPA),[73] which sets guidelines for wind farms in SA. It is designed to prevent third parties, appealing wind farm development approvals. There are four arms to the amendment. Wind farms are envisaged in all rural zones in the state and in these zones, wind farms will be classified as category 2 developments, the classification of which disallows third party appeals. The exception to this is where a turbine falls within 2 km from a dwelling or township zone, in which case it becomes a category 3 development, subject to third party appeals. The issue of visual amenity is to be managed according to a number of criteria including vegetated buffers and set-backs of at least 2 km from urban and township zones and at least 1 km from non-associated dwellings and tourist accommodation. They are required to be regularly spaced, uniform in colour and mounted on tubular towers.[74] They need to minimize the impact on nearby properties and wildlife, through shadow flicker, excessive noise, modifying soils and habitats and bird and bat strike. Finally, certain high value zones with high environmental, scenic and tourist values were identified as areas where wind farms should be minimized.

The abolition of third party appeals has created some concern amongst the community in SA, despite an extensive public consultation process.[75] These actions were deemed necessary to support wind energy development due to the Development Act 1993 prioritizing Development Plans over a legal framework with designated renewable energy targets.

9.4   LESSONS FOR AUSTRALIA

In 2013, the International Renewable Energy Agency (IRENA) produced a list of eight enabling conditions for wind energy after reviewing twelve wind energy markets.[76] They included strong political commitment, a long-term policy framework, clear pricing structures, a supportive finance sector and industry development policy, ability for community buy-in, and priority grid connection. Denmark has had many years of experience to hone their skills in developing a resilient wind energy industry and has well-developed policies in all of these areas. Even though it has been a leader in wind power generation, recently on-shore wind power projects in Denmark have faced increasing local opposition.[77] This resulted in the recent amendments to the Renewable Energy Act 2008.[78]

As this chapter has shown, South Australia is the leading jurisdiction in Australia in wind energy generation but of the eight enabling conditions recommended by IRENA, SA is lacking a supportive finance sector and priority grid connection for wind energy, amongst others.

There are three important lessons that can be learnt from the Danish experience. They include integrated planning across all levels of government;

an industry development policy; and generating a culture of community acceptance.

One of the characteristics of Denmark's integrated planning system is the vertical integration of plans whereby regional planning authorities must respect the framework outlined in the national directive and the municipal plans must comply with the regional planning guidelines.[79] Another characteristic is for the planning authorities to implement their adopted planning guidelines when exercising their authority under the Danish planning legislation. South Australia faces a number of impediments to an integrated planning system. There is a renewable energy policy vacuum at the national level and the planning authorities at the local government level have only to consider their local development plan, ignoring the legislated renewable energy targets, as was illustrated by the decision in *Paltridge*. The solution was for the State government to regulate out third party appeal rights but a more integrated planning system as exists in Denmark would be a solution, more likely to guarantee a longer term wind energy industry. The current situation in South Australia is likely to change if the government changes.

The second lesson to be learnt is the advantage to be gained from an industry development policy. Denmark has had four energy plans from the early 1970s which has led to Denmark creating a strong wind energy industry in terms of export and wind turbine manufacturing.[80] Supporting mechanisms included a feed-in-tariff, comprising a market price element, a compensation for balancing and a government subsidy, as well as R&D subsidies.[81] Additionally, Denmark has had a raft of environmental taxes since the 1980s, including energy taxes designed to cut CO_2 emissions and encourage energy efficiency and renewable energy.[82] Australia does not have a national industry development policy. South Australia established RenewablesSA in 2009,[83] to support the growth in SA's renewable energy industry, as renewable energy had been identified as an important industry for SA's economic future. This intention has not been translated into accompanying developments such as employment and training strategies or accompanying infrastructure development. Without an industry development policy, decisions on approval of wind farms can be blocked on an ad hoc basis. The government's response, as evidenced by its Statewide Wind Farm Planning Policy and the recent Pastoral Land Management and Conservation (Renewable Energy) Amdt Bill 2014, are stop gap measures that may encourage wind farms but a change of government is likely to dismantle these initiatives.

In recent years disenfranchising of the local community has been a hallmark of South Australian wind energy policy[84] and this has been exacerbated coming from a top-down approach. Lessons can be learnt from Denmark where a bottom-up approach has been evident from the very early days, where cooperatives and municipalities owned distribution utilities and power stations.[85] This is one of the hallmarks of Denmark's wind industry and why it has endured. In Australia today, many people are beginning to think about community ownership of distribution utilities and power stations.[86] What lessons in this regard can be learnt from the Danish experience? Community opposition is starting to increase in Denmark. This may be because Denmark is fast running out of space, which has led to the buffer between turbines and dwellings to be only four times the total height of a wind turbine,[87] much less than the 2 km buffer in most Australian states. It has been suggested that strategic planning for potential wind energy areas would help allay individual objections if the proposal complies with the strategic plan.[88] This has been adopted in the recent SA development plan amendment which allowed wind farms in all rural areas except those with high environmental, agricultural, and tourism values.

What lessons can be learnt from the recent amendments to the Danish Renewable Act 2008? The Danish experience illustrates success with its co-ownership scheme, based on the assumption that financial involvement of the local community will have a positive effect on their attitude to wind farms.[89] A mandated 20 per cent must be offered, and those developers who can demonstrate 30 per cent being locally owned will receive an extra price supplement. Individual holdings cannot exceed 5 per cent. Although there have been some concerns, this scheme has stimulated local citizen involvement in projects.[90] The basis of the community benefit scheme is that community acceptance will be enhanced if they are compensated for the degradation of their surroundings. Although applications are somewhat bureaucratic, having to come through local councils, funding has been given for quite wide-ranging projects and local publicity has led to this initiative being seen as a positive gain coming from wind energy projects.[91] Another lesson to be learnt from the Danish experience is to steer away from a scheme compensating for loss of property values. Olsen and Anker give a detailed analysis of the large number of problems resulting from this scheme.[92]

9.5   CONCLUSION

This chapter has examined the energy and planning policies in Denmark and Australia, focusing on South Australia as a case study, with a view to assessing the lessons from Denmark's wind energy industry experience. The longevity of the Danish wind industry can be explained by its strong commitment to renewable energy. At its core is strong political will integrating renewable energy development into all levels of government. Essential support for this includes:

1. an industry development policy which is long-term and which includes strong renewable energy targets, the involvement of both private and public actors, and tax and direct financial incentives; and
2. community acceptance, involving share offers, community ownership, effective consultation, buffer zones and the exclusion of high value areas.

Australia can gain a lot from the Danish experience, particularly in the three areas of integrated planning, industry policy development and community acceptance. South Australia has the political will but there is no integrated political will at the Federal level, with continuing uncertainty over the future of the RET. Industry policy needs to be consolidated and properly supported and community acceptance could be enhanced by supporting a co-ownership scheme and a community benefit scheme.

What of the role of taxation policy? Is a carbon tax necessary? A carbon price alone is not enough to drive investment in renewable energy.[93] What is more important is how the revenue is used. Wind projects in Denmark received a refund from the carbon tax and a partial refund on the energy tax. These refunds effectively doubled the payment to wind projects for the first five years of their operation. In Australia, carbon tax revenue went to fund Australia's Renewable Energy Agency (ARENA), which distributed grants for renewable energy projects and other complementary measures.

The lack of political will at the Federal level has led to the repeal of Australia's carbon tax, the defunding of (ARENA) and uncertainty as to the future of the RET. Despite this, there are pockets of hope among the States and territories of Australia. South Australia's strong record on wind energy can only be enhanced by some of the lessons from the Danish wind energy experience.

NOTES

1. Associate Professor, UNISA Law School.
2. GWEC (2013), http://www.gwec.net/wind-providing-30-of-world-leader-denmarks-electricity/ (accessed 22 April 2015).
3. IRENA-GWEC: 30 Years of Policies for Wind Energy, 59 https://www.irena.org/DocumentDownloads/Publications/GWEC_Denmark.pdf (accessed 22 April 2015).
4. Clean Energy Council (2013), 'Clean Energy Australia Report 2013', 59.

5. Giles Parkinson – reneweconomy http://reneweconomy.com.au/2014/south-australia-could-be-1st-mainland-state-to-100-renewables-17216 (accessed 22 April 2015).
6. IRENA-GWEC, above n3, 55.
7. Blegaa, S., Hvelplund, F., Jensen, J., Josephsen, L., Linderoth, H., Meyer, N.I., Balling, N. and Sørensen, B. (1976), *Sketch of Alternative Danish Energy Plan* (in Danish), Copenhagen: OVE Publishers, and Hvelplund, F., Illum, K., Meyer, N.I., Nørgård, J.S. and Sørensen, B. (1983), *Energy for the Future* (in Danish), Copenhagen: Borgen Publishers.
8. IRENA-GWEC, above n3.
9. Ibid.
10. Ibid.
11. Buen, J. (2006), 'Danish and Norwegian Wind Industry: The relationship between policy instruments, innovation and diffusion', 34 *Energy Policy*, 3887, 3893. It should be noted that energy production in Denmark has a cooperative structure, whereby production units are owned by more than 100 power companies responsible for distribution, and they, in turn are owned by cooperatives or municipalities.
12. In 1988, the newly elected government cut the subsidy by half. However, the return on investment in wind energy was maintained between 15 per cent and 25 per cent, and community-owned wind energy was supported by three principles: (1) The right to connect to the electrical grid; (2) A legal obligation for electrical utilities to purchase wind energy; and (3) A guaranteed fair price (Christianson, n.d., 'Danish Wind Co-ops Can Show Us the Way', http://www.wind-works.org/articles/Russ%20Christianson%20NOW%20Article%201.pdf (accessed 4 May 2015).
13. 1996 Energi 21 – 10 per cent electricity consumption to be covered by 1500 MW of wind power by 2005; 4000 MW offshore wind power by 2030, and 50 per cent of Danish electricity covered by wind power by 2030.
14. IRENA-GWEC, above n3.
15. Ibid., 60.
16. Bolinger (2001) 'Community Wind Power Ownership Schemes and their Relevance to the United States' http://emp.lbl.gov/sites/all/files/REPORT%2048357.pdf (accessed 22 April 2015).
17. IRENA-GWEC, above n3, 60.
18. Ibid.
19. The power companies paid 35 per cent of grid connection costs; and buy excess power from individuals' and cooperatives' turbines at 85 per cent of consumer price.
20. Buen, J., above n11.
21. IRENA-GWEC, above n3, 61.
22. Ibid.
23. Increase the use of renewable energy to 20 per cent of gross energy consumption by 2011.
24. IRENA-GWEC, above n3, 62.
25. Ibid.
26. For new onshore turbines coming online from 1 January 2014 the premium will stand at DKK 0.25/kWh (approximately USD 0.05/kWh) for the first 22 000 full load hours, reduced when the market price of electricity exceeds DKK 0.33/kWh (approximately USD 0.06/kWh), and set to zero when the electricity price reaches DKK 0.58/kWh (approximately USD 0.11/kWh).
27. IRENA-GWEC, above n3, 62.
28. The Danish government (2013), 'The Danish Climate Policy Plan: Towards a low carbon society', August 2013.
29. Ibid., 7.
30. Ibid.
31. Ibid., 14.
32. On the southern coast of Western Australia at Esperance.
33. ABARE (2009), *Energy in Australia 2009*, Department of Resources, Energy and Tourism, Australia.

34. Greg Buckman (n.d.), 'Overseas lessons about Australia's Mandatory Renewable Energy Target and Renewable Energy Target' http://solar.org.au/papers/09papers/141_Buckman%20G.Pdf (accessed 22 April 2015).
35. On 12 December 2007. See http://unfccc.int/kyoto_protocol/status_of_ratification/items/2613.php (accessed 22 April 2015).
36. Thompson, J. (2011), 'Gillard Reveals Carbon Price Scheme', *Australian Broadcasting Corporation*, 11 July, http://www.abc.net.au/news/2011-07-10/gillard-reveals-carbon-price-scheme/2788842 (accessed 22 April 2015), as cited in Bubna-Litic, K. and Stoianoff, N. 'Carbon Pricing and Renewable Energy Innovation: A comparison of Australian, British and Canadian carbon pricing policies', 31 *EPLJ*, 368, 382.
37. Australian government RET Review https://retreview.dpmc.gov.au/ (accessed 22 April 2015).
38. http://www.industry.gov.au/Energy/EnergyMarkets/Documents/ELECTRICITY-PRICES-FACTSHEET.pdf (accessed 22 April 2015).
39. Clean Energy Council, 2013, above n4.
40. Ibid., 5.
41. Bubna-Litic, K. and Chalifour, N. (2012), 'Are Climate Change Policies Fair to Vulnerable Communities? The impact of British Columbia's carbon tax and Australia's carbon pricing policy on indigenous communities', 35 *Dalhousie L.J.*, 127, 171–173.
42. Pettersson and Soderholm, at n 43, 56.
43. Maria Pettersson, and Patrik Soderholm (2011), 'Reforming Wind Power Planning and Policy: Experiences from Nordic countries', CESifo DICE Report 4/2011.
44. Ibid., 54.
45. Renewable Energy Act, Act No1392 of 27 December 2008, ss13–17, as amended by Act No641, 12 June 2013.
46. Ibid., s13(6).
47. Ibid., s13(1).
48. Ibid., s15(1), (2), (4).
49. Ibid., s16(1), (2).
50. Ibid., s13(5).
51. Ibid., s6.
52. Ibid., s7(1).
53. Olsen, B.E. and Anker, H.T. (2014), 'Local Acceptance and the Legal Framework – The Danish Wind Energy Case', Chapter 7 in *Sustainable Energy United in Diversity – Challenges and Approaches in Energy Transition in the European Union*, EELF Series vol. 1.
54. Renewable Energy Act, above n45, s21.
55. ss18–20 http://www.ens.dk/sites/ens.dk/files/supply/renewable-energy/wind-power/onshore-wind-power/Promotion%20of%20Renewable%20Energy%20Act%20-%20extract.pdf (accessed 22 April 2015).
56. s18(1).
57. Climate Change and Greenhouse Gas Emissions Reduction Act 2007, s5(2).
58. See http://www.renewablessa.sa.gov.au/files/140923-retincrease.pdf (accessed 22 April 2015).
59. s33 Development Act 1993 (SA).
60. Wind Farms Ministerial Plan Amendment Report ('Ministerial PAR') of July 2003.
61. [2010] SAERDC 63.
62. Ibid., [55].
63. [2011] SAERDC 23.
64. Objective 44, Development Plan.
65. [2011] SAERDC 23, at [26].
66. Ibid., at [108].
67. Ibid., at [96].
68. *Taralga* v. *Landscape Guardians* [2007] NSWLEC 59.
69. Ibid.

70. [2011] SAERDC 23, at [26].
71. Ibid.
72. Local Government Association of South Australia http://www.lga.sa.gov.au/page. aspx?c=24576 (accessed 22 April 2015).
73. Statewide Wind Farm Development Plan Amendment (DPA https://www.sa.gov.au/__ data/assets/pdf_file/0020/17660/DPA_Minister_Approved_Statewide_Wind_Farms_ DPA_Gazetted_18_October_2012.PDF (accessed 22 April 2015).
74. Ibid.
75. SA Development Policy Advisory Committee, 'Statewide Windfarms Development Plan Amendment – Summary of Consultation and Recommended Amendments Report' July 2012 http://dpac.sa.gov.au/__data/assets/pdf_file/0016/113317/7105343_ Statewide_Wind_Farms_DPA_DPAC_Report_to_the_Minister.PDF   (accessed   22 April 2015).
76. IRENA-GWEC, above n3.
77. Olsen and Anker, above, n53.
78. As amended by Act no. 641 of 12 June 2013.
79. Ibid.
80. IRENA-GWEC, above n3, at 54–63.
81. Ibid.
82. Ibid., 60.
83. See http://www.renewablessa.sa.gov.au/ (accessed 22 April 2015).
84. See *Quinn* v. *Goyder* (2010) SAERDC 63; *Paltridge* v. *District Council of Grant* (2011) SAERDC 23.
85. Pettersson, and Soderholm, above, n 43, at 54.
86. Pingala Power http://www.pingala.org.au/ (accessed 22 April 2015).
87. Olsen and Anker, above n53.
88. Ibid.
89. Ibid.
90. Ibid.
91. Ibid.
92. Ibid.
93. Bubna-Litic and Stoianoff, above n36, at 382.

PART III

Competitiveness considerations

10. Environmental border tax adjustments (BTAs): a forgotten history

Alice Pirlot*

Environmental border tax adjustments (BTAs) – and in particular border carbon adjustments (BCAs) – are regularly discussed as one possible solution in mitigating global environmental challenges, including climate change. The legal scholarship on environmental BTAs usually focuses on the compatibility of these measures with the provisions of the General Agreement on Tariffs and Trade (GATT) and World Trade Organization (WTO) law. This chapter takes a different approach: the objective is to analyse environmental BTAs in light of the 'traditional concept' of non-environmentally specific BTAs. The main hypothesis of this chapter is that the legal analysis of environmental BTAs should better take into consideration the history of traditional BTAs and the legal principles on which this concept relies.

In this short chapter, the concept of 'environmental BTAs' is used to refer to a broad range of environmental measures that have been studied since the 1990s under a variety of names. These concepts include: 'BTA of environmental taxes',[1] 'border adjustments on energy taxes',[2] 'border carbon adjustments'[3] or 'carbon-added tax',[4] etc. This chapter relies on the assumption that environmental BTA studies and proposals have been developed on the basis of the older international trade law concept of BTA. Based on this assumption, this chapter aims at demonstrating that, notwithstanding reference to the concept of BTA, environmental BTA studies and proposals do not always respect the BTA's essence. In other words, it seems as if environmental BTAs have borne the name of BTA but should have been named after other trade-related concepts whose design and key features better match the ideas proposed. The incorrect designation of environmental BTAs may be problematic since, in law, concepts are related to specific legal regimes and consequences. Therefore, when an environmental trade-related measure is erroneously named a BTA, these measures may be – mistakenly – analysed under the legal regime related to the international trade law concept of BTA. Moreover, inaccurate references to the concept of BTA result in a lack of coherence in the literature, which makes it difficult to assess opportunities to introduce environmental BTAs.

This chapter provides an historical analysis of the concept of BTA in order to highlight its main features and distinguish between environmental BTAs that truly respect the essence of the concept of BTA and those that do not. The primary material of the analysis consists of the first 'international' reports on BTAs as well as the preparatory documents to these reports. In particular, the research makes use of the first OECD report devoted to the topic of BTAs (the 1968 OECD Report on 'Tax Adjustments Applied to Exports and Imports in OECD Member countries'[5]), to which the recent literature on environmental BTAs has often forgotten to pay due attention. The analysis of this report sheds light on the roots of the concept of BTA and offers new perspectives from which to examine environmental BTAs.

10.1   RECAP OF THE BTA'S HISTORICAL DEVELOPMENT

The eighteenth century is usually considered the time of both the theoretical and practical foundations of BTAs. On the one hand, David Ricardo (1722–1823) is usually recognized to be the father of BTAs' theoretical development.[6] On the other hand, practical examples of taxes following the BTA mechanism can be found in the legislation of the United States at the end of the eighteenth century.[7] This chapter does not analyse David Ricardo's contribution to BTA history. Neither does it discuss the history of BTAs' practical implementation. Rather, it analyses two of the main important reports on the international trade law concept of BTA, which were issued in the second half of the twentieth century: the 1968 OECD report and the 1970 GATT report.[8]

10.1.1   The 1968 OECD Report

In 1963, the United States asked the Council of the OECD to establish an Ad Hoc Group in order to study the issue of tax adjustments applied by member countries to exports and imports.[9] This request was fueled by the United States' concerns that the planned modifications to the German turnover tax system would have a negative impact on free trade.[10] Consequently, the Council of the OECD demanded the Secretariat analyse the situation of tax adjustments in member countries.[11] In 1964, the OECD

Secretariat released a first 'fact-finding report on border tax adjustments applied by Member Countries to exports and imports' in two parts: the first part analysed the various forms of BTAs as well as their effects, the second part presented the situations in Member countries.[12] In April 1965, a Working Party on Border Tax Adjustments was established.[13] In 1968, the OECD released a report entitled 'Border Tax Adjustments and Tax Structures in OECD Member countries'.[14] This report published in 1968 (hereafter: the '1968 OECD Report') gives an overview of the BTAs and tax structures of OECD member countries in March 1967.

10.1.2 The 1970 GATT Report

In March 1968, at the proposal of the United States, the Council of Representatives established a Working Party on 'Border Tax Adjustments'.[15] As the request was made by the US at the OECD level, this proposal can be explained in light of the new concerns of the United States regarding the potential effects of BTAs on international trade. According to the United States, 'Tax systems had changed considerably since the GATT provisions on border tax adjustments had been drafted and a more sophisticated view of the effects of these would be taken today'.[16] In other words, BTAs – which were not considered to be an important issue at the time of the adoption of GATT provisions – became an essential policy issue for the United States at the end of the 1960s.[17]

The mandate of the Working Party was to examine BTAs in light of the relevant GATT provisions, the practices of the contracting parties and their possible effects on international trade.[18] The United States' hoped-for result was to achieve agreement to a revision – if not a modification – of the GATT provisions on BTAs.[19]

10.1.3 Relationship between the Two Reports

The two reports are interrelated as the GATT Working Party relied on OECD documentation.[20] For example, the definition of BTAs in the OECD report was used in the GATT report.

10.2 HISTORY LESSONS

This section highlights the features of BTAs as they are put forward in the 1968 OECD and 1970 GATT reports. The objective is to explain how the design of so-called 'environmental BTAs' may contradict these distinguishing features. Three main components of BTAs are analysed:

their definition (10.2.1), their rationale (10.2.2) and their legal framework (10.2.3).

10.2.1　BTA Definition

The 1968 OECD Report defines BTAs – also called 'equalisation taxes' in the report[21] – as follows:

> While border tax adjustments may be defined in various ways, it is most convenient for dealing with the problems which they present to regard them as any fiscal measures which put into effect, in whole or in part, the destination principle (i.e. which enable exported products to be relieved of some or all of the tax charged in the exporting country in respect of similar domestic products sold to consumers on the home market and which enable imported products sold to consumers to be charged with some or all of the tax charged in the importing country in respect of similar domestic products).[22]

As already mentioned, this definition was later taken over by the 1970 GATT report. In order to make clear that BTAs should not necessarily take place 'at the border', the GATT Working Party suggested the concept of 'tax adjustments applied to goods entering into international trade' instead of referring to BTAs.[23] BTAs' definition may schematically be presented as shown in Figure 10.1.

BTAs should a priori be limited to 'fiscal measures', excluding 'non-fiscal regulatory measures'. This distinction has usually been taken into account in the literature on environmental BTAs. Authors who analyse non-fiscal proposals usually leave the reference to 'taxes' out of the BTA concept. For example, against the background of climate change, reference is often made to 'border carbon adjustment' instead of 'carbon-related BTAs'.[24]

The definition of the concept of tax is not clear-cut. At the national level, taxes are usually distinguished from charges, fees, etc. on the basis of

Figure 10.1　BTAs' mechanisms

criteria, aimed at ensuring that the adoption of taxes is made in accordance with sufficient constitutional guarantees. In contrast, the GATT does not provide for a definition of taxes. Moreover, GATT case law on the question of whether a measure falls under the 'tax category' or the category of 'regulatory measures' is limited to a few cases.[25] Therefore, there is scope to argue that any market-based measure assumed to be shifted into a product's price could be assimilated to a tax eligible for adjustment.[26]

BTAs cornerstone: taxes on domestic products
The 'taxes charged in respect of similar domestic products' in the national tax system (i.e. the second box in Figure 10.1) are the cornerstone of the BTA design. Indeed, the implementation of the destination principle is inherently linked to the national tax system imposed on domestic products, regardless of the tax system of the countries of import and export. The most important conditions surrounding BTAs' adoption relate to how the national tax system on domestic products is designed, which national products are subject to the tax, etc. As for BTAs on imports, the idea is that the BTAs should mirror the taxes imposed on domestic products. From this perspective, the concept of BTA can be described as a trade concept which puts limits on how domestic taxes may be applied on 'internationally traded goods'. The idea that the tax on imported products should mirror the tax imposed on like domestic products can be illustrated by reference to the case *Japan – Alcoholic Beverages II*, one of the cases related to BTAs on imports. In this case, a differential tax treatment was applied on vodka as well as other distilled spirits and liqueurs in comparison with the tax imposed on shochu (a Japanese alcohol). In other words, the tax on imported products was not mirroring the tax imposed on shochu. This differential tax treatment was deemed to be in violation of the GATT.[27]

In contrast to the 'traditional' definition of BTAs, environmentally related BTAs are sometimes defined by reference to the environmental system of the countries of import and export rather than by reference to the domestic (environmental) tax system of the countries willing to adopt environmental BTAs. Authors sometimes suggest that environmental BTAs should be applied in order to compensate for *the difference* in levels and impact on product price from domestic environmental policies and environmental policies implemented in the countries of import and export. For example, Horn and Mavroidis also state as follows: 'BTAs are typically policy schemes that *threaten* to impose such a tax/tariff should certain conditions be fulfilled. This means that the BTA regimes may affect other countries' policies. This is indeed the idea when they are being imposed to induce other countries to pursue more cooperative climate policies' (emphasis added).[28] According to Belleville, 'Such BTAs are

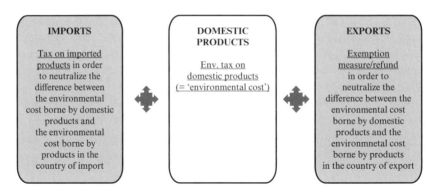

Figure 10.2   Environmental adjustments' proposals

designed to level the playing field between domestic entities and foreign competitors by *assuring that all producers serving the market are paying the same amount under the pertinent government policy*' (emphasis added).[29] In these definitions of carbon-related BTAs, BTAs are aimed at guaranteeing that all products bear a similar 'carbon cost', taking into account the potential higher costs that they would have had to bear, had they been produced in the national territory. The cornerstone of these proposals is the comparison between the environmental costs imposed by national policies on domestic products and the environmental costs borne by products in the countries of import and export (see the scheme in Figure 10.2).

In order to respect the essence of the international trade law concept of BTA, environmentally related BTAs should not be defined as measures used to neutralize differences between countries in how they internalize environmental costs into product price. Such a definition indeed contradicts the intrinsic nature of the traditional concept of BTA: BTAs are imposed on imported products in order to compensate for the tax burden borne by domestic products.

Environmental taxes applied on 'internationally traded goods' in order to internalize the differences in levels of environmental policies within the implementing country should better be named after other trade-related measures, which are also applied as a reaction to other countries' policies, such as anti-dumping measures or countervailing duties.[30]

10.2.2   BTA Rationale

The 1968 OECD and 1970 GATT reports illustrate that the rationale of traditional BTAs has been subject to much discussion. The origin of the two reports is indeed related to the questioning by the United States of the objectives and effects of BTAs. In the reports, it appears clear that proponents of BTAs consider that these measures are necessary to guarantee the neutrality of tax systems.[31] The underlying assumption is that taxes imposed on domestic products are shifted into product price. Under this assumption, BTAs aim at neutralizing the effect of *domestic* taxes on trade exchanges.[32] Here again, it may be derived from the reports that the cornerstone of the BTA design is the reference to the national tax system and not the difference between national and third country tax systems.

In contrast, the need for environmental BTAs is often explained by reference to their objectives of avoiding loss of competitiveness, reducing risks of 'pollution haven' (or 'carbon leakage' in the climate debate) and encouraging third countries to adopt environmental policies as stringent as the ones imposed on the national territory ('leverage').[33] The objectives related to pollution haven and leverage indirectly entail that environmental BTAs are used as a response to third country environmental policy framework. On the one hand, the objective related to pollution haven necessarily relies on the assumption that third countries have less strict environmental policies. In other words, the pollution haven hypothesis implies that environmental BTAs are adopted in light of a comparison between the levels of national and foreign environmental policies. On the other hand, the objective of putting pressure on third countries also involves the assumption that these countries lack environmental policies.[34] As mentioned *supra*, genuine BTAs are designed on the basis of the domestic tax system and not as a response to third country tax systems. Therefore, environmental trade-related measures that are designed as a reaction to other countries' environmental policies should not be called BTAs. Other trade-related concepts such as countervailing duties may better reflect the idea that a country is willing to react to third country policies.

The confusion between these 'environmental trade-related BTAs' and genuine environmental BTAs may be understood by the fact that the concept of 'adjustment' may easily lead one to think that third country (environmental) policies should be 'adjusted' so that imported products be subject to the same requirements as domestic products. Under the traditional concept of BTA with respect to imports, however, the concept of 'adjustment' only means that imported products should be subject to the same tax burden as domestic products, regardless of the tax applied in the country of origin. A similar confusion has arisen over the BTA objective of 'levelling the playing field'.[35] Where traditional BTAs are said to 'level the playing field for imported and domestically produced goods', the balance between imported and domestic goods is assessed in light of the tax burden imposed by the national tax system on domestic products.[36] In the case of environmental BTAs, this same expression ('levelling the playing field') is sometimes used to express the idea that similar 'environ-mental costs' should be borne by domestic and imported products, which is usually evaluated in the light of a comparison between the costs imposed on the domestic territory and abroad.[37] It may be argued that BTAs on imports also rely on a comparison between the taxes imposed on domestic products and the taxes that have been imposed on imported products in the country of export: in the case of traditional BTAs, these taxes would also be assumed to be inexistent. This 'fictive comparison' can however not be assimilated to the case where unilateral trade-related measures would be imposed on countries, on the basis of a real comparison between the level of environmental policies in the country of import and the country of export.

10.2.3   Legal Framework

The two reports list GATT relevant provisions for BTAs. These provisions include: GATT Articles I ('General Most-Favoured-Nation Treatment'), II ('Schedules of Concessions'), III ('National Treatment on Internal Taxation and Regulation'), VI ('Anti-dumping and Countervailing Duties'), VII ('Valuation for Customs Purposes') and Article XVI ('Subsidies').[38] In addition to these articles, the BTA legal framework also includes the Agreement on Subsidies and Countervailing Measures (ASCM), which was enacted after the issuance of the GATT and OECD reports. The interpretation to be given to these various provisions is far from clear-cut. The OECD and GATT reports highlight the points of disagreement between countries at the time. Among the controversial issues discussed by members of the working party was the question of which taxes should be eligible for adjustments, including the question of whether BTAs in respect of 'taxes occultes' (defined as 'the hidden element of a tax in an article, corresponding to the additional tax paid on any of these goods or services'[39]) were compatible with the GATT. The absence of consensus on these issues may be considered an opportunity to argue in favour of environmental BTAs. For example, the absence of agreement as to BTAs in respect of taxes occultes allow for arguing in favour of environmental BTAs on imported products containing certain polluting substances, when these substances are subject to domestic taxes in the national territory.[40]

In contrast to the original concept of BTA, authors do not only discuss 'environmental BTAs' in light of the traditional BTA provisions but also in light of GATT Article XX. It may seem logical since GATT Article XX specifically deals with environmental issues. Article XX is the GATT 'general exceptions' provision allowing WTO Members to adopt measures to protect a range of objectives, including measures 'necessary to protect human, animal or plant life or health' or measures 'relating to the conservation of exhaustible natural resources if such measures are made effective in conjunction with restrictions on domestic production or consumption'.[41] In other words, GATT Article XX allows WTO Members to establish a range of measures which would otherwise be contrary to the GATT. From this perspective, when GATT Article XX becomes the main provision on which environmental BTAs are grounded, it implies that BTAs' traditional legal framework (and related-design) no longer matters. Any measure may be adopted under GATT Article XX as long as the conditions of this Article – regardless of the design requirements mentioned in other GATT provisions – are fulfilled. Consequently, reference to GATT Article XX in the analysis of environmental trade-related measures may reveal that their design does not correspond to the traditional idea behind BTAs.

Only environmental taxes which can truly be analysed under BTAs' original legal framework should be called 'environmental BTAs'. An environmental trade-related measure which distinguishes between countries on the basis of the level of their environmental policies is at first sight contrary to GATT Article I, which requires that 'any advantage, favour, privilege or immunity granted by any contracting party to any product originating in or destined for any other country shall be accorded immediately and unconditionally to the like product originating in or destined for the territories of all other contracting parties'.[42] Consequently, as explained above, such measures should not be labelled as 'environmental BTAs'.

10.3 CONCLUSION

Analysis of the 1968 OECD and 1970 GATT reports on BTAs allows for highlighting the essence of the concept of BTA and comparing it with the concept of environmental BTA that has been developed in the last twenty years. The main recommendation emerging from this study is that the concept of 'environmental BTAs' be limited to fiscal measures that are genuinely based on the design of BTAs as explained in the 1968 OECD and 1970 GATT reports. Such limitation excludes using the concept of 'environmental BTAs' to refer to environmental unilateral trade-related measures aimed at reacting to third countries' lack of commitment to protecting the environment. As for these environmental trade-related measures, this chapter challenges authors to be creative – looking for inspiration in trade-related concepts that better reflect their proposals – in order to rename them.

NOTES

* I would like to thank the staff of the OECD Library and Archives for their great help in the compilation of primary materials for this research. Moreover, I would like to thank the participants and organizers of the Aarhus Conference on 'State Aid, Taxation and Sustainable Growth' (October 2013) as well as the participants and organizers of the 15th Global Conference on Environmental Taxation (Copenhagen, September 2014). Finally, I would like to thank Dr Henri Culot for his challenging comments as well as the anonymous reviewer.

1. See for example, in Paul Demaret and Raoul Stewardson, 'Border Tax Adjustments under GATT and EC Law and General Implications for Environmental Taxes' (1994) 28(4) *JWT* 5; Henrik Horn and Petros Mavroidis, 'To B(TA) or Not to B(TA)? On the Legality and Desirability of Border Tax Adjustments from a Trade Perspective' (2011) 34(11) *The World Economy* 1991; Jon M. Truby, 'Towards Overcoming the Conflict between Environmental Tax Leakage and Border Tax Adjustment Concessions for Developing Countries' (2010–2011) 12 *Vermont Journal of Environmental Law* 149. See also Ben Lockwood and John Whalley, 'Carbon Motivated Border Tax Adjustments: Old Wine in Green Bottles?' (2008) NBER Working Paper No. 14025.

2. See for example, in Frank Biermann and Rainer Brohm, 'Border Adjustments on Energy Taxes: A Possible Tool for European Policymakers in Implementing the Kyoto Protocol?' (2005) 74(2) *Vierteljahrshefte zur Wirtschaftsforschung* S. 249.

3. See for example, in Aaron Cosbey, Susanne Droege, Carolyn Fischer et al., 'A Guide for the Concerned: Guidance on the elaboration and implementation of border carbon adjustment' (2012) 3 *Entwined*; Valentina Durán Medina and Rodrigo Polanco Lazo, 'A Legal View on Border Tax Adjustments and Climate Change: A Latin American Perspective' (2011) 11(3) *Sustainable Development Law and Policy* 29; Olivier Godard, 'L'ajustement aux frontières, condition de la crédibilité d'une politique européenne du climat ambitieuse' (2011) 120 *Revue de l'OFCE* 177; Henrik Horn and Peter C. Mavroidis, 'Border Carbon Adjustments and the WTO', The Research Institute of Industrial Economics, Stockholm, Bruegel, Brussels, Centre for Economic Policy Research London, 14 March 2010, pp. 27–29; Christine Kaufmann and Rolf H. Weber, 'Carbon-Related Border Tax Adjustments: Mitigating Climate Change or Restricting International Trade?' (2011) 10 *World Trade Review* 497.

4. See for example, in Thomas J. Courchene and John R. Allan, 'Climate Change: The Case for a Carbon Tariff/Tax' (March 2008) *Policy Options* 59; Thomas J. Courchene, 'Climate Change, Competitiveness and Environmental Federalism: the Case for a Carbon Tax' (2008) Canada 2020 Speakers' Series; Camillo De Camillis and Malgorzata Goralczyk, 'Towards Stronger Measures for Sustainable Consumption and Production Policies: Proposal of a New Fiscal Framework Based on a Life Cycle Approach' (2013) 18(1) *The International Journal of Life Cycle Assessment* 263; David G. Duff and Margaret MacDonald, 'Towards a Destination-Based Carbon Tax', 14th Global Conference on Environmental Taxation, Kyoto, Japan, 17–19 October 2013; Charles E. McLure, 'The Carbon-Added Tax: An Idea Whose Time Should Never Come' (2010) 3 *Carbon and Climate Law Review* 250.

5. OECD, Border Tax Adjustments and Tax Structures in OECD Member Countries, 1968 (hereafter: 1968 OECD Report).

6. Paul Demaret and Raoul Stewarson, op. cit., 6; John Snape and Jeremy de Souza, *Environmental Taxation Law, Policy, Contexts and Practice* (Ashgate 2006), 9; Terence P. Stewart, Eric P. Salonen and Patrick J. McDonough, 'More Than 50 Years of Trade Rule Discrimination on Taxation: How Trade With China Is Affected' (2007) Trade Lawyers Advisory Group, 24; OECD, Environment Policy Committee and Committee on Fiscal Affairs. Joint Sessions on Taxation and Environment, 2nd Session. Environmental Taxes and Border Tax Adjustments, COM/ENV/EPOC/ DAFFE/CFA(94)31, 27 April 1994, p. 5, para. 9. See also David Ricardo, *The Works and Correspondence of David Ricardo*, vol. 4, Pamphlets and Papers 1815–1823, edited

by Piero Sraffa with the collaboration of M.H. Dobb, Liberty Fund (2005) http://oll.libertyfund.org/title/205/38614/885295 (accessed 21 January 2014).

7. See Gary Clyde and Carol Gabyzon, *Fundamental Tax Reform and Border Tax Adjustments* (1996) Institute for International Economics; Terence P. Stewart, Eric P. Salonen and Patrick J. McDonough, op. cit., p. 23; OECD, Environmental Taxes and Border Tax Adjustments, op. cit., p. 4, para. 7.

8. GATT, Border Tax Adjustments. Report of the Working Party on 2 December 1970, L/3464 (hereafter 1970 GATT Report).

9. See OECD, Council, Minutes of the 49th Meeting held at the Château de la Muette, Paris, on Tuesday, 30 July 1963, C/M(63)15 (Prov.), 16 August 1963, item 154, p. 9. See also OECD, Working Party No. 4 o the Council on Border Tax Adjustments, The United States Submission on Border Tax Adjustments, Paris, 16 February 1966, C/WP4(66)4; OECD, Council, Statement by the United States representative in the OECD Council on the prospective increase of the German Equalisation tax, Paris, 22 May 1962, C(62)91.

10. See OECD, Council, Statement by the United States representative in the OECD Council on the prospective increase of the German Equalisation tax, Paris, 22 May 1962, C(62)91.

11. Ibid., p. 13.

12. OECD Council, Fact-finding report on border tax adjustments applied by member countries to exports and imports (note by the Secretariat of the Council), Paris, 12 October 1964, C(64)137 Part I and Part II. See also OECD Trade Committee, Border Tax Adjustments, Consultation Procedure, Arrangements adopted by the Trade Committee, Paris, 23 June 1967, TC(67)14; OECD, Related Activities Division, Fact-finding report on border tax adjustments applied by member countries to exports and imports, Paris, 13 November 1967.

13. OECD Council, Report by Working Party No. 4 of the Council on Border tax adjust-ments (note by the secretary of the Council), Paris, 25 May 1966, C(66)53. See also OECD Council, Minutes of the 91st Meeting held at the Château de la Muette, on Tuesday, 13 April 1965, at 10.30 a.m., Paris, C/M(65)8(Prov.), 29 April 1965, para. 66, esp. p. 13; OECD Council, Minutes of the 92nd Meeting held at the Château de la Muette, Paris, on Thursday, 29 April 1965, Paris, C/M(65)9(Prov.) Part II, 24 May 1965, para. 74, p. 6; OECD, Border Tax Adjustments. Conclusions of the Executive Committee, Paris, 26 March 1965, CES/65.25.

14. 1968 OECD Report. A list of the most important OECD documents in relation to border tax adjustments can be found in OECD Council, OECD Documentation on Border Tax Adjustments. Request from the Director-General of the GATT (Note by the Secretary-General), Paris, 3 May 1968, C(68)60. See also OECD Council. Fact-Finding Report on Border Tax Adjustments applied by Member Countries to Exports and Imports, Paris, 12 October 1964, C(64) 137 Part I and Part II; OECD, Ad Hoc Group of the Trade Committee, Consultation on Changes in Border Tax Adjustments in Germany, Date of the next meeting, Paris, 28 November 1967.

15. GATT, Border Tax Adjustments. Proposed Terms of References for Working Party, 27 March 1968, C/W/123.

16. GATT, Minutes of Meeting held at the Palais of Nations on 27–28 March 1968, 5 April 1968, C/M/46, 8. See also Terence P. Stewart, Eric P. Salonen and Patrick J. McDonough, op. cit., 33–37.

17. GATT, Working Party on Border Tax Adjustments. Secretariat Note on Meeting of 30 April to 2 May 1968, 17 May 1968, L/3009, Annex, 9 (US Statement).

18. GATT, Border Tax Adjustments, Proposed Terms of References for Working Party, 27 March 1968, C/W/123; GATT, Border Tax Adjustments. Proposed Terms of Reference for Working Party, 28 March 1968, C/W/124. See also GATT, Minutes of Meeting held at the Palais of Nations on 27–28 March 1968, 5 April 1968, C/M/46, 11.

19. GATT, Minutes of the Council meeting held at the Palais des Nations, Geneva on 27 and 28 March 1968, C/M/46, 5 April 1968, pp. 8–9. See also L/3009, Annex, 10; L/3125, Annex, 21.

20. See Jennifer E. Farrell, *The Interface of International Trade Law and Taxation* (26 IBFD Doctoral Series 2013), p. 27, footnote 91. See also GATT, Minutes of Meeting held at the Palais of Nations on 27–28 March 1968, 5 April 1968, C/M/46, 11; OECD, Council, Relations with the GATT Report by the Trade Committee, Paris, 31 October 1961, OECD/C(61)45 and OECD, Council, OECD Documentation on Border Tax Adjustments. Request from the Director-General of the GATT (Note by the Secretary-General), Paris, 3 May 1968, C(68)60.
21. 1968 OECD Report, para. 68, p. 39.
22. 1968 OECD Report, para. 6.
23. 1970 GATT Report, para. 5.
24. Gregory Cook, 'Use of Border Adjustment Measures. A Cement Sector Perspective' (2011) Climate Strategies; Aaron Cosbey et al., op. cit.; Valentina Durán Medina and Rodrigo Polanco Lazo, op. cit.; Olivier Godard, op. cit.; Harro van Asselt and Frank Biermann, 'European Emissions Trading and the International Competitiveness of Energy-Intensive Industries: A Legal and Political Evaluation of Possible Supporting Measures' (2007) 25 *Energy Policy* 497. See also Kateryna Holzer, 'Proposals on Carbon-related Border Adjustments: Prospects for WTO Compliance' (2010) 4(1) Carbon and Climate Law Review, p. 51.
25. On the question whether GATT Article III:2 or III:4 should be applied, see United States – Taxes on Automobiles, Report of the Panel, DS31/R, paras. 5.42–5.43. See also United States – Measures Affecting the Importation, Internal Sale and Use of Tobacco, DS44/5; paras. 73–82; EEC – Measures on Animal Feed Proteins, adopted on 14 March 1978, BISD 25S/49, see paras 3.21–3.36 and para. 4.4. See also EEC – Programme of Minimum Import Prices, Licences and Surety Deposits for Certain Processed Fruits and Vegetables, adopted on 18 October 1978, BISD 25S/68, para. 3.4.
26. On this issue, see Felicity Deane, 'The Border Adjustments of the Australian Clean Energy Package' (2014) 17 *International Trade and Business Law Review*, p. 29, retrieved from http://eprints.qut.edu.au/66938/2/66938.pdf (accessed 23 April 2015); Biswajit Dhar and Kasturi Das, 'The European Union's Proposed Carbon Equalization System: Can it be WTO Compatible?' (2009) RIS Discussion Papers No. 156; Gary Clyde Hufbauer, Steve Charnovitz and Jisun Kim, *Global Warming and the World Trading System* (2009) Peterson Institute for International Economics. Moreover, it could also be argued that the requirements under GATT Articles III:2 and III:4 are similar. In this case, the distinction between tax and regulation would lose its significance.
27. WTO, Appellate Body, Japan – Taxes on Alcoholic Beverages, AB-1996-2, Report of the Appellate Body, WT/DS8/AB/R, WT/DS10/AB/R, WT/DS11/AB/R, 4 October 1996, p. 32: 'that shochu and vodka are like products and that Japan, by taxing imported products in excess of like domestic products in excess of like domestic products, is in violation of its obligations under Article III:2, first sentence, of the General Agreement on Tariffs and Trade 1994'.
28. Henrik Horn and Petros C. Mavroidis, 'To B(TA) or Not to B(TA)? On the Legality and Desirability of Border Tax Adjustments from a Trade Perspective' (2011) *The World Economy*, 1930–1931. See also: See Gavin Goh, 'The World Trade Organization, Kyoto and Energy Tax Adjustments at the Border' (2004) 38 *Journal of World Trade* 2, 398 and 419–422; Warwick J. McKibbin and Peter J. Wilcoxen, 'The Economic and Environmental Effects of Border Tax Adjustments for Climate Policy' (2008/2009) Brookings Trade Forum, p. 1 ('The BTAs would be based on the carbon emissions associated with the production of each imported product, and they would be intended to match the cost increase that would have occurred had the exporting country adopted a climate policy similar to that of the importing country').
29. Mark L. Belleville, 'The Key Stone in the Carbon Tariff Wall: The Alberta Oil Sands and the Legality of Taxing Imports Based on Their Carbon Footprint' (2013) 43 *Environmental Law*, 375. In his article, Belleville acknowledges that 'BTAs differ from typical border taxes (and import tariffs or excise taxes) because a permissible BTA

is truly an 'adjustment' of the charge on an import equal to the tax or charge that the domestic producer of a like product must pay'. See also the confusing definition of Border Carbon Adjustment Measure in: Kommerskollegium (Swedish National Board of Trade), 'Practical Aspects of Border Carbon Adjustment Measures. Using a Trade Facilitation Perspective to Assess Trade Cost', 2010 (5), p. 4: 'border carbon adjustment measures can take two forms: carbon tariffs and a mandatory requirement for importers to hold emissions allowances. A carbon tariff on imports would, in practice, work as fee levied on imports at the border, very much like an ordinary tariff'.

30. We recognize that these concepts also present limits as to the implementation of environmental trade-related measures. See Joost Pauwelyn, 'Carbon leakage measures and border tax adjustment under WTO law', in G. Van Calster and D. Prévost (eds), *Research Handbook on Environment, Health and the WTO* (EE 2013), 448.

31. OECD, Fact-Finding Report on Border Tax Adjustments applied by member countries to exports and imports, Paris, 13 November 1967, p. 3. See also OECD 1968 Report, p. 67, para. 112 and para. 150.

32. 1968 OECD Report, p. 71, para. 120 et al.: 'Most of the arguments either for or against border tax adjustments in respect of consumption taxes centre on the question of the extent to which such taxes are shifted forwards into the price of goods'.

33. See Aaron Cosbey et al., op. cit., p.8. See also M. Condon and A. Ignaciuk, 'Border Carbon Adjustment and International Trade: A Literature Review', *OECD Trade and Environment Working Papers*, 2013/06, OECD Publishing, pp. 5–10; Thomas Cottier and Nashina Shariff, 'International Trade and Climate Change', in G. Van Calster and D. Prévost, *Research Handbook on Environment, Health and the WTO* (EE 2013), pp. 435–436.

34. It could however be argued that this objective may be met even when environmental BTAs are designed regardless of third country policies. Environmental BTAs may indeed serve as an *example* of a measure helping to neutralize the trade effects deriving from the adoption of national environmental taxes, hence encouraging third countries to adopt domestic environmental taxes as well by relieving them from the fear that such measure may have a negative effect on domestic products' price.

35. On the 'level playing field' concept, See also Donald H. Regan, 'How to Think about PPMs (and Climate Change)', in Thomas Cottier, Olga Nartova and Sadeq Z. Bigdeli, *International Trade Regulation and the Mitigation of Climate Change, World Trade Forum* (CUP 2009), p. 110.

36. Wolfgang Schön, 'World Trade Organization Law and Tax Law' (2004) International Bureau of Fiscal Documentation, Bulletin, p. 287.

37. See for example, Tom Manders and Paul Veenendaal, 'Border Tax Adjustments and the EU-ETS. A Quantitative Assessment', October 2008, No. 171, CPB Netherlands Bureau for Economic Policy Analysis, p. 13: 'BTAs are taxes imposed on imports or tax-relief granted to exports, used to level the playing field between taxed domestic industries and untaxed competitors abroad'.

38. GATT, Working Party on Border Adjustments, Meeting of 18–20 June 1968, Note by the Secretariat, 11 July 1968, L/3039, p. 1; GATT, Working Party on Border Tax Adjustments, Note by the Secretariat on 'the GATT Rules on Border Tax Adjustments', Spec(68)55, 31 May 1968. See also 1968 OECD report. The 1968 OECD report only lists Articles III and XVI of the GATT.

39. 1968 OECD report, para. 19.

40. The Superfund case illustrates that such taxes have been implemented in the past: GATT, United States – Taxes on Petroleum and Certain Imported Substances, Report by the Panel, L/6175, 5 June 1987.

41. GATT Article XX, (b) and (g).

42. GATT Article I. Please note that some authors have however suggested that products originating in countries with a low level of environmental policy could be considered 'unlike' to products originating in countries with a high level of environmental policy:

Joost Pauwelyn, op. cit., p. 489: 'the issue is primarily whether, for example, steel from China *made with coal* (subject to a *high* carbon tax or regulation) is "like" domestically produced US steel *using natural gas* (subject to a *lower* carbon tax or regulation, as steel made with natural gas emits less carbon)'. We disagree: it cannot be assumed that a product produced in a country X inherently reflects the environmental policy of this country.

11. Renewable energy: subsidies and taxes as competition distortion*

Rolf H. Weber

11.1 INTRODUCTION

Governmental support for renewable energy production and consumption is an important tool to increase energy efficiency, to reduce carbon emissions and thereby to achieve sustainability objectives. A government can offer financial support in the form of subsidies or tax incentives, such as offering preferential tax treatment for economic operators or imposing higher taxes on the emission-intensive use of energy.[1] However, such measures bear the risk of being not compliant with international trade law: The regulatory framework of the World Trade Organization (WTO Law) enshrines important nondiscrimination principles, which can cause conflicts with environment-protective measures.

WTO Law qualifies electricity as a good leading to the applicability of the General Agreement on Tariffs and Trade (GATT).[2] Therefore, WTO Members are bound by the key disciplines of WTO Law, namely the obligation to accord national and most-favoured nation (MFN) treatment to like products of all WTO Members (Article I and III GATT). With regard to the design of domestic tax schemes in particular, WTO Members are obliged to follow the nondiscrimination-obligations set forth in Article III GATT. As far as subsidies are concerned, WTO Law encompasses general principles stated in Articles VI and XVI GATT as well as detailed specific provisions in the Subsidies and Countervailing Measures (SCM) Agreement.

This contribution looks at the potential scope and design of WTO Law compatible subsidies and taxes introduced by governments to support the production and use of renewable energy.[3] Special emphasis is given to the recent WTO Law case related to a (Canadian) feed-in tariff program that balanced international trade and environmental law for the first time in a distinct manner. Thereby, the elements of admissible subsidies are assessed and the problems of balancing the undistorted competition against environmental needs are discussed; in this connection a particular focus is laid on the justification reasons for applying anti-competitive sustainability measures.

11.2 SUBSIDIZATION OF RENEWABLE ENERGY

11.2.1 Subsidies in WTO Law

According to Article 1.1 of the SCM Agreement a subsidy exists in case of a 'financial contribution by a government or any public body' or 'any form of income or price support' that 'confers a benefit' on a recipient.

A subsidy can be challenged if it is 'specific' (Article 1.1.2 and Article 2 SCM Agreement) and on the basis of positive (in other words, affirmative, objective, credible and verifiable)[4] evidence that it distorts trade or causes 'adverse effects' to the interests of other Members (Article 5 SCM Agreement).

At the time of its incorporation in 1995, the SCM Agreement distinguished three categories of subsidies, namely prohibited ('red light') subsidies, actionable ('yellow light') subsidies and non-actionable ('green light') subsidies. Originally the SCM Agreement also contained an exemption clause for environmental subsidies. However, as of January 1, 2000 the provisions on non-actionable subsidies as well as the exemption expired since WTO Members decided not to extend it.[5]

11.2.2 Elements of Subsidies in View of Renewable Energies

Canada renewable energy case
Measures to promote renewable energies can amount to a subsidy under the SCM Agreement if they are considered to be a 'financial contribution by a government' (Article 1.1 (a)(1) SCM Agreement) and confer a 'benefit' (Article 1.1 (b)(1) SCM Agreement).[6]

The WTO dispute settlement body's first ruling on the compliance of a domestic regulation for the promotion of renewable energies with the SCM Agreement can provide partial clarification with regards to the legal standard to be applied in this context. In Canada Renewable Energy,[7] the WTO Panel and Appellate Body had to assess the compliance of a feed-in tariff (FIT) program introduced by Ontario based on two substantive grounds, namely (1) the claim of violating the provisions on National Treatment (Article III:4 GATT and Article 2.1 of the Agreement on Trade-Related Investment Measures) and (2) the claim of constituting a prohibited subsidy under Article 3.1(b) SCM Agreement.

Whereas the Panel and Appellate Body acknowledged the legitimacy of the objectives of the FIT program, it nevertheless ruled that the local content requirements favored domestic renewable energy equipment and therefore violated the National Treatment provisions.[8] However, neither the WTO Panel nor the Appellate Body (AB) could confirm the existence of a subsidy despite a thorough examination of the submitted claims and arguments. Even though an eventual illegal subsidization was not excluded, both WTO judicial organs refrained from taking a clear decision, arguing that it would have been the burden of the complainants to submit sufficient evidence for factual findings.[9] Since the WTO AB will most likely be confronted with the question of whether a feed-in tariff is a subsidy in the near future again it appears worthwhile to analyze the Canada Renewable Energy case in more detail.[10]

Financial contribution by a government
The term 'public body' in Article 1.1(a)(1) of the SCM Agreement is regularly interpreted in a broad way. A body can be considered public if its management is accountable to the government and exercises delegated responsibilities to perform a public function or service.[11]

Equally, the term 'financial contribution' has a wide meaning referring to the transfer of certain economic resources from a government or a public body to recipients such as enterprises and industries.[12] Article 1.1(a)(1) SCM Agreement enumerates four possible forms of a financial contribution namely: (1) a direct transfer of funds, (2) foregone or not collected government revenue being otherwise due (such as taxes), (3) provision of goods or services other than general infrastructure or purchase of goods by a government and (4) payments to a funding mechanism.

In Canada Renewable Energy the WTO AB defined 'public body' in line with the previous jurisprudence[13] as an 'entity that exercises authority vested in it by a government' for the performance of governmental functions[14] and accordingly found that this requirement was met since several governmental agencies and state-related bodies were responsible for the comprehensive industrial program.[15]

With regard to whether the FIT program constitutes a 'financial contribution', the Panel found that 'the appropriate legal characterization to be given . . . is as "government purchases of goods" under Article 1.1(a)(1)(iii) SCM Agreement' since the government purchased electricity produced from renewable resources and had it delivered into the system to grant a diversified supply mix.[16] The AB upheld the Panel's finding about the legal characterization of the FIT scheme and further clarified that 'that a transaction may fall under more than one type of financial contribution'.[17]

Benefit-analysis and market delineation

A benefit (Article 1.1(a)(2) SCM Agreement) is deemed to exist when the financial contribution places the recipient in a more advantageous position ('better off') than without governmental intervention.[18] This benefit-analysis requires an identification of the applicable market,[19] which is often done by way of comparison of the conditions of the government-favored producers with those of the other producers in the same market.

In the case at hand, the Panel found that the relevant market was a single market of electricity generated from all sources of energy, rather than a separate renewable energy market.[20] However, the AB reversed this finding and developed a novel conceptual interpretation distinguishing between government intervention that creates new markets (that would otherwise not exist) and government intervention in markets that already exist.[21] According to the AB 'where a government creates a market, it cannot be said that the government intervention distorts the market, as there would not be a market if the government would not have created it'.[22] The AB held that the creation of markets by governments does not in and of itself give rise to subsidies.[23] With regard to the relevant market, the AB found the 'benefit benchmarks for wind- and solar PV-generated electricity should be found in the markets for wind- and solar PV-generated'.[24] The AB, however, did not complete the benefit-analysis since it would have been the complainant's burden to establish a *prima facie* case and to submit the facts to determine a benchmark market and, consequently, a benefit.[25]

11.2.3   Assessment

The first decision by the WTO AB in the context of renewable energy support and subsidies has attracted major attention and was confronted with critical observations: The major concern consists in the appreciation that the WTO AB seemingly wanted to avoid a clear ruling on whether the FIT program must be qualified as a subsidy or not ('we cannot determine whether the challenged measures confer a benefit ... and whether they constitute prohibited subsidies').[26] Obviously, this creates uncertainty for governments and for investors in renewable energies, particularly since this issue is likely to return in WTO adjudication.[27]

The WTO AB's opinion that the governmental regulator had created a new market leaves it open how a market analysis should be conducted.[28] Other commentators find it problematic that according to the WTO AB (1) supply side factors such as the cost structures between different electricity generating technologies and (2) the supply mix reflecting a government's policy for energy security have to be taken into account for the relevant market.[29] The question remains unanswered whether renewable energy markets will be able to compete with electricity from conventional electricity sources on a purely financial basis without government intervention.[30] Further open issues also merit attention:[31] How can it be determined whether a green market is in the process of formation or has already been established in order to assess a governmental preference as subsidy? Does the existence of previous or concurrent programs with similar objectives have a bearing on this dichotomy? Should temporal aspects, such as the duration of a program, be taken into account?

However, notwithstanding these uncertainties, it is worth pointing out that the existence of a financial contribution and the respective benefits do not automatically qualify climate-related subsidies as illegal measures under WTO Law.[32] If green subsidies are designed in a proper way without any import substitution or export promotion elements legal challenges are less likely to be successful.

11.2.4 Outlook

The procedure has shown that the assessment of subsidies in the renewable energy market can become quite complex and that an adjustment of the international trade rules improving the supportiveness with international environmental law remains a burning political task.[33] A need to have more debates on renewable energy incentives in different committees in the WTO can hardly be contested. As long as no such movement is successful the WTO AB will either have to limit the financial promotion of renewable energy or find creative interpretations of the existing WTO Law.

11.2.5 Annex: Regional Level

Recently, the governmental support has also been challenged in the European Union. On July 1, 2014, the Court of Justice (CJ) decided that a Swedish support scheme promoting green energy production was compatible with EU Law.[34] The CJ came to the conclusion that the Swedish support scheme is capable of hindering imports of electricity from other Member States (in the given case Finland). Furthermore, the possibility for producers of green electricity from Sweden to sell their certificates together with the electricity that they produce, as a package, would facilitate their business prospects; as a result, the scheme constitutes a restriction of the free movements of goods.[35] The importance of the case, however, consists in the fact that this restriction was justifiable based on the specific exemption clause of Article 36 TFEU.[36]

11.3   TAXES AND RENEWABLE ENERGY

11.3.1   Taxes in WTO Law

The WTO Law does not define the term 'tax' but its notion is understood in a rather broad way, encompassing direct and indirect payments to the government as well as direct and indirect tax reliefs granted by the government. WTO Law acknowledges that national tax schemes can have the same effects on trade as tariffs and amount to subsidies. Thus, WTO Member's preferential tax schemes have often been subject to disputes before the WTO AB,[37] but so far none of these disputes has concerned environmental taxation schemes; however, with the increasing use of taxes as a fiscal incentive instrument, the situation might change in the future.

11.3.2   Assessment of Taxes in View of the National Treatment Principle

Governments, with regard to taxes, need to take into account the general principles of WTO Law, in particular the national treatment obligation. The relevant provisions state that WTO Members shall not apply taxes in a protectionist manner (Article III:1 GATT) and that Members shall not levy higher taxes on imported products than on 'like', 'directly competitive' or 'substitutable' domestic products (Article III:2 GATT). Whereas judicial interpretation considered Article III:1 GATT to be a principle without normative force,[38] Article III:2 GATT contains specific obligations concerning the design of a domestic tax: A tax measure is considered inconsistent with Article III:2 if it taxes 'like' foreign products 'in excess' of domestic ones, or if it taxes 'directly competitive or substitutable' foreign products 'not similarly' and 'so as to afford protection to domestic production'.[39]

Likeness of 'green' and 'grey' energy
The first sentence of Article III:2 GATT contains two elements: the 'likeness' of the taxed products and the whether the foreign product is taxed 'in excess of' the domestic one.[40] Whereas the latter one can be determined through a comparison of the actual tax burden of the products (in other words, the calculation of the tax/price-ratio),[41] the determination of the likeness of two products is often controversial.

Generally, the likeness under Article III GATT is determined based on four criteria: (1) the product's end-uses in a given market; (2) consumers' tastes and habits, (3) the product's properties, nature and quality and (4) its tariff classification.[42] Aside from the criteria of 'consumer preferences' the GATT, contrary to EU-law,[43] does not take into consideration process and production methods (PPMs) when determining the likeness of two products. PPMs concern differences in terms of the production process which, however, do not necessarily affect the appearance of the final products in question. Thus, it is not undisputed as to whether this criterion, which is of particular interest in the context of environmental measures, should suffice to render two products 'unlike'. For such reasons, it appears appropriate to assess the likeness on a case-by-case basis.[44]

The question of the likeness of 'green' and 'grey' energy has so far never been subject to WTO jurisprudence. If the WTO AB would maintain its traditionally broad interpretation for the assessment of likeness also in the context of energy, it appears to be probable that 'green' and 'grey' energy would be seen as 'like' products: They fall in the same tariff classification category (HS 2716.00, 'Electrical Energy'), they share the same end use and they cannot be distinguished based on physical characteristics.

The only criterion which might allow a differentiation is the 'consumer preference' applied by the WTO AB in the EC Asbestos case;[45] however, contrary to energy production, in the asbestos situation a direct link between the products and their health effects was given. Nevertheless, in view of consumer preferences it could be argued that a competitive relationship between 'green' and 'grey' electricity does exist.[46] The fact that electricity is not a tangible good and is not visible for consumers strengthens the need to take PPM into consideration in order to carry out an appropriate comparison between 'green' and 'grey' electricity.[47] This is further reinforced by the AB's finding that likeness in the context of Article III:2 GATT first sentence should be construed narrowly since the second sentence provides for a separate and distinctive consideration.[48] This assessment might also be based on the comparable arguments of the WTO AB in the Canada Renewable Energy case;[49] if 'green' and 'grey' energy would amount to different markets, the likeness of the two products could be hardly assumed.[50]

Competitiveness and substitutability of 'green' and 'grey' energy
Even if the taxed products are not considered to be like, the tax measure at issue can still be in breach of the national treatment principle: the *Ad* Article to Article III:2 GATT second sentence further states that Members shall not apply taxes on 'directly competitive or substitutable products' in a way 'not similar' and 'so as to afford protection to domestic production'.

The analysis of whether two products are 'directly competitive or substitutable' has to be conducted on a case-by-case basis considering not only the physical characteristics or consumer-preferences[51] but also the relevant 'marketplace', in particular the cross-price elasticity of the products.[52] However, in the case of renewable energy, the recent findings brought uncertainty over the question whether the wholesale electricity market should be considered or if there is a single market for renewable energy.

Furthermore, the AB stated that 'supply-side factors suggest that wind power and solar PV producers of electricity cannot compete with other electricity producers because of differences in cost structures and operating costs and characteristics'.[53] This reasoning regarding the SCM Agreement might indicate that the relationship between renewable and conventional energies cannot be considered to be 'directly competitive or substitutable' under Article III:2 GATT.

With regard to the second criterion ('not similarly taxed') the AB clarified that this requirement goes further than 'in excess of' in Article III:2 GATT first sentence, where 'even the smallest amount of 'excess' is too much'.[54] Therefore, the degree of the preferential tax treatment for renewable must be 'more than *de minimis*' to be considered 'not similarly taxed'.[55]

Finally, the WTO AB clarified that the assessment of the third criterion ('so as to afford protection to domestic production') 'requires a comprehensive and objective analysis of the structure and application of the measure in question on domestic as compared to imported products'.[56] In Japan Alcoholic Beverages II the AB upheld the Panel's finding that the tax measure at issue was applied so as to afford protection since it failed to guarantee competitive conditions for directly competitive or substitutable foreign products.[57] Since governmental support for renewable energy usually only aspires to 'level the playing field' it is not likely that a preferential tax treatment scheme would be found to restrict the market access for foreign non-renewable energy. However, this strongly depends on the design and the modalities of the tax scheme at issue and would have to be determined on a case-by-case basis.

Conclusion

Recent case law concerning renewable energy in the context of subsidies suggests that the WTO AB might deviate from the traditionally broad interpretation of likeness. The adoption of a narrow legal standard (as was suggested also in Japan Alcoholic Beverages II)[58] for likeness would lead to the consequence that 'green' and 'grey' electricity would not be classified as like products. The same result would be achieved in case of following an approach that takes into consideration PPM when determining the likeness of two products: When focusing on production methods, energy generated from renewable resources could hardly be considered the same as electricity generated from fossil fuel resoucres or nuclear power.

In analyzing the 'competitiveness' and 'substitutability', the WTO AB would have to assess the conditions of the relevant market. In this regard, the recent case law leads to uncertainties concerning the applicable market benchmark: If a Panel entrusted with an analysis of non-renewable and renewable energies under Article III:2 GATT would, in analogy to the AB in the recent Canada Renewable Energy case, find that there is no wholesale electricity market, 'green' and 'grey' energy could hardly be considered 'directly competitive or substitutable'.

11.3.3 Assessment of Taxes in View of Actionable Subsidies

Preferential tax treatment possibly amounts to a subsidy under WTO Law if it is considered a 'financial contribution by the government' which 'confers a benefit'. To be considered as non-compliant with WTO Law, a tax scheme would further have to be specific and cause an adverse effect on the interest of other Members.[59]

Taxes are typically levied by the government and thus the criterion of the subsidizing entity is regularly fulfilled. The assessment of the 'financial contribution' might be more difficult since preferential tax treatment is not a direct fiscal contribution. Taxes are listed under the concept of 'government revenue that is otherwise due is forgone or not collected' in Article 1.1(a)(1)(ii) SCM Agreement. However, the term 'otherwise due' is vague and thus afflicted with legal uncertainty.[60]

In assessing whether there is 'government revenue that is otherwise due' the WTO has to compare the tax treatment applicable to the alleged subsidy recipients to the taxes that would have been raised 'otherwise'.[61] According to the WTO AB in US FSC the applicable benchmark for the 'otherwise due'-test is the 'tax rules applied by the Member in question':[62] Only if the tax treatment at issue deviates from the general rule of taxation insofar as to 'constitute an exception to this rule'[63] it can be considered 'otherwise due' and challenged under the SCM Agreement.[64] In cases where a 'general rule for taxation' cannot be identified the 'fiscal treatment for legitimately comparable income' can serve as the normative benchmark.[65] This benchmark analysis should also take into consideration logic and objective reasons behind the differential treatment.[66] However, the question if and to which degree a different tax rate can be justified by environmental concerns is highly controversial and not yet clarified by jurisprudence.[67]

Third, the contested tax scheme has to 'confer a benefit' within the meaning of Article 1.1(b) SCM Agreement on the allegedly subsidized taxpayer or the recipient of a tax exemption. As already noted[68] the 'benefit' is calculated on the basis of a relevant-market-analysis and is deemed to exist if the recipient is 'better of' with the favorable tax treatment or the tax exemption rather than without it. In respect of the assessment of the challenged 'benefit' in the context of renewable energies similar considerations must be taken into account as done by the WTO AB in the Canada Renewable Energy case; in particular, the question arises whether a market is newly created or corrected by the tax regime.[69] Furthermore, an analysis needs to be conducted as to the situation of the renewable energy suppliers both with and without financial contribution.[70]

11.4 JUSTIFICATION OF TRADE DISTORTING SUBSIDIES AND TAXES

11.4.1 Article XX of the GATT

Trade restrictive measures can generally be justified, if specific interests are given which call for the protection of political, social or cultural objectives. However, in order not to jeopardize the legalization of cross-border trade, the exceptions must be interpreted in a narrow way.[71]

In the context of renewable energy, the main justification reasons concern the conservation of exhaustible natural resources (Article XX (g) GATT) and the protection of human, animal or plant life and health (Article XX (b) GATT).[72]

In order to fulfill the criteria of Article XX (b) GATT, a national measures distorting cross-border trade have to meet a necessity test,[73] in other words, a weighting and balancing process to find out whether less restrictive measures would be suitable to achieve the envisaged national interest.[74] Interpretation elements are (1) the relative importance of the policy objective, (2) the contribution of the measure to the achievement of the ends sought (sustainability), and (3) the effect of the measure on trade.[75] Article XX (g) GATT, however, requires only that the measure at issue be related to the conservation of exhaustible natural resources, which implies a weaker material link between the trade restrictive domestic measure and the justifying objective.

Furthermore, Article XX GATT encompasses an introductory provision ('Chapeau'), which has been constantly interpreted by the WTO AB as containing three standards, fairly broad in scope and reach, namely (1) the avoidance of arbitrary discrimination (2) as well as unjustifiable discrimination (3) and of a disguised restriction on international trade.[76]

In theory, both exceptions are applicable in the given field, however, since the direct link between 'green' electricity and health is not close, some reluctance in the assumption that the WTO AB would easily apply this provision appears to be justified.[77]

11.4.2 Application of Article XX GATT on Subsidies and Taxes

Looking from a formal perspective, Article XX GATT can apply if subsidies or taxes do not comply with the national treatment principle. In case of a violation of the SCM Agreement the assessment is less clear since the SCM Agreement is a special law and its Article 32.1[78] states the prevailing force of the respective special law. Nevertheless, legal doctrine argues that Article XX GATT should be taken into account if there is sufficient evidence that the introduced measures (taxes or subsidies) are primarily aiming at the conservation of exhausting natural resources or the protection of life and health.[79]

A justification by a national legislator will only be successful if the objective with which a subsidy or a tax is introduced is clearly determined. As mentioned, the subsidy must be a necessary means to protect the environment or lead to a reduction of risks for human, animal or plant life or health. Generally, therefore, the previous practice of the WTO AB appears to be reluctant in accepting the fulfillment of the conditions contained in Article XX GATT, however, the application of the justification provisions has become more flexible during the recent past.

11.4.3 Annex: Regional Level

In the mentioned Swedish renewable energy case, the CJ ruled that the caused restriction on the import of electricity is justified by the objective of promoting the use of renewable energy sources in order to protect the environment and to combat climate change. In the Court's opinion, the measures promoting the transition to green energy justifiably target the production stage rather than the consumption stage. Furthermore, according to the Court the support scheme is necessary in order to foster, from a long-term perspective, investments in green energy.[80] Consequently, on the European level, governmental measures supporting renewable energy seem to be more acceptable as in international trade law.

11.5 OUTLOOK

In the past, countries only had limited tools to encourage industries to adopt greener technologies or to promote environmentally preferable products. In addition, the practice of the WTO AB was quite inflexible in accepting the justification reasons as of Article XX GATT in environmental matters.

In the context of renewable energies (having gained importance after the nuclear power disaster in Japan) the WTO AB in the recent case Canada Renewable Energy assessed the treatment of subsidies more flexibly by arguing that the wholesale energy market was an irrelevant market for the benefit-analysis. Even if the regulatory measure in the given situation has not been considered as being in compliance with the national treatment principle of the WTO Law the conclusion can be drawn from the decision, provided a detailed analysis is executed, that along the chosen approach it seems to be possible that environmentally friendly subsidies and taxes could be (partly) allowed again.

As a consequence, the Canada Renewable Energy decision appears as a positive sign towards an improved conservation of environmental sustainability. However, a precise delineation of the relevant market is necessary, based on the characteristics in the given circumstances. In addition, the WTO Law disciplines (most favored nation principle and national treatment principle) need to be carefully assessed in the design of subsidies and taxes and finally the mentioned justification reasons must be evaluated.

Notwithstanding the fact that the first relevant decision of the WTO AB addressing renewable energy does give some hope in respect of a broader consideration of environmental protection and sustainability considerations, AB practice alone cannot solve the existing tensions between international trade and international environmental law. Therefore, WTO Law needs to be appropriately adjusted. In this sense, a number of WTO Members officially started negotiations for a plurilateral agreement related to environmental goods on July 8, 2014.[81] The respective countries would reach 86 percent coverage in respect of the envisaged environmental goods. The aim consists in abolishing any import taxes on these goods and to increase the volume of cross-border trade with (expected volume: USD 1 billion per year).

Consequently, assessing the present situation, the prospects for reconciling international trade law with environment and sustainability objectives appear to be improving. But continuing efforts are needed to find an adequate equilibrium between the differing policies.

NOTES

*   The author would like to thank Rika Koch, MLaw, University of Zurich for her valuable support in the finalization of this chapter.
1.   The present contribution analyzes subsidies and taxes promoting renewable energy. Other climate change mitigation measures are border tax adjustments and emission trading schemes; to these measures see Kaufmann and Weber (2011).
2.   Cf. Classification No. 2716.00 of the Harmonized System (HS) and the GATT Schedules of Concessions list, in which electricity is denoted as a good.

3. For a general overview see also Weber (2014), 612–619 and Condon and Sinha (2013), 52–91.
4. See Appellate Body Report, United States Anti Dumping Measures at Certain Hot-Rolled Steel Products from Japan, WT/DS184/AB/R (adopted July 24, 2001), para. 192.
5. See Weber (2014), 617; Hsueh (2013), 530–531; Condon (2009), 901–902.
6. For an overview in relation to renewable energy and climate change issues see Condon and Sinha (2013), 5761 and 208–210; Howse (2010), 12–15; Rubini (2012).
7. Appellate Body Report, Canada Certain Measures Affecting the Renewable Energy Generation Sector; Canada Measures Relating to the Feed-in Tariff Program, WT/DS412/AB/R, WT/DS426/AB/R (adopted May 24, 2013); Panel Reports Canada Certain Measures Affecting the Renewable Energy Generation Sector; Canada Measures Relating to the Feed-in Tariff Program, WT/DS412R, WT/DS426R (adopted May 24, 2013). The Appellate Body and the Panel issued their reports on these two disputes in the form of a single document.
8. See AB Report, Canada Renewable Energy (fn 6), paras. 5.79, 5.84, 6.1; Panel Report, Canada Renewable Energy (fn 6), paras. 8.6 and 8.7; the National Treatment issue will not be discussed in connection with the subsidies hereinafter, but only related to taxes (see section 11.0).
9. See section 11.2.2.
10. At the moment, four other cases are pending, namely DS419 (China), DS452 (European Union), DS456 (India) and DS459 (European Union).
11. See also Appellate Body Report, United States Definitive Anti-dumping and Countervailing Duties on Certain Products from China, WT/DS379/AB/R (adopted March 25, 2011), para. 320.
12. See also Panel Report, United States Measures Treating Export Restraints as Subsidies, WT/DS194/R (adopted August 23, 2001), paras. 8.65 and 8.73.
13. See for example AB Report, anti-dumping and countervailing duties (fn 11), para. 320.
14. *Idem*, paras. 309/10 and 316.
15. Shadikhodjaev (2013), 870.
16. Panel Report, Canada Renewable Energy (fn 6), paras. 7.169–7.185 and 7.222–7.241.
17. AB Report, Canada Renewable Energy (fn 6), paras. 5.118–5.139.
18. See Panel Report, Canada Measures Affecting the Export of Civilian Aircraft, WT/DS70/RW (adopted May 9, 2000), para. 9.112. and para. 9.120, as upheld by the Appellate Body Report, WT/DS70/AB/R, paras. 153 ff.
19. See also AB Report, Canada Aircraft (fn 17), paras. 154–157.
20. AB Report, Canada Renewable Energy (fn 6), para. 5.196.
21. *Idem*, para. 5.188.
22. *Idem*.
23. *Idem*, para. 5.190; Shadikhodjaev (2014), 9.
24. *Idem*, para. 5.190.
25. *Idem*, para. 5.219.
26. *Idem*, para. 5.246.
27. Casier and Moerenhout (2013), 2/3.
28. This approach might lead regulators to move to the design of new markets in order to avoid the application of the benchmarking method.
29. Casier and Moerenhout (2013), 4.
30. The question remains whether the market design model is sustainable and does not underestimate structural dynamics.
31. See also Shadikhodjaev (2013), 877.
32. *Idem*.
33. Casier and Moerenhout (2013), 6.
34. Case C-573/12, Ålands Vindkraft AB Energimyndigheten, judgment given on July 1, 2014, not yet reported.
35. *Idem*, paras. 56–75.
36. See section 11.0.

37. See for example Appellate Body Report, Japan Taxes on Alcoholic Beverages, WT/DS8/AB/R, WT/DS10/AB/R, WT/DS11/AB/R (October 4, 1996), Appellate Body Report, Chile Taxes on Alcoholic Beverages, WT/DS87/AB/R; WT/DS110/AB/R (December 13, 1999), Appellate Body Report, Korea Taxes on Alcoholic Beverages, WT/DS75/AB/R, WT/DS84/AB/R (adopted January 18, 1999).
38. Panel Reports, United States Measures Affecting Alcoholic and Malt Beverages, DS23/R – 39S/206 (adopted June 19, 1992), para. 5.2, reiterated by Panel Reports United States Standards for Reformulated and Conventional Gasoline, WT/DS2/R (adopted January 29, 1996), para. 6.71.
39. AB Report, Japan Alcoholic Beverages II (fn 37), 18/19 and 24.
40. AB Report, Japan Alcoholic Beverages II (fn 37), 18/19.
41. Panel Report, Japan Alcoholic Beverages II (fn 37), para. 6.24 ff. as confirmed by AB Report, Japan – Alcoholic Beverages II (fn 37), 223.
42. AB Report, Japan Alcoholics II (fn 37), 20, with reference to the Report of the Working Party on Border Tax Adjustments, *BISD* 18S/97, para. 18, reiterated by the Panel Report, European Communities Measures Affecting Asbestos and Products Containing Asbestos, WT/DS135/AB/R (adopted April 5, 2001), paras. 8.130 and 8.132.
43. See Outokumpu Oy, C-213/96, Judgment of April 2, 1998.
44. Cf. AB Report, EC Asbestos (fn 43), para. 8.101, 8.123; see also, AB Report, United States Import Prohibition of Certain Shrimp and Shrimp Products, WT/DS58/AB/R (adopted October 12, 1998), with regard to PPMs in the context of environmental measures.
45. AB Report, EC Asbestos (fn 42), para. 102; see also Condon/Sinha (2013), 67–70.
46. Cottier et al. (2014), 32/33; Condon and Sinha (2013), 67, Howse (2009), 3.
47. Howse (2009), 3.
48. AB Report, Japan Alcoholic Beverages II (fn 38), 20/21.
49. AB Report, Canada Renewable Energies (fn 7), para. 5.63.
50. See also Cottier et al. (2014), 33.
51. In this regard the Panel in Korea Alcoholic Beverages (fn 37), para. 120, stated that 'The object and purpose of Article III confirms that the scope of the term "directly competitive or substitutable" cannot be limited to situations where consumers already regard products as alternatives.'
52. Panel Report, Japan—Alcoholic Beverages II (fn 37), para. 6.22, confirmed by AB Report, Japan Alcoholic Beverages II (fn 37), 25.
53. AB Reports Canada Renewable Energy (fn 7), para. 51174 and para. 5.236.
54. AB Report, Japan Alcoholic Beverages II (fn 37), 23.
55. *Idem*, 27.
56. *Idem*, 20.
57. *Idem*, 31.
58. *Idem*, 20/21.
59. See section 11.0.
60. Rubini (2012), 9.
61. Appellate Body Report, United States Tax Treatment to 'Foreign Sales Corporations', WT/DS108/AB/R (adopted March 20, 2000), para. 90.
62. *Idem*.
63. Panel Report, US Measures affecting the Trade in Large Civil Aircraft (2nd complaint), WT/DS353/R (March 31, 2011), para. 7.121.
64. Rubini (2012), 9.
65. AB Report, US—FSC (fn61), paras. 91 and 98.
66. Cottier et al. (2014), 45, with reference to Appellate Body Report, US Large Civil Aircraft (2nd complaint), WT/DS353/AB/R (March 12, 2012), para. 831.
67. For further details see Rubini (2012), 9ff., for the discussion in the context of Article III:2 GATT ('so as to afford protection') see section 11.3.2.
68. See section 11.2.2.
69. See section 11.2.2.

70. Cottier et al. (2014), 46.
71. Weber and Burri (2012), 129.
72. Condon and Sinha (2013), 71–73; in the context of Border Tax Adjustments see Kaufmann and Weber (2011), 511–513.
73. Condon and Sinha (2013), 75; Kaufmann and Weber (2011), 513/14; an extensive discussion of the necessity test is now contained in the Appellate Body Report in European Communities Measures Prohibiting the Importation and Marketing of Seal Products, WT/DS400,401/AB/R (adopted June 18, 2014), paras. 5.207–5.230.
74. See also Appellate Body Report, Brazil Measures Affecting Imports of Retreaded Tyres, WT/DS332/AB/R (adopted December 17, 2007), para. 101.
75. Weber and Burri (2012), 134 with further references.
76. For further details see Kaufmann and Weber (2011), 515–520.
77. See also Condon and Sinha (2013), 61–62.
78. See footnote 56 to Article 32.1 of the SCM Agreement.
79. Howse (2010), 17/18, with further references; for a more critical view see Shadikhodjaev (2014), 21 ff.
80. See Case C-573/12, Ålands Vindkraft AB Energimyndigheten (fn 34), paras. 76–119.
81. WTO Environmental Goods Agreement (EGA).

REFERENCES

Casier, Lisbeth and Moerenhout, Tom (2013), 'WTO Members, Not the Appellate Body, Need to Clarify Boundaries in Renewable Energy Support', *International Institute for Sustainable Development*, July 2013, retrieved from http://www.iisd. org (accessed April 23, 2015).

Condon, Bradley J. (2009), 'Climate Change and Unresolved Issues in WTO Law', *Journal of International Economic Law*, 12 (2009), 895–926.

Condon, Bradley J. and Sinha, Tapen (2013), *The Role of Climate Change in Global Economic Governance*, Oxford: Oxford University Press.

Cottier, Thomas, Espa, Ilaria, Hirsbrunner, Simon, Holzer, Kateryna and Payosova, Tetyana (2014), 'Differential Taxation of Electricity: Assessing the Compatibility with WTO Law, EU Law and the Swiss-EEC Free Trade Agreement', *Report to the Federal Finance Administration of the Swiss Government*, retrieved from http://www. efv.admin.ch/e/downloads/finanzpolitik_grundlagen/els/Differentiatial%20_Taxa tion_e.pdf?lang=de&msg-id=50122 (accessed April 23, 2015).

Howse, Robert (2009), 'World Trade Law and Renewable Energy: The Case of Non-tariff Barriers', *Study for the United Nations Conference on Trade and Development (UNCTAD), United Nations Publications 2009*, retrieved from http://unctad.org/en/docs/ditcted20085_en.pdf (accessed April 23, 2015).

Howse, Robert (2010), 'Climate Mitigation Subsidies and the WTO Legal Framework: A Policy Analysis', *Published by the International Institute for Sustainable Development*, retrieved from http://www.iisd.org (accessed April 23, 2015).

Hsueh, Ching-Wen (2013), 'A Greener Trade Agreement: Approaches to Environmental Issues in the TPP Negotiations', *Asian Journal of WTO and International Health Law and Policy*, 8 (2013), 521–542.

Kaufmann, Christine and Weber, Rolf H. (2011), 'Carbon-related Border Tax Adjustment: Mitigating Climate Change or Restricting International Trade?', *World Trade Review*, 10 (2011), 497–525.

Rubini, Luca (2012), 'Ain't Wastin' Time No More: Subsidies for Renewable Energy, the SCM Agreement, Policy Space and Law Reform', *Journal of International Economic Law*, 1–55.

Shadikhodjaev, Sherzod (2013), 'First WTO Judicial Review of Climate Change Subsidy Issues', *The American Journal of International Law*, 107 (2013), 864–878.

Shadikhodjaev, Sherzod (2014), 'Renewable Energy and Government Support: Time to "Green" the SCM Agreement?', *World Trade Review*, published online on October 27, 2014, 1–28, retrieved from http://journals.cambridge.org/abstract_S1474745614000317 (accessed April 23, 2015).

Weber, Rolf H. (2014), 'Designing Trade Rules to Promote Climate Sustainability', *Journal of Energy and Power*, 8 (2014), 612–619.

Weber, Rolf H. and Burri, Mira (2012), *Classification of Services in the Digital Economy*, Zurich: Springer.

12. The impact of environmental tax on enterprise competitiveness in China

Jian Wu, Yujiao Mao* and Xingjie Guo

12.1 THE UPCOMING REFORM OF ENVIRONMENT TAX IN CHINA

China's Pollution Levy System (PLS) has been implemented for more than 30 years. Under the context of environmental fiscal reform, the PLS was considered to be reformed into an environmental tax by three ministries (Ministry of Finance, Ministry of Environmental Protection and State Taxation Administration) since the 11th Five-Year Plan period (2005–2010). The first legislation draft was formulated and submitted to the State Council to formally initiate the legislation process in November 2013. With this reform, we expect to see a higher price on pollution as well as differences in many other aspects such as a unified rate across regions and different revenue-recycling effects. This chapter will discuss the industrial impact of the increased price rate on pollution due to this reform.

Many studies predicted the macro effect of environmental tax in an economy. But what will be the micro-level impact of this tax on the competitiveness of enterprises? This chapter will take enterprises of four industries in a city in China (City S) as a case study, to understand the micro-level impact of environment tax on enterprises, by using the Environment-Competitiveness Matrix (ECM). City S is a typical industrial city located in Jing-Jin-Ji Area, a heavily polluted region. It has a population of 10.16 million with 58 billion USD of GDP and dominant second industry (48.6 per cent in overall economic structure) in 2010. We chose four typical industries in City S to study: power, iron and steel, cement and the pharmaceutical industry. The new environmental tax may target the emission of three pollutants: sulfur dioxide (SO_2), nitrogen oxides (NO_X), and wastewater.

The rest of the chapter consists of four sections: section 12.2 is a review of related studies; section 12.3 is about the methodology and data of this study; section 12.4 is the analysis, and section 12.5 presents the conclusions and some policy implications.

12.2   IMPACT OF ENVIRONMENTAL TAX ON ENTERPRISE COMPETITIVENESS

There are various understandings and definitions of the concept of competitiveness. In this study, we take it that 'Competitive Advantage' is an advantage that a firm has over its competitors. There are two dimensions in understanding the competitive advantages – comparative advantage and differential advantage. Comparative advantage, or cost advantage, is a firm's ability to produce a good or service at a lower cost than its competitors, which enables the firm to sell its goods or services at a lower price than its competitors or to generate a larger margin of sales. A differential advantage is created when a firm's products or services differ from its competitors and are seen as better than a competitor's products by customers.

As environmental tax is one of the market-based regulatory tools, early studies about the impact of environment regulation on the competitiveness of enterprises could shed some light on the current situation. There are mainly two streams of opinions concerning the impact of environmental regulation on the competitiveness of enterprises. One is the traditional opinion that environmental regulation constrains the competitiveness of enterprise; the other is the 'Porter Hypothesis',[1] which claims that appropriate environmental regulation can stimulate the enterprise's innovation, thus improving its competitiveness.

The scholars who support the traditional view mainly examine it by econometric methods. Barbara and McConnell (1990)[2] analyzed five pollution industries in the United States and found a negative correlation between stringency of a regulatory (measured by the pollution control cost) and the enterprise's production efficiency; Gray and Shadbegian (1995)[3] analyzed the pulp and paper, petroleum refining, as well as the iron and steel industries in the United States and argued that the more rigorous environmental regulation is, the heavier regulatory burden the enterprise will shoulder and thus the lower its productivity will be. Generally, enterprises improved environmental performance at the expense of production performance. Jaffe et al. (1995)[4] studied the Swedish pulp and paper industry and found a negative correlation between environmental regulation and the competitiveness of enterprises.

Scholars who support the 'Porter Hypothesis' did their research mainly through case study, among which the representative researches are as follows: Slater and Angel (2000)[5] reported that the enterprises equipped with green technology have more advantages over others in terms of innovation, efficiency, earlier-mover and so on. Barbara and McConnell (1990)[6] analyzed the direct impact of the environmental regulation on five heavily polluted industries, and found that the cost of pollution abatement has negative effects on productivity. Murty and Kumar (2003)[7] introduced output distance function into production function and found a negative correlation between stringency of the sewage control standard and enterprises' production efficiency based on the research of the Indian industry. However, their case study lacks universal applicability with its certain particularity, and the precondition of the 'Porter Hypothesis' seems to be too idealistic, which makes the view less convincing.

Regarding the impact of environmental tax on competitiveness, there are some early discussions about the impact of cost internalization.[8] Only with the implementation of environmental tax in some EU countries, more evidence came out to support quantitative empirical study. COMETR provides an ex-post assessment of experiences and competitiveness impacts of using carbon-energy taxes as an instrument of an Environmental Tax Reform (ETR).[9] But few empirical studies conducted the ex-ante evaluation of the competitiveness impact of environmental tax.

This chapter uses empirical analysis to understand the potential impact of environmental tax on the competitiveness of some sensitive industries, by taking some case studies of enterprises in China.

12.3   METHODOLOGY AND APPROACH

12.3.1   Policy Scenarios

Our policy scenario includes an environment tax with low, medium and high tax rate and some supporting policies. The low tax rate refers to the current rate of pollution levy; the medium tax rate is based on the pollution abatement cost, which is about twice the current rate of pollution levy; the high tax rate is based on environmental damage, which is about four-and-a-half times the current rate of pollution levy.

To date, there has been no consensus on supporting policy design within the policymaking community. Potential policies range from recycling environment tax revenue (such as by subsidizing pollution costs, or reducing corporate income tax) to information disclosure policies. We try to understand the potential of some policies that will not have a direct cost impact, in offsetting the negative cost impact by tax. Therefore, we only analyze the potential for different enterprises to enhance competitiveness through general differentiation strategy under some supporting policy such as information disclosure.

12.3.2 Determinants of the Impact of Environmental Tax on the Competitiveness of Enterprises

The way we look at the mechanism of how an environmental tax makes an impact on enterprises' competitiveness is inspired by relevant studies attempting to understand the impact of environmental regulation on the competitiveness of enterprises. Qu (2000)[10] pointed out that environmental regulation affects the industry's competitiveness through cost effects and differentiation effects. Environmental regulation may increase or decrease the production cost, therefore creating the cost advantage or disadvantage. When products are classified according to their environmental characteristics, the positive effect of differentiation is achieved.

Cost dimension

As Fu (2002)[11] discussed, the impact of environmental tax on competitiveness of enterprises through imposing a cost depends largely on the characteristics of the enterprises, such as the scale of environmental externalities, technology and profitability, and so on (which will decide a firm's ability to absorb the cost and the ability to pass on the cost to consumers).

The competitiveness impact made by an environmental tax through cost will be explained in two dimensions: net increase of cost caused by environmental tax (C1) and the importance of cost in competitiveness of enterprises (C2). C1 depends on the scale of environmental externalities,[12] as well as the technical capability of enterprises. The scale of environmental externalities can be measured by factors of pollution intensity (X1) and pollution cost (X2); technology capability of enterprise is represented by enterprise scale and investment ability (X3, X4), production capacity (X5), current pollution control ability (X6) and some other factors. C2 represents the impact on the competitiveness of enterprises under cost change, which could be measured by two factors, namely the ability of enterprises to absorb cost and then to pass on the cost to consumers. The former can be measured by indexes such as cost structure (X7), profitability (X8), and value added (X9) while the latter mainly depends on market share (X10), and price elasticity (X11).

In order to understand how all these indices make impact on cost and further on competitiveness, we use principal component analysis (PCA) method to convert these multiple correlated factors into the two factors (C1, C2) that impact cost.

The basic idea of principal component analysis is as follows:

$$\begin{cases} Y_1 = l_{11}X_1 + l_{12}X_2 + \cdots + l_{1p}X_p \\ Y_2 = l_{21}X_1 + l_{22}X_2 + \cdots + l_{2p}X_p \\ \quad \cdots \cdots \\ Y_m = l_{m1}X_1 + l_{m2}X_2 + \cdots + l_{mp}X_p \end{cases} \tag{12.1}$$

Where X_1, X_2, ..., X_p are original variable indices, Y_1, Y_2, ... , Y_m (m<p) are new variable indices. If there are the following relations between the two indices, namely Y_i is an index uncorrelated with Y_1, Y_2, ..., Y_{i-1} ($i \le m$) and has the biggest variance in all the linear combination of X_1, X_2, ..., X_p, then the new variable indices Y_1, Y_2, ..., Y_m (m < p) are called the 1st, 2nd, ..., n^{th} principal component of original variable indices X_1, X_2, ..., X_p, (i = 1,2, ... ,m; j = 1,2 ... ,p) is the load of original variable X_j (j = 1,2 ... ,p) on principal component Y_i(i = 1,2 ... ,m). Accordingly, the load $l$ij and comprehensive score (set to F) can be derived mathematically.

Differentiation dimension
An environment tax reform may also make indirect impact on firm's competitiveness through creating product differentiation, by introducing some supporting policy. Environmental characteristics of a product may respond to consumers' environmental preference, and thus gain more consumers' votes. If at the point of introducing the environmental tax, some supporting or complementary policy, such as environmental tax-related information disclosure to distinguish environment-friendly enterprises or products, could bring more advantage through a positive differentiation effect.

Therefore, the differential impacts on enterprises of levying environmental tax can be summarized as: the importance of differentiation on competitiveness (D1) and the importance of environmental factors in differentiation (D2). D1 is reflected by the homogeneity of product, geographical position, time of entry, and business coverage in the production chain; D2 reflects the relationship between differentiation and environment, and depends on customer's environment preference or sensitivity, and how close the product is to the final consumer (the stage of a product in full product chain).

Since the indicators in differentiation analysis are relatively abstract, we undertake qualitative analysis through interviewing industrial experts. We invited 2–3 local industrial experts from each industry to assess the differentiation potential of each enterprise with three scales (low/medium/ high) based on the index we mentioned above. By using a subjective scoring method, we could achieve full ranking of the enterprises on each dimension and understand the enterprises' positioning in a differentiation

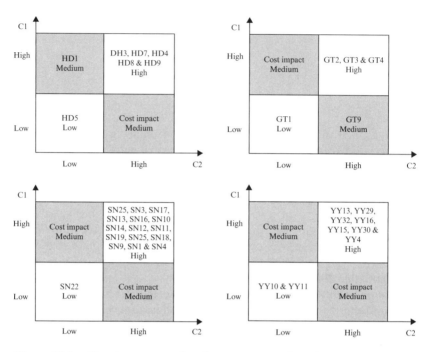

Figure 12.1   Cost impact matrix of power, iron and steel, cement and
pharmaceutical industry in City S

matrix. With these analyses, we are able to judge whether there is a potential to offset the negative impact of cost increase on competitiveness by
creating differentiation through introducing some potential supporting
policy along with an environment tax.

12.3.3   Environment Competitiveness Matrix (ECM)

Alanen (1996)[13] created an environment-competitiveness matrix (ECM)
to analyze effects of environmental regulation on competitiveness. Su and
Chen (2009)[14] divided the existing industries into the different areas of
the ECM matrix. To date, the matrix has not been applied to a particular
industry: we apply the ECM for each industry, as shown in Figure 12.1.
   First, we create a Cost Impact Matrix with horizontal and vertical axes
representing the net cost increment caused by environmental tax and the
importance of cost in competitiveness of enterprises, respectively. Any
enterprise will get a position based on its performance on these two dimensions. Similarly, a differentiation matrix, with the horizontal and vertical
axes representing the importance of differentiation on competitiveness

and importance of environmental factors in differentiation, respectively, is worked out to capture the potential differentiation impact along with environmental tax reform.

After we assess the positioning of each enterprise on cost dimension and differentiation dimension, respectively, all the results are plugged into the ECM, thus determining the overall impact of environmental tax on enterprises.

In ECM, the horizontal axis represents the potential differentiation impact on competitiveness; the vertical axis represents environmental tax's negative cost impact on competitiveness. The Matrix is divided into four quadrants:

1. Status Quo: environmental tax has little negative impact on enterprises' cost, the positive product differentiation effect it may cause is also very small, the environment tax has little impact on the competitiveness of enterprises, and enterprises will maintain the status quo.
2. Challenge: in contrast to the lower left corner, environmental tax will cause enterprises' costs to rise considerably. At the same time it can also offer better opportunities for enterprises to achieve the differentiation effect. At this point, the impact of environmental tax on the competitiveness of enterprises is uncertain; the result depends on the effect of an environmental management strategy, environmental tax itself and other supporting policies, and so on, thus it is a challenge for enterprises.
3. Threat: environmental tax will cause enterprises' costs to rise considerably, however there is little room for differentiation, thus bringing threat to the competitiveness of enterprises.
4. Opportunity: environmental tax will not bring high costs to enterprises, but will bring enterprise profit opportunities through differentiation, thus providing good opportunities for enterprises to improve competitiveness.

12.3.4   Data Processing

We selected four heavy pollution industries in City S: power, iron and steel, cement and the pharmaceutical industry. All of the enterprises are from highly polluting and energy-intensive industries, so they should be considered under environmental tax policy. Thirty-eight enterprises among these four industries have full a dataset on all indices we measured. Their coverage among all four industries is: nine enterprises from the pharmaceutical industry, seven enterprises from the power industry, five enterprises from the iron and steel industry, as well as 17 enterprises from the cement industry. Although the sample number is not large, it covers all important industries, different ownership structure (state owned/controlling enterprise, foreign capital and joint ventures, private enterprises) and scale (small, medium and large scale) in City S, thus the data has good representation.

We collected data of pollutant discharge, enterprises' general information and financial status in 2011. We chose pollution emission intensity, pollution control ability, pollution cost, fixed assets, the number of employee and enterprise revenue as six explanatory variables of net cost increment caused by environmental tax (C1), set as X1, X2, X3, X4, X5 and X6; we chose environment cost structure, profitability, additional value of product, and market share as four explanatory variables of C2, set as X7, X8, X9 and X10. We used SPSS 16.0 to calculate the correlation coefficient matrix, eigenvalue and contribution rate of variables, and determined the number of principal components. Based on the above principle, we calculated principal component loads of C1 and C2 dimensions in the four industries of City S, that is, principal main component equations' coefficients, while the composite score of each enterprise value was calculated using the expression F under three scenarios of tax rate, and then ranked the enterprise according to the value.

12.4   EMPIRICAL RESULTS

12.4.1   Cost Impact

On the C1 dimension, based on the comprehensive score (F) we calculated, the enterprises are ranked in descending order under different tax rate scenarios. In this ranking, the higher the comprehensive principal component values are, the less an enterprise is affected by cost and thus more competitive advantages; the lower, the more an enterprise is affected by cost. Similarly, we obtain the enterprise ranking in the dimension of the importance of cost in the competitiveness of enterprises (C2).

We synthesize the results from two cost dimensions to figure out every enterprise's position in the cost impact matrix (Figure 12.1). We find that: (1) In terms of power enterprises, cost impact on enterprise HD5 is low, cost impact on enterprise HD1 is medium, cost impacts on enterprises HD3, HD4, HD7, HD8 and HD9 are high. (2) In terms of iron and steel enterprises, cost impact on enterprise GT1 is low, cost impact on enterprise GT9 is medium and cost impacts on enterprises GT2, GT3 and GT4 are high. (3) In terms of cement enterprises, cost impact on enterprise SN22 is low, cost impacts on enterprises SN1, SN2, SN3, SN4, SN9, SN10, SN11,

SN12, SN13, SN14, SN16, SN17, SN18, SN19 are high. (4) In terms of medicine enterprises, cost impacts on enterprises YY10 and YY11 are low, cost impacts on enterprises YY4, YY13, YY15, YY16, YY29, YY30 and YY32 are high.

Besides, the positioning of each enterprise remained almost unchanged under different tax rate scenarios, although the principal variables that make an impact could be different.

12.4.2   Differentiation Potential

Based on the experts' interview, we have determined the position of each enterprise in the differential matrix (Figure 12.2). Results are as follows:

1. There are some common characteristics for each industry that may affect the differentiation potential. The products in the power industry are highly homogenized and in a middle position in the industrial chain, thus the positive differentiation effect is limited. There are more types of products in the iron and steel industry and the cement industry, however the products are in a middle position in the industrial chain, thus their positive differentiation effects are medium. There are many types of products in the pharmaceutical industry, the degree of homogenization is relatively low and the products are at the end of the industrial chain, its positive differentiation effect is significant. From the perspective of demand, as the government's demand for environment-friendly products is relatively strong, there are certain positive differentiation effects.
2. Power industry: the positive differentiation effects of enterprises HD1 and HD3 are medium and the effects of enterprises HD5,HD7, HD4, HD8 and HD9 are low.
3. Iron and steel industry: the positive differentiation effects of enterprises GT1 and GT9 are high, the effects of enterprises GT2 and GT3 are medium and the effects of enterprise GT4 is poor.
4. Cement industry: the positive differentiation effects of enterprises SN2, SN9, SN12, SN13 and SN14 are high, the effects of enterprises SN1, SN3, SN10, SN16, SN17, SN18, SN19, SN20 and SN22 are medium and the effects of enterprises SN4, SN11 and SN25 are poor.
5. Pharmaceutical industry: the positive differentiation effects of enterprises YY4, YY10, YY11, YY16, YY30 and YY32 are high and the effects of enterprises YY13, YY15 and YY29 are medium.

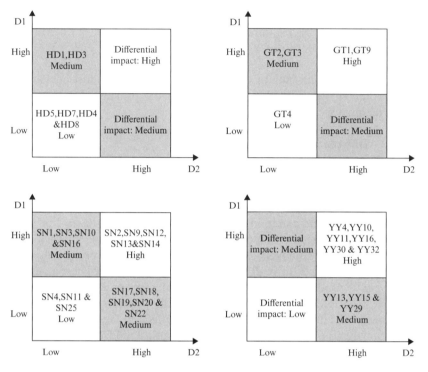

Figure 12.2   Differentiation matrix of power, iron and steel, cement and pharmaceutical industries in City S

12.4.3   Overall Impact

In view of Figures 12.1 and 12.2, we can determine the positions of enterprises in ECM (Figure 12.3), and find out about the current state of each enterprise: threat, challenge, status quo or opportunity. The results show that for enterprises in different industries, the impacts of environmental taxes on competitiveness vary a lot.

Power industry
Environmental tax will not bring opportunities to any power enterprises and most of the enterprises are vulnerable to threat (including enterprises HD4, HD7, HD8 and HD9). Though enterprise HD3 does not suffer explicit threat, it is in a stage between threat and challenge, facing a relatively pressing situation. The influences of environmental tax on enterprises HD5 and HD1 are not remarkable. Specifically, the enterprises under threat are endowed with two features: one is small in scale, such as

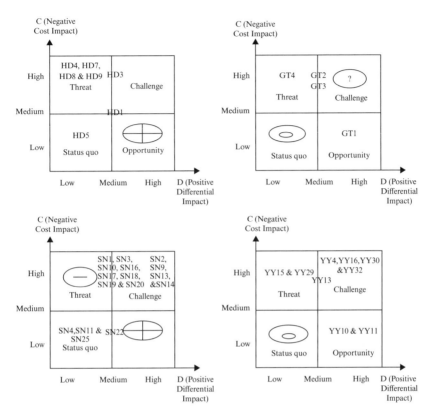

Figure 12.3 ECM of power, iron and steel, cement and pharmaceutical industries in City S

HD3, HD4 and HD7, and the other is that investment in pollution control is too low, such as enterprise HD9.

Power enterprises are key taxpayers of environmental tax in the future, for they are the main source of sulfur dioxide emissions where their emissions account for about half of the total emissions. Therefore the levying of environmental tax is bound to place great cost rising pressure on power enterprises. What is more, for the reason that the electricity price is regulated by the government, enterprises are not entitled to decide the price, thus the environmental tax exerts tremendous adverse influence on the enterprise cost.

Iron and steel industry
Enterprise GT4 is the most vulnerable enterprise to the threat, followed by enterprises GT2 and GT3, while enterprises GT1 and GT9 are faced with

opportunity, in general, the iron and steel industry is less threatened by environmental tax. Threatened enterprises have two characteristics: one is small in scale, such as enterprise GT3, production of GT1 is five hundred times more than its production; the second one is that they lack pollution cost, such as the emissions of GT2 are about one-fifth of GT1, but the pollution facility's operating cost is less than 1/400 of GT1, the input–output ratio is far below the average level of the industry.

Cement industry

The enterprises that are especially vulnerable to the threat are enterprises SN1, SN3, SN10, SN16, SN17, SN18, SN19 and SN20. Enterprises that are not greatly affected are enterprises SN4, SN11 and SN25, enterprise SN22 may receive some positive effects, enterprises SN2, SN9, SN12, SN13 and SN14 will face challenge. Overall, cement enterprises are more vulnerable to the threat of environmental tax; the levying of environmental tax and the rising tax rate has a considerable negative impact on enterprise costs. Enterprises which are not greatly affected by environmental tax or even get positive impacts have two characteristics: one is having a strong ability in pollution control, such as enterprises SN4 and SN22; the other is these enterprises are relatively large in scale, such as enterprise SN25.

Pharmaceutical industry

Enterprises YY15 and YY29 are especially vulnerable to the threat, followed by YY13, enterprises YY10 and YY11 will be faced with opportunities, enterprises YY4, YY16, YY30, and YY32 will face challenges: in general, the pharmaceutical industry is less threatened by environmental tax. Enterprises under threat have two characteristics: one is the nature of private enterprises; the other is that additional value of products is relatively low, such as enterprise YY29.

To sum up, the power industry and the cement industry are more vulnerable to the threat of environmental tax, and the iron and steel industry and the pharmaceutical industry are less threatened by environmental taxes. Enterprises that are more vulnerable to the threat generally have following characteristics: (1) small-scale, hence a weak ability to internalize cost; (2) low pollution costs, limited existing pollution control facilities, and more discharge of pollutants than other enterprises.

12.5   CONCLUSIONS

The chapter studies the impact of environmental tax on the competitiveness of enterprises. We analyze the impact of environmental tax on the competitiveness of enterprises from two dimensions: cost and product differentiation. Environmental tax directly affects cost in two aspects: net increment of cost caused by environmental tax (C1) and the importance of cost in competitiveness of enterprises (C2); the impact of levying environmental tax on enterprises' product differentiation can be summarized as: importance of differentiation on competitiveness (D1) and importance of environmental factors in differentiation (D2). We analyze the four industries in a case city in China (represented by City S) based on the environment-competitiveness matrix (ECM), and finally judging the positioning of enterprises in ECM. The following conclusions have been reached:

1. Under all the three scenarios of tax rate, there is little difference between the principal component scores of corporations in power, iron and steel, cement and pharmaceutical industries. Therefore tax rate does not change the overall positioning of enterprises in the cost impact matrix.
2. The overall positioning of enterprises in the ECM of the four industries shows that the power industry and the cement industry are more vulnerable to the threat of environmental tax, and the iron and steel industry and the pharmaceutical industry are less threatened by environmental tax. The common features of the threatened corporations are: small-scale hence a weak ability to internalize cost, low pollution costs, limited existing pollution control facilities, and more discharge of pollutants than other enterprises.

Based on the findings above, the chapter puts forward the following suggestions:

1. Small-scale corporations are most vulnerable to the threat of environmental tax. These enterprises are usually weak in absorbing increased cost, thus will face great pressure. In order to avoid short-run macroeconomic disruption, for example, employment, it may worth providing some short-run relief to them in the early stage of this policy, especially for the cement industry. We suggest the government sets a lower tax rate for small-scale corporations, just as the VAT tax rate setting system. However, small-scale enterprises could also be in the grey zone of environmental regulation, which will break the fair competition due to failure of environmental tax enforcement. Therefore, when the levying of environmental tax becomes more systematical and mature, the environmental tax rate of small-scale taxpayers should also be gradually restored to normal levels to form a unified tax rate among

all taxpayers. Environmental enforcement should be further strengthened under a tax system.

2. The corporations with inadequate pollution control input are also more vulnerable to the threat of environmental tax. These corporations are generally privately owned, with less fiscal subsidy by the government, weaker social responsibility consciousness and less constraint from government compulsory administrative measures. Also, the pollution control facilities in these corporations are limited. At the beginning of environmental tax, it is suggested that the government can encourage these corporations to increase investment in pollution control facilities by means of fiscal subsidy, bank interest rate discounts and the preferential tax of facilities (for example, offering them exemption from VAT), or encouraging equipment manufacturers to sell pollution treatment equipment to the pollution corporations through financing lease, installment and other feasible approaches.

3. For the power industry, their products are of high homogeneity; positive differentiation effects seldom occur in clean corporations, and thus undermine the persistence of corporations' emission reduction behaviours. Therefore, the government can produce positive differentiation effects for environmentally friendly corporations by disclosing environment information or even providing clean power generation corporations priority in access to the grid, thus motivating pollution control and clean production of the enterprises in the industry.

NOTES

1. Porter, M.E. (1990). *The Competitive Advantage of Nations*, London: MacMillan.
2. Barbara, A.J. and V.D. McConnell (1990). The Impact of Environmental Regulations on Industry Productivity: Direct and Indirect Effects. *Journal of Environmental Economics and Management*, 18, 50–65.
3. Gray, W. and B. Shadbegian (1995). Pollution Abatement Cost, Regulation and Plant Level Productivity. NBER Working Paper, No. 4994.
4. Jaffe, A.B., S.R. Peterson, P.R. Portney and R.N. Stavins (1995). Environmental Regulations and the competitiveness of US Manufacturing: What Does the Evidence Tell Us? *Journal of Economics Literature*, 33, 132–163.
5. Slater, J. and I.T. Angel (2000). The Impact and Implications of Environmentally Linked Strategies on Competitive Advantage: A Study of Malaysian Companies. *Journal of Business Research*, 47(1), 75–89.
6. Barbera, A.J. and V.D. McConnell (1990). The Impact of Environmental Regulations on Industry Productivity: Direct and Indirect effects. *Journal of Environmental Economics and Management*, 18, 50–65.
7. Murty, M.N. and S. Kumar (2003). Win–Win Opportunities and Environmental Regulation: Testing of Porter Hypothesis for Indian Manufacturing Industries. *Journal of Environmental Management*, 67, 139–144.
8. Alanen, L. (1996). The Impact of Environmental Cost Internalization on Sectorial

Competitiveness: A New Conceptual Framework. UNCTAD Discussion Papers, No. 119.
9. Andersen, M.S., T. Barker, E. Christie, P. Ekins, J.F. Gerald, J. Jilkova, S. Junankar, M. Landesmann, H. Pollitt, R. Salmons, S. Scott and S. Speck (eds) (2007). Competitiveness Effects of Environmental Tax Reforms (COMETR), Final report to the European Commission, National Environmental Research institute, University of Aarhus, 543 pp.
10. Qu, R. (2000). A New Angle to Understand the Environmental Protection and International Competitiveness. *China Industrial Economy*, 9, 59–63.
11. Fu, J. (2002). Internalizing Environmental Cost and Industrial Competitiveness. *China Industrial Economy*, 6, 37–44.
12. Wang, L.J. and Zhao, X.P. (2010). The Impact Analysis of Environmental Regulation on Enterprise Competitiveness. *Xi'an SHiyou University Journal* (JCR Social Science Edition), 19, 1.
13. See n8.
14. Su, Q. and X. Chen (2009). The International Competitiveness Impact of Environmental Regulation on Chinese Industries. *Value Engineering*, 1, 30–33.

PART IV

Strategic considerations

13. Reclaiming the 'T' word: ways of improving communication and public acceptance of environmental fiscal reform in Europe

Jacqueline Cottrell

13.1 INTRODUCTION

This chapter examines some recent research findings from behavioural economics and looks at how these might be used to improve the way in which environmental fiscal reform (EFR) in general, and environmental taxation in particular, is designed and communicated.

The premise of the chapter, which is a research output of the FRE-Communicate project,[1] is that improved communication can enhance the prospects for the implementation of EFR by improving public understanding of its benefits and advantages in comparison with other policy instruments.

Both practical experience and research have demonstrated that one of the most fundamental barriers to the implementation of EFR is a general lack of knowledge about EFR amongst policymakers, stakeholders, for example, in the business sector, the media and the general public. In response to this, the project sets out to communicate what EFR is about in an accessible way and to develop a number of different communication strategies targeting diverse audiences.

This chapter will introduce current attitudes and responses to EFR and examine research into the acceptance of taxation and EFR measures, before making a series of recommendations for communications efforts in the future.

13.2　ATTITUDES TOWARDS THE ENVIRONMENT AND FISCAL MEASURES IN THE EU

13.2.1　Paradoxical Survey Results

Research and opinion polls have shown that the polluter pays principle is met with broad support among electorates (see for example, PETRAS 2002; Green Fiscal Commission 2009). However, this does not seem to feed into a general understanding that environmental taxes are a means of realizing the polluter pays principle – indeed, opinion polls have revealed that many EU citizens at least do not understand the connection at all (see for example, Federal Environment Agency 2004; PETRAS 2002). Perhaps this goes some way to explaining the results of a 2011 EU-wide survey of attitudes towards the environment, which found that, when respondents were asked to suggest what should be the top three priorities for citizens in their daily lives for environmental protection, only 2 per cent overall opted for 'pay a little more in taxes to help protect the environment' (European Commission 2011).

However, even if the connection between the polluter pays principle and EFR is not clear to electorates, there is also a broad body of opinion that EFR instruments are among the most efficient to tackle environmental problems, particularly those of a diffuse nature. The International Panel on Climate Change (IPCC), international organizations such as the World Bank, the International Monetary Fund (IMF), the Organisation for Economic Co-operation and Development (OECD), and various European institutions and indeed state governments all acknowledge this fact and have stated so in documents and in the press.[2]

In spite of this broad body of opinion in favour of EFR, environment simply does not seem to be a priority for many in the current economic climate – a factor likely to feed into opposition to EFR measures. This is reflected by an EU-wide survey in spring 2013, which showed that only 4 per cent of the population identified environment, climate and energy as one of the two most important issues facing their country (European Commission 2013).

The underlying reason for this lack of interest might be – and this is highlighted in the statements of some policymakers in recent years – that environment is less of political priority in times of crisis. Since 2008, when the financial crisis began, an overriding focus on growth, and the need to restart ailing EU economies, seems to have distracted governments from environmental policy and undermined their commitment to green taxation – a classic case of a perceived conflict between growth and environment.[3] However, in 2011, 95 per cent of Europeans described protecting the environment as important to them personally and 80 per cent believed that the efficient use of natural resources and environmental protection can boost economic growth (European Commission, 2011). Similarly, a 2014 poll of 2,000 people in the UK revealed support of 72 per cent of those polled to agree a global deal to address climate change.[4] Such statistics do not reflect a European electorate convinced that growth should take precedent over environment in times of economic downturn.

Research has also found that willingness to pay for climate change mitigation may be much higher than is generally assumed. For example, motivated by their recognition of responsibility for emissions, statements by air travellers about their willingness to pay to offset their emissions suggest that about €23 billion in offsets could be generated annually from aviation passengers worldwide to mitigate emissions in other sectors (Brouwer et al. 2008).

In the face of this seemingly contradictory evidence – widespread support for the polluter pays principle and lack of support for environmental taxation, a widely held belief that environmental policy can boost Europe's economy alongside apparent acceptance of a narrow focus on growth at the expense of the environment – this chapter will try to tease out the root causes of opposition to EFR in general and environmental taxation in particular, as well as suggest a number of ways in which this opposition can be mitigated.

13.2.2   Initial Assumptions: First Steps towards an Explanation

What might the solution to these misunderstandings be? Many researchers and members of the policymaking community have suggested that improved clarity, more transparency and clearer policy communication may be the key to boosting political acceptance and thus overcoming at least one of the barriers to EFR. For this reason, this chapter will focus on the notion that improving the chances of EFR being implemented in many EU countries is 'basically a matter of how the policy is framed and communicated to the public' (Jagers and Hammar 2009: 224) and will suggest some ways in which this can be done.

One of the challenges to an investigation of this nature is that perceptions of EFR differ significantly across Europe – there is no 'one size fits all solution'. Nonetheless, there seems to be potential in exploring how the framework conditions for the implementation of EFR can be enhanced. Taking current research and findings from behavioural economics into account, the chapter will try to suggest what form this framing could take in the European context. It will also consider what kind of shift in perceptions and understanding of EFR can improve its acceptability.

13.3   NEGATIVE PERCEPTIONS OF ENVIRONMENTAL FISCAL REFORM – AND POSSIBLE EXPLANATIONS

13.3.1   Geographical Variations in Acceptability of Taxation

The way in which European citizens perceive taxation and the degree to which they are tax averse, or accepting of taxation, varies by country. Harring (2013) suggests it is reasonable to assume that particularly those countries with relatively high levels of taxation are likely to have higher levels of acceptance of environmental taxation than countries with lower levels of taxation. Indeed, as shown in Figures 13.1 and 13.2, there does seem to be a correlation between European countries with high tax revenues as a percentage of GDP and those countries where acceptance for economic instruments for environmental policy is highest, although this correlation does not necessarily indicate a causal relationship.

In geographical terms: Even a cursory glance at revenues raised from environmental taxation in the EU reveals that as a general rule, green taxes raise considerably more revenues in countries in Northern Europe (particularly Scandinavia and Benelux) than in Southern or Eastern Europe (see for example, Eurostat 2014). Harring (2013) has suggested two main reasons for these regional variations: First, higher perceived levels of corruption and lower levels of trust in government result in lower acceptance of taxation and EFR in Southern and Eastern Europe; Second, more unequal societies are more concerned about distributional impacts and thus tend to be more opposed to measures which might have a negative impact.

Regional differences open up the possibility of identifying trends and commonalities within and between European countries to account for differing levels of acceptance and rates of implementation.

13.3.2   Tax Aversion and Fiscal Illusion

One obvious explanation for low rates of acceptance of taxation in general and environmental taxation in particular is that some – or even many – people do not like paying taxes. This problem is compounded by the problem economists refer to as 'fiscal illusion' – 'the notion that systematic misperception of key fiscal parameters may significantly distort fiscal choices by the electorate' (Oates 1988, 65). Simply put: Fiscal illusion leads to people tending to estimate the amount of taxes they pay inaccurately, and to underestimate taxes not directly levied on income.

In a similar vein, research has shown that electorates also tend to

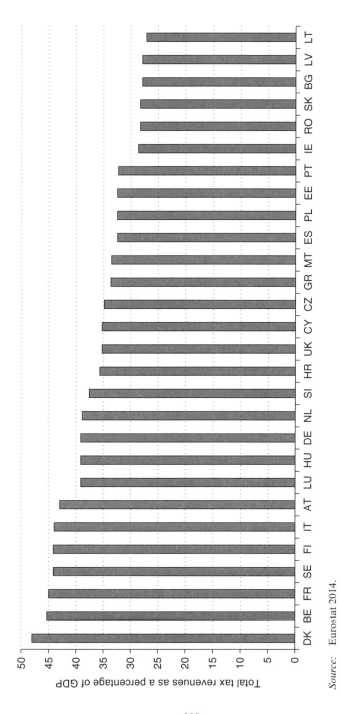

Source: Eurostat 2014.

Figure 13.1 Total tax revenues as a percentage of GDP in EU countries in 2012

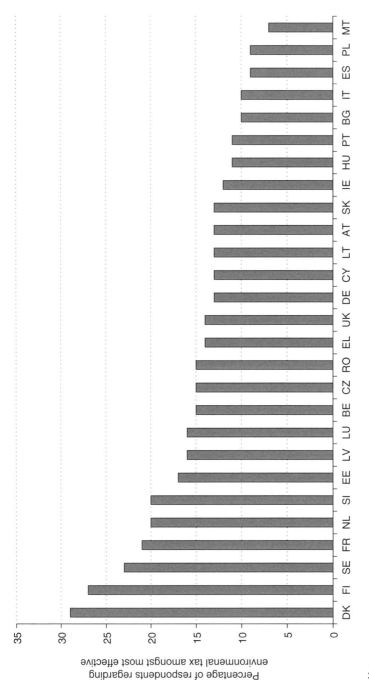

Notes:
For this survey, respondents were asked to identify the two most effective ways of tackling environmental problems from a choice of: Introducing heavier fines for offenders; Ensuring better enforcement of existing environmental legislation: Providing more information on environmental issues; Offering higher financial incentives (for example, tax breaks, subsidies) to industry, commerce and citizens who protect the environment; Introducing stricter environmental legislation; Introducing and increasing taxation on environmentally damaging activities.

Source: European Commission (2008).

Figure 13.2 Percentage of population in selected EU countries that perceives economic instruments as one of the most effective policy instruments

overestimate costs related to environmental taxes while underestimating cost of alternative measures, such as regulation (Jagers and Hammar 2009). Such inaccuracies and misconceptions are also evident in polling and focus groups, which have shown that people tend to believe that they will be worse off under a green tax shift, even when faced by evidence to the contrary (Green Fiscal Commission 2009). Indeed, it has been shown that subjects are more than twice as likely to vote against taxation when it is in their material self-interest (tax-averse 'mistakes') than they are to vote in favour of taxation when it is not in their self-interest (tax-loving 'mistakes') (Kallbekken et al. 2011). It is possible that these kinds of responses are linked to a behavioural phenomenon referred to as loss aversion, which reveals that people tend to value losses higher than gains (Fryer et al. 2012). Ways of designing EFR instruments to address these biases are proposed in section 13.4.

13.3.3 Lack of Trust in Government Institutions and Corruption

Research and polling in several countries has revealed that trust in government and in the revenue neutrality of green tax shifting in practice are important factors in boosting confidence and support for EFR instruments, and that conversely, lack of trust in governments leads to reduced support for EFR measures (Green Fiscal Commission 2009; Harring 2013; PETRAS 2002). Indeed, lack of trust in government has been shown to be a key impediment to EFR in many countries, even in Denmark, where EFR measures have been implemented on a larger scale than almost anywhere else in the world (PETRAS 2002).

13.3.4 Perceptions of EFR Measures as Unfair and Regressive

One of the strongest arguments against EFR is that it is regressive – although, depending on other changes in the tax system, or on the compensation measures put in place at the same time, this may or not be the case in practice. Certainly, well-designed measures can be expected to alleviate the vast majority of concerns – and in relation to transport fuels, assumptions that increased taxation will have regressive impacts have been largely discredited (see for example, Vivid Economics 2012; Sterner and Morris 2013; Kosonen 2012). Nevertheless, a dominant perception of EFR measures appears to be that they will have a regressive effect and thus, such measures are often opposed for fairness reasons (PETRAS 2002; Green Fiscal Commission 2009). Conversely, progressive environmental taxes, such as aviation taxation targeting frequent flyers, are met with general support in focus groups and opinion polls (Green Fiscal

Commission 2009). Fairness arguments seem to be important when communicating EFR.

Harring has suggested that assumptions about unfairness also influence whether EFR measures are perceived as effective and thus preferable. He suggests that, in more unequal societies where the regressive effect is potentially larger, economic instruments are less popular than in more equal societies, where regressive impacts in general are less of a concern (Harring 2013).

13.3.5 Perceptions of EFR as 'Coercive' and 'Punitive'

In general, certain kinds of policy measures tend to command more support than others. For example, more coercive 'push' measures appear to be less accepted than less coercive 'pull' ones, as the former are regarded as an infringement on personal freedom. Acceptability seems to be greater when a policy targets behaviours which can be changed at a low (social/economic) cost, and when the policy is in line with strong social norms. If this is not the case, then there is a risk that a measure comes to be regarded as a punishment for people behaving in a socially acceptable way (de Groot and Schuitema 2012). These findings have been echoed elsewhere, and a significant source of resistance to EFR appears to be that it is often seen as 'punitive' (Green Fiscal Commission 2009).

Some possible responses to these perceptions of EFR measures as coercive, unfair, regressive and mistrusted ('stealth taxes') are proposed below, exploring ways of improving policy design and policy communication – framing – to overcome barriers and facilitate the broader implementation of EFR measures.

13.4 IMPROVING POLICY DESIGN

Design has a critical influence on policy acceptance, and can make carbon taxation socially acceptable to the majority of the population, for example, by taking perceptions of fairness, transparency, accountability and effectiveness into account (Bristow et al. 2010). Many studies have demonstrated that perceived effectiveness of policies is an important determinant of their acceptability, and moreover that policy design has an influence on perceptions of how effective a particular policy is (de Groot and Schuitema 2012; Brouwer et al. 2008; Harring 2013). Thus, improved policy design feeds into, and indeed is an integral part of, improved communication – as examined in detail in the series of recommendations, below.

13.4.1 Earmarking and Tax Shifting – Linking Revenue Recycling to Policy Priorities

There is a broad body of evidence that earmarking and tax shifting can be a helpful way of reducing resistance to environmental taxation and can enhance the implementing environment for EFR (see for example, Kallbekken et al., 2010, Green Fiscal Commission, 2009; Kallbekken et al. 2011).

Apparent preferences for earmarking are probably related to a limited understanding of the economic theories underlying green tax shifting among the general public. Unfortunately, explaining efficiency and welfare gains to non-economists is not easy, because it relies on a specific vocabulary unfamiliar to the general public.

For many, it is also not clear why or how green taxation can act as a steering mechanism and thus change behaviour and in this way have a positive environmental impact, no matter what the revenues are used for (PETRAS 2002). Members of the general public tend to accept the premise that if revenues from an environmental tax flow into the general budget, then this is a so-called 'stealth tax', which has nothing to do with the environment. For this reason, earmarking of tax revenues is generally preferred by non-economists, because it increases the perceived effectiveness of an environmental tax and thus enhances its legitimacy as an environmental rather than a fiscal policy instrument (Sælen and Kallbekken 2011).

Support for earmarking has been demonstrated in many different contexts. The UK Green Fiscal Commission identified a significant increase in support for a green tax shift – from 51 per cent to 73 per cent – if revenue was spent on projects to directly reduce carbon dioxide emissions (Green Fiscal Commission 2009). In the eye of the taxpayer, earmarking seems to help establish the environmental credentials of a measure and make clear that it is not simply a revenue-raising measure (Kallbekken et al. 2011). Of course, increased support can also be explained in part by expectations that earmarking will benefit taxpayers, and thus will be in the voters' self-interest (Sælen and Kallbekken 2011).

On the other hand, revenue recycling can secure the survival of EFR measures in times of opposition and can to some extent enhance acceptance, if it targets the highest priority concern in a particular country, for example, unemployment and revenues raised are used to deal with policy priorities. When the Ecotax was introduced in 1999 in Germany, an absolute policy priority for Chancellor Schröder and the electorate was to tackle unemployment. Almost 90 per cent of Ecotax revenues were used to reduce social security contributions. In spite of some opposition and protests in 2000, the government held its course and prioritized tackling unemployment above responding to protests.

The most preferable instrument design, then, is one that includes sufficient earmarking to reduce opposition and enhance policy acceptance, while also recycling revenues to reduce other distortive taxes. The petrE project[5] – Productivity and Environmental Tax Reform in Europe, commissioned by the Anglo-German Foundation and led by Paul Ekins – modelled greenhouse gas emissions reduction scenarios to 2020 and found that the best model, in terms of impacts on GDP and the carbon price needed to meet EU targets, was 90 per cent revenue recycling combined with 10 per cent investment in green technologies in the power generation, transport and housing sectors (Ekins 2009).

13.4.2 Creating Trust in EFR Instruments – Accountability and Transparency

Another route to boosting the acceptability of EFR is to foster trust in how revenues are spent by creating an independent organization to administer funds (as called for by many respondents in the 2002 PETRAS project). This enhances accountability and transparency and mitigates concerns that ETR measures are simply 'stealth taxes'. This is the case in Denmark, where the non-profit enterprise Energinet.dk is funded by a proportion of funds raised from energy bills (by means of the Public Services Obligation tariff). Similarly, the UK Carbon Trust was originally created to manage a proportion of revenues raised by the Climate Change Levy.

If all tax and expenditures relating to the environment are communicated transparently, this can also foster trust in EFR policies. If they are not, however, this can be extremely counterproductive. In Germany, for example, energy bills often list the electricity tax and the 'renewable energy surcharge' (EEG – feed-in tariff), but fail to include a cost breakdown for coal and nuclear energy – even though figures suggest that a 'conventional energy surcharge' would be almost three times higher than the EEG (Küchler et al. 2012). Similarly, in the UK in 2013 ongoing political discussions about rising energy bills have focused on green taxation, which in fact makes up about 6 per cent of household gas and 11 per cent of household electricity energy bills, and is spent on government programmes to save energy, reduce emissions and fund social programmes (Ofgem 2013).

The potential benefits of increased transparency in, for example, energy pricing have been highlighted by many international organizations, including the World Bank, IMF, OECD and APEC. A recent global survey of environmental policy experts also highlighted the need to reframe policy debates on subsidies and energy prices to increase transparency (Tamanini 2013).

13.4.3 Facilitating Behavioural Change and Protecting the Vulnerable

EFR measures introduced alongside improved provision of services to facilitate behavioural change, for example, fuel tax rises in parallel with better public transport, can also be expected to enhance public support (Cherry et al. 2011). Making alternatives easily available can help address fairness concerns. In terms of protecting the vulnerable – earmarking has been shown in laboratory experiments to be preferred if revenues are targeted to relatively narrowly defined groups, rather than recycled in a general way – thus meeting to some extent fears that EFR measures are regressive and thus unfair (Kallbekken et al. 2011).

For fairness and social justice reasons, the direct negative effect of EFR measures on household incomes should always be taken into consideration in policy design and addressed. From a purely theoretical point of view, it is better to compensate independently of an environmental tax to retain the incentive effect, and to compensate individuals and households elsewhere in the tax and/or benefits system. Ultimately, the overall progressivity of taxation and social security should be the focus of policymakers, rather than the progressive impact of each particular instrument. While this is more challenging for policymakers, particularly in terms of communication, there are two very strong arguments in favour of this approach. First, reduced tax rates or exemptions, as mentioned above, undermine EFR's incentive effect. Second, impacts of green taxes may vary as much (or more) as a result of household characteristics which are not income-related than as a result of different household incomes (see Vivid Economics 2012).

Some EFR measures are generally progressive, such as reform of company car taxation, aviation taxes, and transport taxation (see for example, Kosonen 2012). Other EFR measures more likely to have regressive impacts can be compensated elsewhere in the tax system or designed to have a progressive impact, for example, by charging a lower rate of taxation on the first units of consumption, while charging higher rates on higher levels of energy use.

13.5 IMPROVING THE IMAGE OF EFR: NEW WAYS OF FRAMING THE DEBATE

Better policy design, with more thought given to how to address the many biases and misconceptions surrounding EFR measures when conceptualizing policy, seems to be one route to increase rates of implementation of EFR. Design which increases trust in particular instruments and improves transparency of revenue transfers should, if instruments are effective in environmental and fiscal terms, lead to improved perceptions of EFR and increase faith among the general public in the efficacy of such measures.

On the other hand, the findings of section 13.2 also revealed a number of misunderstandings which may require responses other than improved policy design. Low acceptance of tax measures and a lack of understanding of the underlying principles of EFR were also highlighted as reasons for the low rates of implementation of EFR and the unpopularity of green taxation. Dealing with these relatively entrenched attitudes towards EFR instruments is not an easy task. At least part of the solution might be to communicate the benefits, potential and underlying rationale of EFR measures in a clear and transparent way. This requires that we reframe discussions and rethink many of our communications approaches to environmental policy.

13.5.1   Evolving Vocabularies

There is a great deal of evidence that the language used to describe policy can have a profound impact on acceptability – particularly in the case of tax instruments (Cherry et al. 2011: 94). An easy way to reframe the debate is for governments to refer to EFR measures using different vocabulary. For example, a carbon-energy tax on industry in the UK is known as the 'Climate Change Levy' (CCL), while Australia's carbon pricing scheme met with new levels of unpopularity once the scheme was dubbed a 'carbon tax'. In the same vein, cap-and-trade schemes tend to be more accepted than carbon taxation.

The negative connotations associated with the word 'tax', particularly in some countries, have undermined attempts to implement green taxes. Thus, using alternative vocabularies where feasible, for example, tariff, cess, charge, fee, levy, certainly merits consideration. However, such approaches run the risk of being criticized for being somehow dishonest and skirting the issue. Those communicating should make a deliberate decision, in view of the political and social context, whether such a move will be welcomed or leave a particular instrument vulnerable to attack. A balance needs to be found between mitigating tax aversion and transparency.

13.5.2   Shifting Emphasis to Benefits and Incentives

A stronger focus on the positive benefits of EFR, rather than the penalties associated with it, can also increase the public acceptability of green taxes

(Green Fiscal Commission 2009). Pull measures (carrots) are perceived to be more acceptable than push measures (sticks, such as taxes), regardless whether they are aimed at high or low-cost behaviour (de Groot and Schuitema 2012). Thus, a stronger focus on incentives as well as penalties, such as bonus-malus schemes, or measures which actively reward those who attempt to reduce consumption, might also be a means of boosting support (PETRAS 2002).

Taking advantage of this preference for carrots rather than sticks could go much further than communications and also influence policy design – for example, by applying the findings of behavioural economics in a more targeted way (see for example, Bridle et al. 2013). This could mean redesigning EFR measures so that they function in very different ways – for example, by visibly distributing revenues *before* taxes are imposed. This may sound farfetched, but reform of fossil fuel subsidies in Iran was realized in this way – first, bank accounts for vulnerable households were set up and funds transferred, then energy subsidies were withdrawn (see for example, Guillaume et al. 2011).

13.5.3 Presenting EFR Measures in the Broader Context of Policy Choice

As noted above in section 13.2.2, populations tend to find it difficult to compare the costs of different taxes or environmental policies. It is not sufficient to know in isolation that in theory EFR is the most 'efficient' option. Instead (environmental) fiscal policy should be presented and communicated as a series of choices, each of which has an intended effect and actual cost to the state and the individual (see for example, Jagers and Hammar 2009).

This approach was followed by a 2012 study commissioned by Green Budget Europe and the European Climate Foundation, which compared the macroeconomic impacts of carbon-energy taxation with VAT and direct taxation as a means of meeting fiscal deficits (Vivid Economics 2012). The report demonstrated convincingly that of the three tax increases, carbon-energy taxation was the most preferable policy option. If electorates are presented policy alternatives in a broader context, as a choice between different options with different costs and benefits, it will be much easier for them to make informed choices about which policies they support.

13.5.4 Reconfiguring the Fairness Debate

Fairness concerns are one of the most significant obstacles to EFR. Usually, when EFR is discussed – and when populations form opinions about EFR as a policy instrument – the discussion focuses on equality of economic *outcomes*. If this approach is used, then ETR is unfair, because some are more affected than others. However, those paying environmental taxation are required to do so because they choose to be *polluters* and their *behaviour* has a causal link to pollution and environmental damage. EFR is simply a policy measure to ensure that *polluters* pay for the damage they cause.

The latter approach to environmental damage is usual in the climate change debate, where climate justice foresees mitigation actions related to *equity* (i.e. those who pollute have a moral responsibility to take action), rather than *equality* (fairness of economic outcomes) (Jagers and Hammar 2009). Taking causal responsibility as a marker of fairness in environmental policy is a means of clarifying the thinking behind EFR. If framed in this way – clearly and distinctly as a fair means to make polluters pay for their behaviour – EFR is likely to be met with higher rates of acceptance.

A further reason to focus on the polluter pays principle is that many opinion polls in Europe have shown that support for it is generally strong, while at the same time, support for environmental taxation is weak, highlighting a lack of understanding that the two concepts are closely linked. The German Environment Ministry conducted an opinion poll in 2004 which looked quite specifically at support for the Ecotax. In this survey, 73 per cent agreed or partly agreed that the Ecotax in Germany was discriminatory, socially unfair and essentially a revenue-raising measure and 69 per cent agreed that it did not contribute to solving environmental problems. Ironically, in the same questionnaire, 80 per cent agreed or partly agreed that it is only fair that those who pollute less pay less tax – essentially an expression of support for the polluter pays principle (BMU 2004).

What such opinion polls seem to show – and similar results have been found in the PETRAS project, which looked at several countries in Europe, by Eurobarometer polling, and by the Green Fiscal Commission in the UK – is that environmental taxation and environmental fiscal reform are not linked in the minds of the majority of the population with the polluter pays principle – *and that if they were, support and acceptance for green fiscal measures would increase significantly*.

13.6   CONCLUSIONS

The above has highlighted a number of reasons why EFR is not met with such high levels of acceptability as environmental regulation. It has also suggested some possible directions of travel for the future design of EFR measures, and has highlighted a number of lessons learned for the future communication and framing of EFR.

These arguments can be distilled into a number of lessons learned for future policy design and the development of communications strategies:

1. *Earmarking and tax shifting – linking revenue recycling to policy priorities.* Earmarking can increase public trust in policy, enhance transparency of expenditure and might even 'mitigate the baggage associated with the t-word' (Kallbekken et al. 2011: 63). Linking revenue recycling to policy priorities can ensure policy stability. A combination of both is most effective (Ekins 2009).
2. *Creating trust in government.* Mistrust in how governments spend EFR revenues results in opposition. The creation of an independent body to manage revenues can reduce opposition and ensure transparency and accountability.
3. *Facilitating change and protecting the vulnerable.* Policy should be designed to deal with these concerns effectively, while policymakers should also endeavour to make clear that regressive impacts can be overstated.
4. *Evolving vocabularies.* EFR should be framed in a transparent way that reflects its impacts on individuals and the state in comparison with other instruments.
5. *Shifting emphasis towards rewards and benefits.* The perceived coercive nature of EFR 'sticks' can reduce acceptance, while EFR 'carrots', for example, rewards for good environmental behaviour, can increase it. Policymakers should explore novel ways of designing policies which take this into account.
6. *Presenting EFR and other measures as a policy choice.* Governments should be called upon to transparently present the cost of all fiscal and environment-related policies so that electorates can compare their actual cost and make decisions about which policies they support on that basis.
7. *Reconfiguring the fairness debate.* EFR is often perceived as unfair, and is met with low levels of acceptance as a result. Discussions about fairness should focus on equity and the polluter pays principle – EFR measures are not 'blind' and it does not make sense to discuss them as if they are.
8. *Framing.* Finally and most importantly, to appeal to a broader audience, EFR should be framed in a way which emphasizes fairness (equity) and the realization of the polluter pays principle.

If these factors are taken into account during the development and communication of EFR, it is reasonable to assume that this will boost public acceptance of EFR and over time, increase rates of implementation of EFR measures.

NOTES

1. For more information on the project, which is funded by the Velux/Villum Foundations and led by Green Budget Europe in cooperation with the Danish Ecological Council and Professor Paul Ekins of University College London, please see: http://www.foes.de/inter nationales/green-budget-europe/gbe-projekte/fre-communicate/ (accessed 15 January 2014).
2. See for example, the fifth IPCC report http://www.ipcc.ch/index.htm, the World-Bank led carbon pricing leadership coalition endorsed by 73 countries and over 1,00 companies http://www.worldbank.org/en/news/press-release/2014/09/22/73-countries-1000-companies-investors-support-price-carbon, the IMF's promotion of EFR on its website http://www.imf.org/external/pubs/ft/survey/so/2014/pol073114a.htm and the OECD's extensive research on EFR http://www.oecd.org/env/tools-evaluation/48178034.pdf (all accessed 21 November 2014).
3. This was exemplified by a scandal in 2013 in the UK, where it was rumoured that the Prime Minister, David Cameron, had called on his party aides to 'get rid of all the green crap', in other words, remove green taxes on domestic energy consumers. For an analysis see (retrieved 21 November 2014): http://www.theguardian.com/environment/2013/nov/21/david-cameron-green-crap-comments-storm.
4. For more information please see: https://www.gov.uk/government/news/public-want-rgent-global-action-to-tackle-climate-change (retrieved 28 November 2014).
5. See http://www.petre.org.uk/.

BIBLIOGRAPHY

Bridle, R., Collings, J., Cottrell, J.L. and Leopold, A. (2013), Communication Best Practices for Renewable Energy (RE-COMMUNICATE) – scoping study, International Energy Agency Renewable Energy Technology Deployment, Paris.
Bristow, A., Mark Wardman, M., Zanni. A. and Chintakayala, P. (2010), 'Public acceptability of personal carbon trading and carbon tax', *Ecological Economics*, 69: 1824–1837.
Brouwer R., Brander, L. and Van Beukering, P. (2008), 'A convenient truth: air travel passengers' willingness to pay to offset their CO_2 emissions', *Climatic Change*, 90: 299–313.
Bundesministerium für Umwelt, Naturschutz und Reaktorsicherheit (BMU) (2004), Umweltbewusstsein in Deutschland 2004, Berlin. Retrieved 7 November 2013 from http://www.umweltbundesamt.de/publikationen/fpdf-l/2792.pdf.
Cherry, T., Kallbekken, S. and Kroll, S. (2012), 'The acceptability of efficiency-enhancing environmental taxes, subsidies and regulation: An experimental investigation', *Environmental Science and Policy*, 16: 90–96.
de Groot, J. and Schuitema, G. (2012), 'How to make the unpopular popular? Policy characteristics, social norms and the acceptability of environmental policies', *Environmental Science and Policy*, 19–20: 100–107.
Ekins, P. (2009), *Resource Productivity, Environmental Tax Reform and Sustainable Growth in Europe*, Anglo-German Foundation for the Study of Industrial Society.
European Commission (2008), *Special Eurobarometer 295, Wave 68.2: Attitudes of European Citizens Towards the Environment*. Retrieved from http://ec.europa.eu/public_opinion/archives/ebs/ebs_295_en.pdf (accessed 1 May 2015).

European Commission (2011), *Attitudes of European Citizens towards the Environment*, Special Eurobarometer 365, Brussels.

European Commission (2013), *Eurobarometer*, Brussels. Retrieved from http://ec.europa.eu/public_opinion/index_en.htm (accessed 15 January 2014).

Eurostat (2014), *Taxation Trends in the European Union: Data for the Member States, Iceland and Norway – Report and Annexes*, retrieved from http://ec.europa.eu/taxation_customs/taxation/gen_info/economic_analysis/tax_structures/index_en.htm (accessed 29 April 2015).

Federal Environment Agency (2004), *Umweltpolitik: Umweltbewusstsein in Deutschland 2004 (Environmental Policy: Environmental Awareness in Germany)*, retrieved from http://www.umweltbundesamt.de/sites/default/files/medien/pub likation/long/2792.pdf (accessed 21 November 2014).

Fryer, R.G., Levitt, S.D., List, J. and Sadoff, S. (2012), Enhancing the efficacy of teacher incentives through loss aversion: A field experiment. NBER Working Paper No. 18237.

Green Fiscal Commission (2009), *The Case for Green Fiscal Reform: Final Report of the UK Green Fiscal Commission*, London 2009. Retrieved from http://www.greenfiscalcommission.org.uk/images/uploads/GFC_FinalReport.pdf (accessed 15 January 2014).

Guillaume, D., Zytek, R. and Reza Farzin, M. (2011), Iran – the chronicles of the subsidy reform, IMF Working Paper 11/167, Washington.

Harring, N. (2013), 'Corruption, inequalities and the perceived effectiveness of economic pro-environmental policy instruments: A European cross-national study', *Environmental Science and Policy*, 39: 119–128.

Jagers, S. and Hammar, H. (2009), 'Environmental taxation for good and for bad: The efficiency and legitimacy of Sweden's carbon tax', *Environmental Politics*, 18(2), March: 218–237.

Kallbekken, S., Kroll, S. and Cherry, T. (2010), 'Pigouvian tax aversion and inequity aversion in the lab', *Economics Bulletin*, 30(3): 1914–1921.

Kallbekken, S. and Kroll, S. and Cherry, T. (2011), 'Do you not like Pigou, or do you not understand him? Tax aversion and revenue recycling in the lab', *Journal of Environmental Economics and Management*, 62: 53–64.

Kosonen, K. (2012), Regressivity of Environmental Taxation: Myth or Reality?, Taxation Papers: Working Paper no.32, European Union, 2012.

Küchler, S. and Meyer, B. (2012), *The Full Costs of Power Generation: A comparison of subsidies and societal cost of renewable and conventional energy sources*, German Wind Energy Association (BWE) and Greenpeace Energy, 2012.

Oates, W. E. 1988. 'On the Nature and Measurement of Fiscal Illusion: A Survey' in Brennan, G., Grewel, S. and Groenwegen, P. (eds), *Taxation and Fiscal Federalism: Essays in Honour of Russel Mathews* (pp. 65–82), Sydney: Australian National University Press.

Ofgem (2013), *Updated: Household Energy Bills Explained*, London, July 2013, retrieved from https://www.ofgem.gov.uk/ofgem-publications/64006/household energybillsexplaineddudjuly2013web.pdf (accessed 7 November 2013).

PETRAS (2002), *Environmental Tax Reform: What Does Europe Think? Policies for Ecological Tax Reform: Assessment of Social Responses*, a Framework 5 Project: EVGI-CT-1999-0004, March, 2002.

Sælen, H. and Kallbekken, S. (2011), 'A choice experiment on fuel taxation and earmarking in Norway', *Ecological Economics*, 70: 2181–2190.

Sterner, T. and Morris, D. (2013), Defying Conventional Wisdom: Distributional

Impacts of Fuel Taxes, Mistral Indigo Policy Paper 1, June 2013. Retrieved from http://indigo.ivl.se/download/18.57d279e13f33d0117e56d/1371715642677/Defying%20Conventional%20Wisdom.pdf (accessed 8 November 2013).

Tamanini, J. (2013), *White Paper Communications and Green Economic Growth*, Washington.

Vivid Economics (2012), *Carbon Taxation and Fiscal Consolidation: the Potential of Carbon Pricing to Reduce Europe's Fiscal Deficits*, London: Vivid Economics.

14. Regulatory taxes as an instrument to foster sustainability transitions: an exploratory analysis

Kris Bachus and Frederic Vanswijgenhoven

14.1 INTRODUCTION

Modern society faces several persistent sustainability problems. The diversity in scale, time and space makes it challenging to solve them. There are different research strands engaged in finding solutions for such contemporary sustainability challenges. For this chapter two disciplines are particularly relevant. The theory of the internalization of externalities using regulatory taxation, elaborated by Pigou (1932) and transitions thinking, which partly evolved out of complexity theory.

Although both research strands try to answer partly similar research questions, there seems to be a discrepancy between the solutions presented by the two disciplines. It appears that the theory of internalization is mainly concerned with abatement of current environmental damage, which results in a focus on short-term objectives instead of the long-term objectives inherent to transition studies whereby multiple generations are involved.

Although initially transition researchers regarded taxes (among other regulatory instruments) as not applicable because of the uncertainty associated with transitions (Geels et al., 2004), more recent studies show an interest in taxes as an instrument for supporting sustainability transitions. Geels (2012), for example, indicates that taxes could be used as an incremental step in low-carbon transitions. Chappin (2011) explicitly examines the role of carbon taxation in energy transition simulations, as does Van den Bergh (2013) with regard to regulation in general. The theoretical implications, however, have not been thoroughly elaborated to date. This chapter aims to fill that gap by exploring the relationship between regulatory taxation and sustainability transitions by analyzing the potential of taxation as an instrument to support sustainability transitions. Our research focuses primarily on the environmental aspects of the sustainability transition.[1]

More specifically, this chapter examines on which levels and in which phases of a sustainability transition potential effects of regulatory taxes can be expected with regard to the progress towards a sustainable transition goal. The robustness of this theoretical framework is then tested on a case study: the Flemish/Belgian energy system. That system clearly shows the characteristics of a socio-technical system and is linked to long-term sustainability challenges. Because of the complexity of the power division in Belgium, it is necessary to include both the nation of Belgium and its subnational region of Flanders into the analysis. Case study interviews and a focus group with academics were used to discuss the connections between taxation and transitions.

The chapter is organized as follows. Section 14.2 presents some useful concepts and theories with regard to sustainability transitions. In section 14.3 a brief summary is given of regulatory taxation theory. Section 14.4 gives an overview of the energy system in Flanders/Belgium. Sections 14.5 and 14.6 are devoted to the results and discussion. Finally, in section 14.7 we set out some conclusions for the research area.

14.2 TRANSITION THEORY

A transition can be seen as a radical and structural change in a societal system. Such a societal system addresses particular public needs (Rotmans and De Haan, 2011). A more appropriate term for such a system is a socio-technical system. A socio-technical system consists of a physical and a social component, and it consists of three building blocks: *structures*, *culture* and *practices*.[2] The structure of the system includes the institutional, physical, legal and economic aspects of the performed societal function (De Haan, 2010). The cultural component consists of cognitive, normative and ideological aspects covered by the functioning of the system. The practices, which interact with the structure and the culture, include routines, habits and procedures applied by the actors in the societal system.

One important characteristic of socio-technical systems is complexity, which is the result of adaptation behavior by the system. The system adapts to its environment as well to changing public priorities (Loorbach, 2007). This implies that a socio-technical system is in continuous evolution (Rotmans and Loorbach, 2009). Loorbach and Wijsman (2013) distinguish a shift from one dynamic system balance to another dynamic balance. However, the evolution can be restricted by choices made in the past, which results in path dependencies.

Changes need to be integrated in an overarching process whereby different domains of the system are evolving (Kemp, 1994; Kemp and Loorbach, 2006). This process involves economic, cultural, ecological and institutional developments on different levels (Rotmans, 2006; Rotmans and Loorbach, 2009). These different levels are translated into a *multi-level perspective* (Geels, 2005), introducing three levels: landscape, regime and niches (Grin et al., 2011). The landscape consists of elements such as macroeconomic trends, international political culture, demographic developments and the natural environment. On this level changes tend to occur at low pace. Kemp and Loorbach (2006) emphasize that the landscape is to a large extent autonomous. As such the landscape forms a broad context in which the system is evolving (Geels and Schot, 2007). The regime and niches on the other hand are part of the socio-technical system. The regime is designated as the dominant constellation in the system, which resists the niches. The latter form alternatives for the dominant regime and are believed to replace the regime and install a new dominant regime (Rotmans and Loorbach, 2009).

Applying those terms to our case study of the energy system will make them easier to understand. The landscape, which forms the context for the energy system, consists of international geopolitical evolutions, relations or events, such as natural disasters or a global economic crisis, which influences energy prices. As a result, the prices on the world market are an autonomous factor for the actors in the energy system. Fossil-fuel based energy products and energy-intensive industries form the regime of the energy system. Some examples of niches are renewable energy production and energy-efficient technologies such as heat pumps.

The process of change is neither linear nor sequential; there are periods of rapid change interspersed with slow moving dynamics (Rotmans and De Haan, 2011). Despite the variability in pace, the process of change is a gradual one. This implies that there are multiple phases in a transition, as indicated by the so-called *multi-phase perspective*. There are four phases in a transition: predevelopment, take-off, breakthrough/acceleration and stabilization. Different actors experiment with innovations in the predevelopment phase. During the take-off phase a window opens up as a result of different developments on different levels (Loorbach et al., 2010). When niches respond to those developments, structural changes can be enforced, which become visible in the acceleration phase. The developments can no longer be reversed. In the last phase, the stabilization phase, a new dynamic balance is reached (Avelino and Rotmans, 2009).

Transitions can be seen as a result of endogenous and exogenous developments. The latter are displayed at the landscape level. The endogenous developments originate out of the other two levels, the regime and the niches.

There are three groups of conditions for change (Rotmans and De Haan, 2011). The first group consists of changes on the landscape level that put pressure on the position of the regime, so-called *tensions*. The second group contains developments arising because of inadequate or inconsistent functioning of the regime, which is labelled as *stress*. Third, when niches become valid competitors for the regime or displace the need for the product/service of the regime, this is called *pressure*. Tensions will result in *reconstellation*, stress will result in *adaptation* and pressure will result in *empowerment*. It is important to notice that adaptation can result in the regime adopting niches' structures, practices or culture although this does not result in a transition but rather in a transformation. A chain of patterns subsequently creates certain transition paths (De Haan, 2010). To summarize, conditions push patterns, which form chains, which results in transition paths. As mentioned before with regard to path dependency, following a certain path will narrow down the number of choices that can be made in a later stage.

There are different actors involved in a transition process. Geels et al. (2004) give an indication of different groups of actors: public authorities, companies, universities and knowledge institutions, civil society organizations and intermediates. The latter are organizations that have a facilitating role between the government and other actors. Each of these actors has their own norms, values and preferences (Berkhout et al., 2004).

In the next section some characteristics of regulatory taxes and their meaning for transition research are set forth.

14.3   REGULATORY TAX THEORY

Public authorities are part of the regime but also play a role in the development of niches (Annema et al., 2013). This implies that public authorities can accelerate or slow down system innovations. In our research the focus lies on the possibility to accelerate system innovations by means of regulatory taxation. On which *level* can regulatory taxes have an effect? In which *phases* can regulatory taxes have an effect, as to say can regulatory taxes help us to reach the next transition phase? When the government taxes less sustainable regime elements, a substitution effect could occur, giving an advantage to the sustainable niche elements. The result is more competitive niches and thus pressure on the system. As mentioned in the previous section, that pressure could lead to empowerment, enabling niches to rise and become a viable competitor for the regime.

In this research regulatory taxes are defined as taxes that are designed with the primary purpose of influencing the behavior of citizens and not

---

BOX 14.1   DOUBLE DIVIDEND: FACT OR FICTION?

The concept of a double dividend finds its origin in the 1990s and is considered an important topic in environmental economics today. Goulder's (1994) distinction between a *weak* and *strong* form of *double dividend* received a lot of attention. While the existence of the first form was broadly recognized by the research community, the second has created a divide between those in favor and those opposing the theory. If an environmental fiscal reform results in zero or negative gross costs, this effect is called a *strong double dividend* (Bachus et al., 2004). The proponents point to the efficiency gains as a result of the shift (Pierce, 1991). The opponents of the strong double dividend theory (Bovenberg and de Mooij, 1994; Bovenberg and van der Ploeg, 1994; Parry, 1995) claim that environmental taxes would not alleviate, but instead exacerbate pre-existing tax distortions.

---

to increase government revenues, as is the case with traditional taxes. In this chapter, our focus is on taxes with an environmental objective, so on (Pigouvian) environmental taxation.[3] The strength of regulatory taxes lies in their static and dynamic efficiency. Taxes are statically efficient because the greatest reduction efforts are made at lowest abatement costs (Sandmo, 2000). Because undesired behavior remains subject to the environmental tax, the taxpayer will seek new methods to reduce his impact on his surroundings, this is called dynamic efficiency. Besides efficient, regulatory taxes are also considered effective because of the behavioral changes that come about in case of a well-designed environmental tax (Bachus, 2011). A fourth advantage of taxes is the fact that they raise government revenues. Finally, there is the possibility of realizing a *double dividend*, although some scholars contest this effect (see Box 14.1). This double dividend could be a consequence of an environmental tax reform (Speck and Gee, 2011).

Our research does not elaborate on subsidies as an instrument for sustainable transitions. Bachus (2011) identifies four reasons why subsidies should be used with caution in environmental policy. First, despite their high political feasibility, subsidies burden the government's budget. The efficiency of subsidies is also questionable, as a portion of the target population would have changed its behavior despite of the absence of subsidies. Third, in contrast with taxes, it is the victims (taxpayers) who pay for abatement measures. Moreover, subsidizing production will result in overproduction and overconsumption. This leads to the possibility of a *rebound effect* when the subsidized product still has harmful effects.[4]

An important remark with respect to regulatory taxes concerns price elasticities. Demand price elasticities can change over time due to the emergence or development of substitutes (Lipsey and Chrystal, 2007). This implies that the price elasticity of a product/service in absolute numbers will rise over time (Pindyck and Rubinfield, 2009). Baranzini and Weber (2013) for example found evidence for higher elasticities for gasoline in the long run compared with the short run. Supply price elasticities also change over time, as producers need to make decisions about investments and need to take into account new competitors. Previous statements would indicate that the potential of regulating taxes rises as time continues.

In the next section, we apply some of the theoretical insights provided in the previous paragraphs to the selected case study.

14.4   CASE STUDY: THE ENERGY SYSTEM IN FLANDERS/BELGIUM

The energy system in general faces different persistent sustainability problems. Lagendijk and Verbong (2010) distinguish four problems: (1) depletion of energy supplies, (2) emissions, (3) affordability and (4) dependence on unstable regions. We developed a long-term vision for the transition to a sustainable Belgian/Flemish energy system, based on Belgian and Flemish government documents and an analysis of publications by relevant stakeholders. The long-term vision contains the following four central elements: (1) decarbonizing the energy system, (2) preserving affordability of energy, (3) maintaining sufficient energy supply and (4) ensuring competitiveness of companies. This long-term vision should be further translated into operational objectives. However, certain objectives seem to be partly contradicting each other, which contribute to the complexity of the energy transition.

A radical system change is needed to achieve the transition objectives mentioned above. The need for radical change of the Belgian/Flemish energy system becomes more apparent if we take a look at the state of the energy market. Figure 14.1 gives an overview of the energy market in Flanders/Belgium in 2011.

Figure 14.1 clearly shows that carbon-intensive energy products are the present dominant regime. Belgium relies heavily on nuclear power for electricity production, which can be considered part of the dominant regime. At the moment there are no regulatory environmental taxes in force with regard to energy; only traditional revenue-raising taxes are in place. Three groups of existing energy taxes can be distinguished: (1) excise duties, primarily on carbon-based energy products, (2) federal contributions for gas and electricity and (3) the nuclear rent tax.

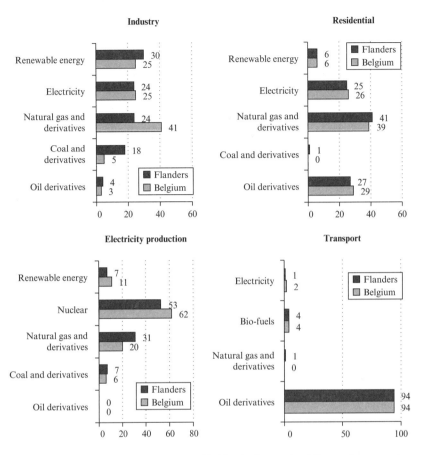

Source: Own compilation of statistics provided by the International Energy Agency and VITO (Energy balance for Flanders).

Figure 14.1   Overview energy market Flanders/Belgium: distribution
of consumption of energy sources used in different sectors
(percent, 2011)

14.5   RESULTS

In the following two subsections the outcome of our analysis are put forth with regard to the potential influence of regulatory taxes on the development of the structure (14.5.1), the culture and the practices (14.5.2) of a socio-technical system. The barriers for the use of regulatory taxes as an instrument for the governance of sustainability transitions are discussed in the last subsection (14.5.3). At the end of each subsection some insights relevant to the case study are presented.

14.5.1   Structure

It is obvious that fulfilling the transition goals requires adaptation of the existing energy system structure. The regime and the niches share some structure elements, such as the electricity transport networks. However, structures can be regarded as regime elements. The structures of several socio-technical systems are to a significant extent defined by the availability of technology. The question that follows is: can regulatory taxes have an effect on the availability of niche technologies so that less sustainable regime structures are replaced?

To answer this question, we introduce a third theoretical framework into the analysis, namely the theory of diffusion of technologies and technology life cycle. Rogers defines diffusion as a process through which an innovation is propagated throughout time to the members of the society (Rogers, 2003: 5–6). Furthermore, it appears to be a kind of societal change whereby the structure and functioning of a society is adapted. This definition has a clear resemblance with the definition of a transition.

The technology life cycle consists of four phases: (1) research and development, (2) growth (3) maturity and (4) saturation (Gao et al., 2013). The technology life cycle curve is similar to the S-shaped curve of the multiphase model of sustainability transitions, as is shown in Figure 14.2.

There is a possibility to apply taxes on regime technologies, as previously mentioned, in order to decrease the price ratio between the sustainable technologies, offered by the niches, and the (usually cheaper) environmentally less sound technologies. According to the respondents of our interviews, the appropriate moment to implement this tax would be on the boundary between the take-off phase and the acceleration phase (see Figure 14.2) so that upscaling of the more environmentally friendly technology can take place. During the acceleration phase the tax should be retained to further support the growth of the niches' technology.

We conclude that a tax on less sustainable technologies can result in the adoption of more sustainable technologies, which can speed up the transition process. Figure 14.2 shows the graphic representation of this conclusion.

The saturation phase may be followed by a decay phase, during which the adoption of the technology declines when the value of the technology declines. This devaluation can be the result of declining revenues. According to Geels (2004), those declining revenues constitute an internal problem for the regime, which can result in stress. In the ideal situation,

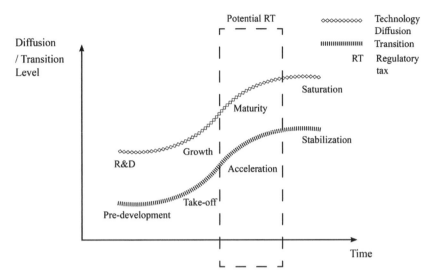

Source: Own compilation building on theories by Gao et al. (2013: 400) and Rogers (2003: 11).

Figure 14.2   Transition and technology diffusion

this is the moment a new transition process sets in, as is illustrated in Figure 14.3. As such, a sustainable technology takes over the dominant position of the former, less sustainable, technology, leading to a new dynamic equilibrium.

The above situation can be found in the Belgian energy sector with regard to nuclear power plants. The nuclear facilities do not have to deal with declining returns because they earn rents (Verbruggen, 2013), which facilitates a technology lock-in (Geels and Schot, 2007). Since April 2003, producers of electricity who control nuclear facilities need to pay a lump-sum tax to the federal government.[5] The nuclear tax is not a regulatory tax but it could have a regulatory effect if this tax ensures that producers of electricity make new investments and update the structure of the system. The rents earned by the producers are an indication of a price-inelastic demand and supply of energy products (Cooper, 2007). Consequently, a regulatory tax may have only a modest impact on energy prices in theory. The solution for this problem is introducing high tax rates. But high tax rates result in higher energy prices, which may jeopardize the other transition goals of affordability and competitiveness. Compensation mechanisms can be put in place to mitigate those undesired side-effects.

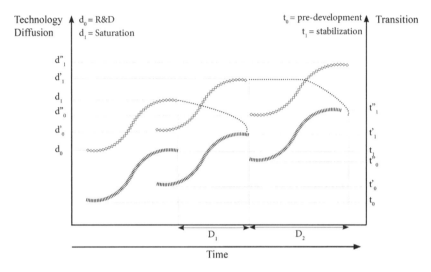

Figure 14.3   Influence of stress

14.5.2   Culture and Practices

Obviously, regulatory taxes will have an impact on the practices within a system. As elaborated on in the existing literature on taxation, the goal of regulatory taxes is to make citizens change their behavior, their practices. In this case the goal is to convince people to adopt niche practices by taxing less sustainable regime practices. The whole instrument of regulatory taxation implicitly builds on the assumption of a rational consumer who weighs the benefits and costs of his behavior (rational choice theory). Other theories, such as the social practices theory, oppose this view. According to that theory a *practice* is routine behavior, which consists of different elements that are connected to each other: physical activities, mental activities, objects and their use and several forms of knowledge (Reckwitz, 2002). Naus et al. (2014), for example, already used this framework to study the influence of information flows on energy practices. Nevertheless, Geels and Schot (2007) confirm that rationality should be considered as one of the foundational paradigms of the multi-level perspective. Furthermore, regulatory taxes could be part of a policy package, which includes a focus on creating awareness about less sustainable behavior, thus overcoming to some degree the hurdle of the actor's lack of information or knowledge. Furthermore, 'culture' is not as straightforward as it seems. However, changing practices could cause a shift in culture towards more sustainable ideas according to our interviewees.

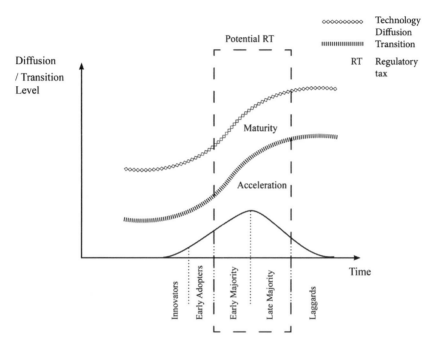

Figure 14.4   Public acceptance

14.5.3   Barriers

A first barrier is the discussion about competitiveness. This discussion refers to the potential existence of *carbon leakage*. Second, public acceptance for environmental taxes is generally low. The theory of diffusion of innovations can again shed some light onto this issue. Certain groups of consumers are more receptive to innovative technologies and thus do not need persuasion via regulatory taxes. Figure 14.4 shows the groups who should be persuaded via taxes. The innovators and the early adopters can shape public support, although the degree of this support is case specific.

A market situation with low prices for energy products at the international markets can be seen as an additional specific barrier for the use of regulatory taxes to accelerate the transition of the Flemish/Belgian energy system. Indeed, low prices result in lower investment rates in sustainable renewable energy, provoking the need for high tax rates.

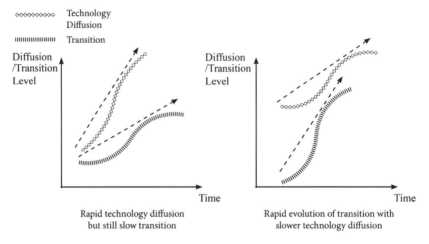

Figure 14.5   *S-curves*

14.6   DISCUSSION

First, a substantive remark, previous figures always show identical curves for the transition process and the technology diffusion process. Because of the complexity of transitions, as set forth in section 14.2, it would be incorrect to assume that technology would be the only driver of a transition process. As illustrated in Figure 14.5, major progress in the diffusion process could result in minor progress in the transition process, and vice versa.

We extended the two theoretical frameworks that form the basis of this research by adding insights from other theoretical perspectives, such as the diffusion of innovations and rational choice theory. However, certain elements of the impact of taxation on the transition cycle are still unexplored and need more comprehensive research, possibly with the introduction of more theoretical angles. The relevance of issues such as power, political economy insights and governance aspects are just a few examples of additional frameworks that could be included in future analyses.

14.7   CONCLUSIONS

Our analysis provides indications that regulatory taxes should not be ignored as potential instruments for enhancing sustainability transitions. We have shown that the structure of a socio-technical system could be influenced by the introduction of a regulatory tax. Primarily the element of niches' technologies, as a part of the structure, could benefit from rising prices of dominant regime technologies that are a consequence of the implementation of a regulatory tax.[6] Niches becoming more competitive result in pressure on the regime, which could induce an acceleration leading to a next step in the transition process. The best moment for implementing a regulatory tax with regard to technology would be between the take-off phase and the acceleration phase. The influence of regulatory taxes on the culture and the practices of the socio-technical system is less distinct. Instinctively, respondents agree that regulatory taxes will have an impact on the culture and practices. However, our theoretical framework for assessing this hypothesis is still immature. The barriers are not clear-cut either. Barriers for the use of regulatory taxation as an instrument for transition governance are case specific, although some general barriers for taxation like, for example, competitiveness and public support issues, can be highlighted. Further research may contribute to develop a theoretical framework for evaluating the impact of regulatory taxation on the occurrence and the speed of sustainability transitions.

NOTES

1. Although the same type of analysis could also be done focusing on social and economic aspects of sustainability transitions, those variants are not part of the scope of this chapter.
2. For example: the mobility system is a socio-technical system consisting of structure (for example, roads, car technologies), culture (for example, the expectation that we can get into our car and drive to any point at any time with almost unlimited flexibility) and practices (for example, the daily routine to take the car, drop off the children at school and then drive to work).
3. Note that regulatory environmental taxes and environmentally related taxes are different concepts (Bruvoll, 2009). The latter, as defined by the OECD (2001), refers to the *tax base* as a distinguishing feature, whereas the definition of the former includes the *objective* of the measure as the sole criterion. Regulatory environmental taxation is a more narrow term than environmentally related taxation: an excise tax on gasoline is a good example of an environmentally related tax (tax base is environmentally relevant) that is not a regulatory environmental tax (objective is not to improve the environment, but to raise government revenues).
4. For example: a subsidy for a fuel-efficient car may lead to more distance travelled by car, or to the purchase of more cars; in both cases the positive environmental impact of the more efficient car is (partly or fully) hollowed-out by both detrimental effects.
5. Federal law of April 11, 2003 concerning the facilities for the dismantling of nuclear power plants.
6. For example, the tax level on the purchase of a diesel-driven car could be significantly higher than an electrical car.

REFERENCES

Annema, J.A., Van den Brink, R., and Walta, L. (2013). Transport technology to reduce transport's negative impacts. In Van Wee, B., Annema, J.A., and Banister, D. (eds), *The Transport System and Transport Policy* (pp. 163–206). Cheltenham, UK and Northampton, MA, USA: Edward Elgar Publishing.

Avelino, F., and Rotmans, J. (2009). Power in transition—an interdisciplinary framework to study power in relation to structural change. *European Journal of Social Theory*, 12(4), 543–569.

Bachus, K. (2011). Instrumenten voor klimaatbeleid: een multilevelperspectief. In De Clercq, M., Albrecht, J., and Verbeke, T. (eds), *Glokaal beleid in Europa. Lokaal beleid voor een globale markt: concurrentie of coördinatie binnen de EU?* (pp. 289–313). Leuven: Acco.

Bachus, K., Defloor, B., and Van Ootegem, L. (2004). *Indicatoren voor de vergroening van de fiscaliteit in Vlaanderen*. Brussel: MIRA.

Baranzini, A., and Weber, S. (2013). Elasticities of gasoline demand in Switzerland. *Energy Policy*, 63, 674–680.

Berkhout, F., Smith, A., and Stirling, A. (2004). Socio-technological regimes and transition contexts. In Elzen, B., Geels, F.W., and Green, K. (eds), *System Innovation and the Transition to Sustainability* (pp. 48–75). Cheltenham, UK and Northampton, MA, USA: Edward Elgar Publishing.

Bovenberg, A.L. and de Mooij, R.A. (1994). Environmental levies and distortionary taxation, *The American Economic Review*, 84, 1085–1089.

Bovenberg, A.L. and van der Ploeg F. (1994). Environmental policy, public finance and the labour market in a second-best world, *Journal of Public Economics*, 55, 349–390.

Bruvoll, A. (2009). *On the measurement of environmental taxes* (Working Paper 559). Kongsvinger: Statistics Norway.

Chappin, E.J.L. (2011). *Simulating Energy Transitions* [PhD Thesis]. Delft: Technische Universiteit Delft.

Cooper, M.N. (2007). The failure of federal authorities to protect American energy consumers from market power and other abusive practices. *Loyola Consumer Law*, 19(4), 315–411.

De Haan, H. (2010). *Towards Transition Theory* [PhD Thesis]. Rotterdam: Erasmus Universiteit Rotterdam.

Frantzeskaki, N., and de Haan, H. (2009). Transitions: Two steps from theory to policy. *Futures*, 41, 593–606.

Gao, L., Porter, A.L., Wang, J., Fang, S., Zhang, X., Ma, T., Wang, W., and Huang, L. (2013). Technology life cycle analysis method based on patent documents. *Technological Forecasting and Social Change*, 80, 398–407.

Geels, F.W. (2004). Understanding system innovations: A critical literature review and a conceptual synthesis. In Elzen, B., Geels, F.W., and Green, K. (eds), *System Innovation and the Transition to Sustainability* (pp. 19–47). Cheltenham, UK and Northampton, MA, USA: Edward Elgar Publishing.

Geels, F.W. (2005). *Technological Transitions and System Innovations*. Cheltenham, UK and Northampton, MA, USA: Edward Elgar Publishing.

Geels, F.W. (2012). A socio-technical analysis of low-carbon transitions: Introducing the multi-level perspective into transport studies. *Journal of Transport Geography*, 24, 471–482.

Geels, F.W., and Schot, J. (2007). Typology of sociotechnical transition pathways. *Research Policy*, 36, 399–417.

Geels, F.W., Elzen, B., and Green, K. (2004). General introduction: System innovation and transitions to sustainability. In Elzen, B., Geels, F.W., and Green, K. (eds), *System Innovation and the Transition to Sustainability*. Cheltenham, UK and Northampton, MA, USA: Edward Elgar Publishing.

Goulder, L.H. (1994). Environmental taxation and the double dividend. A reader's guide. *National Bureau of Economic Research Working Paper*, 4896, 41 p.

Grin, J., Rotmans, J., and Schot, J. (2011). *Transitions to Sustainable Development*. New York: Routledge.

Haupt, R., Kloyer, M., and Lange, M. (2007). Patent indicators for the technology life cycle development. *Research Policy*, 36, 387–398.

Kemp, R. (1994). Technology and the transition to environmental sustainability. *Futures*, 26, 1023–1046.

Kemp, R., and Loorbach, D. (2006). Transition management: A reflexive governance approach. In Voß, J., Bauknecht, D., and Kemp, R. (eds), *Reflexive Governance for Sustainable Development* (pp. 103–130). Cheltenham, UK and Northampton, MA, USA: Edward Elgar Publishing.

Lagendijk, V, and Verbong, G. (2010). Setting the stage for the energy transition. In Verbong, G., and Loorbach, D. (eds), *Governing the Energy Transition* (pp. 51–74). New York: Routledge.

Lipsey, R.G., and Chrystal, K.A. (2007). *Economics*. New York: Oxford University Press.

Loorbach, D. (2007). *Transition Management, New Mode of Governance for Sustainbable Development*. Utrecht: International Books.

Loorbach, D., and Wijsman, K. (2013). Business transition management: Exploring a new role for business in sustainability transitions. *Journal of Cleaner Production*, 45, 20–28.

Loorbach, D., Frantzeskaki, N., and Thissen, W. (2010). Introduction to the special section: Infrastructures and transitions. *Technological Forecasting and Social Change*, 77, 1195–1202.

Naus, J., Spaargaren, G., van Vliet, B.J.M., and van der Horst, H.M. (2014). Smart grids, information flows and emerging domestic energy practices. *Energy Policy*, 68, 436–446.

Organisation for Economic Co-operation and Development (2001). *Environmentally Related Taxes in OECD Countries—Issues and Strategies*. Paris: OECD.

Pierce, D. (1991). The role of carbon taxes in adjusting to global warming. *Economic Journal of Applied Economics*, 101, 938–948.

Pigou, A.C. (1932). *The Economics of Welfare* (4th edn). London: Macmillan.

Pindyck, R.S., and Rubinfield, D.L. (2009). *Microeconomics* (7th edn). New Jersey: Pearson Education.

Reckwitz, A. (2002). Toward a theory of social practices: A development in culturalist theorizing. *European Journal of Social Theory*, 5, 243–263.

Rogers, E.M. (2003). *Diffusion of Innovations*. New York: Free Press.

Rotmans, J. (2006). *Societal Innovation: Between Dream and Reality Lies Complexity*. Rotterdam: RSM Erasmus University.

Rotmans, J., and De Haan, J.H. (2011). Patterns in transitions: Understanding complex chains of change. *Technological Forecasting and Social Change*, 78, 90–102.

Rotmans, J., and Loorbach, D. (2009). Complexity and transition management. *Journal of Industrial Ecology*, 13(2), 184–196.

Sandmo, A. (2000). *The Public Economics of the Environment*. New York: Oxford University Press.

Speck, S., and Gee, D. (2011). Implications of environmental tax reforms: Revisited. In Kreiser, L., Sirisom, J., Ashiabor, H., and Milne, J.E. (eds), *Environmental Taxation and Climate Change: Achieving Environmental Sustainability through Fiscal Policy* (pp. 19–34). Cheltenham, UK and Northampton, MA, USA: Edward Elgar Publishing.

Van den Bergh, J. (2013). Policies to enhance economic feasibility of a sustainable energy transition. *PNAS*, 110(7), 2436–2437.

Verbruggen, A. (2013). Belgian nuclear power life extension and fuss about nuclear rents. *Energy Policy*, 60, 91–97.

15. Resilience based policy for groundwater protection

Deborah L. Jarvie

15.1 INTRODUCTION

Water management in the twenty-first century requires a new and innovative framework in order to address the growing needs and diverse usage of this essential resource. This chapter is part of a larger doctoral study examining the protection of groundwater during unconventional natural gas (UNG) extraction. While economic benefits are recognized from the practice of UNG production, environmental concerns have also been raised, and as stated by Sprohge et al. (2012: 97), '[i]f these environmental concerns are handled properly, hydraulic fracturing drilling may be one of the biggest technological innovations of all time. If these concerns are not handled properly, serious environmental degradation may take place in our lifetime'. This study thus explores the notion of how to properly handle the environmental concerns that pertain to groundwater, examining the role of *environmental tax incentives* in the complex socio-ecological framework surrounding this particular energy–water nexus.

The intention of this chapter is not to reiterate the processes of UNG extraction, the economic benefits from production, nor the specific concerns, but rather to present the proposition that there is a need for policy designed within a systems framework based on the construct of *resilience*[1] in complex socio-ecological systems. The need to move away from traditional, static environmental regulatory schemes is discussed at length in the literature[2] as the knowledge of complexities within socio-ecological systems continues to grow. Within this discussion, there is increasing support for the use of taxation as a means to protect the environment,[3] a theory brought to light in the middle of the twentieth century by the English economist, Arthur Cecil Pigou—the 'intellectual father of environmental taxes' (Milne and Andersen, 2012: 4). Environmental taxation is typically based on theories and concepts from economics, law, and finance

(Milne, 2012), and this study suggests that these categories be expanded to include that of 'resilience' within complex systems.

15.2 INTRODUCING ECOSYSTEM ANALYSIS INTO POLICY DESIGN

Figure 15.1 (from Scheffer et al., 2001) illustrates the temporal effects of changing conditions in an ecosystem. Boxes a and b depict the gradual

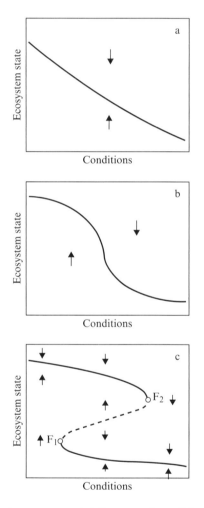

Figure 15.1   Shifts in ecosystems[4] (diagrams from Scheffer et al., 2001)

change in an ecosystem's state as it is affected by a given condition. Box a shows a steady adjustment to the condition, while Box b illustrates a more sudden decline in the state of the system. Box c, on the other hand, shows a 'flip' in the system to an alternative state once the point of resilience has been reduced to an unsustainable point (F_2). The section between F_2 and F_1 represents an unstable region, or '"catastrophic" transition to the lower branch' (Scheffer et al., 2001: 591).

Command and control regulations are typically designed with the intention of mitigating impacts, like those shown on the trajectory towards an F_2 outcome, or worse yet, an F_1 position. However, socio-ecological interactions are often irreversible and impact long timelines (Pindyck, 2007),[5] thus commanding that policy be designed around these characteristics and within a framework capable of encapsulating the dynamics of the spatial and temporal system. Holling and Meffe (1996: 329) state that '[t]he command-and-control approach implicitly assumes that the problem is well-bounded, clearly defined, relatively simple, and generally linear with respect to cause and effect. But when these same methods of control are applied to a complex, nonlinear, and poorly understood natural world, and when the same predictable outcomes are expected but rarely obtained, severe ecological, social, and economic repercussions result'. In a discussion as to why some systems thrive and others do not, Ostrom (2009: 420) addresses the challenge of carrying out the 'identification and analysis of relationships among multiple levels of these complex systems at different spatial and temporal scales'.

Senge (1990) points out that the most common method of dealing with situations is by reacting to events and that a more useful process exists in the determination of long-term patterns of behavior, with the most powerful method for understanding and resolving issues being through the understanding of the system's structure. Coghlan and Brannick (2001: 100) further support Senge's views on the systems approach as 'hold[ing] the key to integrating intuition and reason because intuition goes beyond linear thinking to recognize patterns, draw analogies and solve problems creatively'.

To illustrate the various systems and regulatory concerns, Figure 15.2, developed in this study, presents an introductory framework of the components and relationships between (1) economic and ecological systems and (2) the issues of policy theory and enactment.[6] The construct of resilience is recognized in the model as an essential element of effective design, recognizing the fact that systems are ambiguous, nonlinear, complex and capable of shifting to alternative steady states if resilience is weakened.

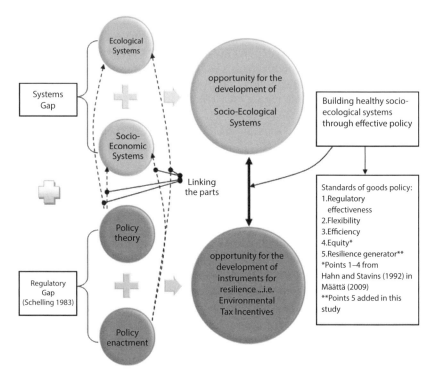

*Figure 15.2   An exploration of dynamic systems and environmental policy
in a framework for the resilience of groundwater*

15.3   SHIFTING TOWARDS A RESILIENCE BASED FRAMEWORK

> Policies and management that apply fixed rules for achieving constant yields . . .
> independent of scale, lead to systems that gradually lose resilience, i.e., to ones
> that suddenly break down in the face of disturbances that previously could be
> absorbed.
>
> (Holling and Meffe, 1996; Holling, 1986)

Many current policy mixes are the result of poor planning and haphazard
'policy layering', 'developed without any real sense of an overall con-
scious design' (del Rio and Howlett, 2013: 4). Carpenter et al. (2009) state
that, 'Because they are not easily computable, many important aspects
do not find their way into the models that dominate policy decisions.
Instead, the dominant models are a patchwork of rigorous but fragmented

information'. These authors also state that, '[t]he stronger the dominant view, and the more completely it dominates, the greater the myopia of what could otherwise be a broad problem-solving-team'. As such, this dependence on past statistical data and unreliable models, and the inability to ask the proper questions, prevents policymakers from foreseeing future 'shocks' to systems.[7]

A policy mix capable of mitigating these types of shocks, based on theories of resilience, complexity, system dynamics, and environmental tax incentives for innovation recognizes that traditional command and control measures are no longer sufficient to address all of the intricacies of socio-ecological systems. Gunningham and Grabosky (2004: 4) suggest that 'in the majority of circumstances, the use of multiple rather than single policy instruments, and a broader range of regulatory actors, will produce better regulation'.[8] However, debates concerning regulatory mixes often consider only two alternatives; those of 'all government-imposed regulations', or 'full-swing market determination when allocating scarce resources' (Ayres and Braithwaite, 1992). Del Rio and Howlett (2013) address the lack of attention to the complexity of policy 'bundles', suggesting that actual policy design has typically attempted to structure itself on the notion of a single policy instrument thus 'forc[ing] complex situations into the more simple mold required for Tinbergens' simple case rule[9] to apply' (p. 3, citing Knudson, 2009). Munda et al. (1994: 111) also address this 'tendency to make reality fit the model' in their discussion of policy design, suggesting that there is a need for a multi-criteria evaluation for environmental policy and management.

Thus a paradigm shift (Kuhn, 1962)—one from the current '*reality fitting the model*' to a new '*models fitting reality*'—is required. As there is no prescription for the optimal mix nor any one best solution, but rather alternatives to choose from and solutions to be analyzed within those alternatives, a challenge exists with regard to (1) sifting through the various policy instruments, (2) determining their respective strengths and weaknesses, (3) structuring their design and implementation, and (4) measuring their effectiveness and efficiency. To address this complex issue, a policy mix for the resilience of groundwater has been identified in this study (Figure 15.3), recognizing the need for multiple regulatory[10] instruments.

Environmental tax incentives are highlighted in Figure 15.3, as it is this element of the policy mix which is proposed here to be that most capable of providing the motivations necessary for the innovation required to protect the resilience of groundwater.

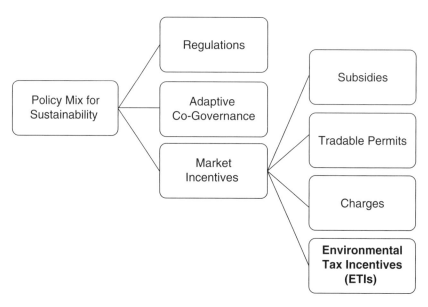

Figure 15.3   Range of policy instruments for the resilience of groundwater

15.4   ENVIRONMENTAL TAX INCENTIVES IN THE POLICY MIX

> Indeed, it is hardly disputed nowadays that environmental taxes can be of critical importance to the inducement and diffusion of new technologies, or 'technological change' for short.
>
> (Vollebergh, 2012: 360)

Sharpe and Long (2012: 21) discuss the need for increased innovation for environmental protection in natural resource industries, stating that '[t]here is evidence . . . to suggest that firms may not invest enough in environmental technologies without the right incentives'. Drawing on the Porter Hypothesis,[11] they support the idea that properly designed environmental policy may actually be beneficial to firms, rather than a hindrance (which has been the traditional viewpoint). The OECD (2001) suggests that in addition to the removal of environmentally damaging subsidies and tax provisions, the employment of a more effective use of technology is necessary to address the concerns of (1) production patterns, (2) consumption patterns, and (3) efficiency gains; and to meet the objectives of (1) maintaining ecosystems, (2) decoupling environmental pressures from economic growth, (3) enhancing social and environmental quality of life, and (4) improving governance and cooperation.

To foster the innovation necessary to mitigate negative impacts and thus better protect the resilience of the system, specific mechanisms capable of providing these incentives for innovation are required. Canada's Oil Sands Innovation Alliance (COSIA, 2012) states in its *Water Environmental Priority Area* (EPA) that it 'is looking for innovative and sustainable solutions to reduce water use and increase water recycling rates at oil sands mining and in situ operations without causing negative environmental impacts in other areas'.

This study examines provisions within the Canadian Income Tax Act in which there exists the potential for innovation for water protection. One of these provisions—scientific research and experimental development (SR&ED)—is presented here to illustrate this point. To begin, Section 248(1) of the Act defines SR&ED as:

'scientific research and experimental development' means systematic investigation or search that is carried out in a field of science or technology by means of experiment or analysis and that is

(a) basic research, namely, work undertaken for the advancement of scientific knowledge without a specific practical application in view,

(b) applied research, namely, work undertaken for the advancement of scientific knowledge with a specific practical application in view, or

(c) experimental development, namely, work undertaken for the purpose of achieving technological advancement for the purpose of creating new, or improving existing, materials, devices, products or processes, including incremental improvements thereto,

(Income Tax Act, RSC 1985, c. 1 (5th Supp.) as amended (herein referred to as 'the Act'). Unless otherwise stated, stautory references in this article are to the Act., Subsection 248(1).)

Within this definition, Paragraph (c) includes 'technological advancements' and thus can potentially provide monetary incentives for water protection, as SR&ED offers deductions and tax credits dependent on the provisions of the Act. While Paragraph 248(1)(h) of the Act explicitly excludes SR&ED for the 'prospecting, exploring or drilling for, or producing, minerals, petroleum or natural gas', technological advancements or incremental improvements to current processes for water protection may be argued to fall outside of this restriction.

This is but one example of an environmental tax incentive whereby resilience can be facilitated through a bridging of economics and the environment, and other incentives examined in the study include accelerated capital cost allowance, the Canadian Renewable and Conservation Expense, and flow-through shares. Revisiting an earlier comment, policy must shift to a model that fits reality. Tax incentives based on the complexities of socio-ecological systems present an opportunity to drive innovative

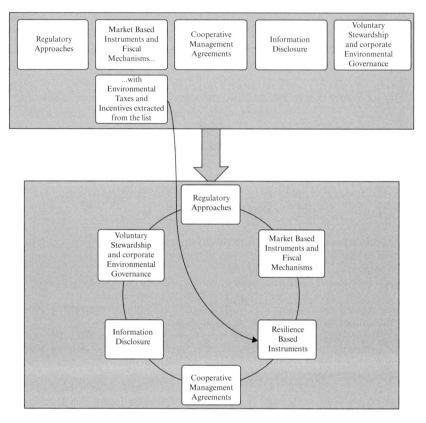

Figure 15.4   The addition of 'Resilience Based Instruments' to the mix of environmental policy tools[12]

practices in the direction of sustainable conservation, while also providing economic benefits.

15.5   CONCLUDING THOUGHTS

> Policy design includes the creation of entirely new strategies, structures, and decision rules. (Sterman, 2000: 104)

We are unquestionably in a time of uncertainty and rapid ecological change (Gunderson et al., 2010), and as such, determining the optimal mix of policy instruments for groundwater protection poses itself as both necessary and complicated. Conventional scientific solutions and traditional government policies may not be able to provide 'effective long-term management' (Turnpenny et al., 2009), and thus a new era of policy is deserving of consideration. A policy mix inclusive of environmental tax incentives based on innovation for resilience (Figure 15.4)—carefully designed to address competitive effects, the political environment, revenue recycling, the tax base, and the distinction between charges and credits—will be essential to meet the challenges of the twenty-first century.

NOTES

1. The concept of resilience described here is that as defined from an ecological perspective by the likes of Berkes and Folke (1998), Carpenter et al. (2009), Folke et al. (2010) and Walker et al. (2004).
2. The need for a shift away from traditional command and control regulations is discussed by the likes of, for example, Baldwin et al. (2012), De Schutter and Lenoble (2010), Gunningham and Grabosky (2004) and Holley et al. (2012).
3. Andersen (1994), Baumol and Oates (1988), de Mooij and Vollebergh (1995), Enevoldsen (2005), Fullerton et al. (2008), Gunningham and Grabosky (2004), Määttä (2006), Milne (2004), OECD (2001), Stavins (2003) and Wallart (1999) are among a growing body of contributors to the literature on environmental taxation.
4. Adapted by permission from Macmillan Publishers Ltd: *Nature*, Scheffer et al., copyright (2001).
5. Pindyck (2007) refers to the chemical contamination of water supplies as one example whereby long-term effects are ignored when short-term net-present value calculations are used in policymaking based on cost–benefit.
6. The larger study proposes that there exists both a systems gap and a regulatory gap. The need for a policy mix designed around the construct of resilience is proposed as an essential mechanism to narrow these gaps.
7. The authors cite Hurricane Katrina in the US, the depletion of ozone at the South Pole, and depleted fisheries as examples where faulty predictions have indirectly led to catastrophic results.
8. The idea that there is a need for a comprehensive policy mix for effective policy design is supported in the literature by the likes of del Rio and Howlett (2013), Gunningham (2009), Hessing et al. (2005), Gunningham and Grabosky (2004), Fullerton (2001), Munda et al. (1994), Hahn and Stavins (1992) and Tinbergen (1952), to name but a few.
9. Tinbergen (1952) originally laid the foundation for the idea that the number of instruments should equal the number of policy goals, theorizing that having more targets than instruments makes targets incompatible, and implementing more instruments than targets provides for 'alternatives'; in other words, a different instrument or combination thereof could be chosen than that which was intended. However, even Tinbergen recognized that some goals would require sub-policies due to side-effects that might occur (del Rio and Howlett, 2013).
10. The term *regulation* is used interchangeably in this study (as it is in the literature) to mean both (a) regulation at a high level, for example, encompassing an entire range of policy instruments; and (b) regulation at a specific level, referring to specific instruments such as command and control directives.
11. Porter and van der Linde (1995) introduced the idea that well-designed regulations could actually enhance a company's innovation and profits, a theory that became known as the Porter Hypothesis. This thought was contrary to the preceding literature concerning regulations for environmental externalities (Ambec et al., 2011), which proposed that regulations would negatively affect the profits of a company.

12. This policy framework has been designed based on the policy categories stated in the *Alberta Environment and Sustainable Resource Development: 'The range of environmental policy tools'* (Government of Alberta, 1995–2014) with the addition of 'Resilience Based Instruments' added here.

REFERENCES

Ambec, S., Cohen, M.A., Elgie, S., and Lanoie, P. (2011). The Porter Hypothesis at 20: Can Environmental Regulation Enhance Innovation and Competitiveness? (pp. 28): Resources for the Future, retrieved from http://www.rff.org/documents/RFF-DP-11-01.pdf (accessed April 24, 2015).

Andersen, M.S. (1994). *Governance by Green Taxes: Making Pollution Prevention Pay*. Manchester, UK: Manchester University Press.

Ayres, I., and Braithwaite, J. (1992). *Responsive Regulation: Transcending the Deregulation Debate*. New York, Oxford: Oxford University Press.

Baldwin, R., Cave, M., and Lodge, M. (2012). *Understanding Regulation: Theory, Strategy, and Practice* (2nd edn). New York: Oxford University Press.

Baumol, W.J., and Oates, W.E. (1988). *The Theory of Environmental Policy* (2nd edn). Cambridge: Cambridge University Press (Original work published 1975).

Berkes, F., and Folke, C. (eds). (1998). *Linking Social and Ecological Systems*. Cambridge: Cambridge University Press.

Carpenter, S.R., Folke, C., Scheffer, M., and Westley, F.R. (2009). Resilience: accounting for the noncomputable. *Ecology and Society*, 14(1), online.

Coghlan, D., and Brannick, T. (2001). *Doing Action Research in Your Own Organisation*. London, UK: Sage.

COSIA (2012). Canada's Oil Sands Innovation Alliance, retrieved from http://www.cosia.ca (accessed April 24, 2015).

de Mooij, R.A., and Vollebergh, H.R.J. (1995). Prospects for European Environmental Tax Reform. In F.J. Dietz, H.R.J. Vollebergh and J.L. de Vries (eds), *Environment, Incentives and the Common Market* (pp. 139–159). Dordrecht: Springer Science + Business Media.

De Schutter, O., and Lenoble, J. (2010). *Reflexive Governance: Redefining the Public Interest in a Pluralistic World*. Oxford and Portland, Oregon: Hart Publishing.

del Rio, P., and Howlett, M. (2013). Beyond the 'Tinbergen Rule' in policy design: Matching tools and goals in policy portfolios. *Annual Review of Policy Design*, 1, 1–16.

Enevoldsen, M. (2005). *The Theory of Environmental Agreements and Taxes*. Cheltenham, UK and Northampton, MA, USA: Edward Elgar Publishing.

Folke, C., Carpenter, S., Walker, B., Scheffer, M., Chapin, T., and Rockström, J. (2010). Resilience thinking: Integrating resilience, adaptability and transformability. *Ecology and Society*, 15(4), retrieved from http://www.ecologyandsociety.org/vol15/iss4/art20/ (accessed April 24, 2015).

Fullerton, D. (2001). A framework to compare environmental policies. *Southern Economic Journal*, 68(2), 224–248.

Fullerton, D., Leicester, A., and Smith, S. (2008). Environmental taxes. *NBER Working Paper Series*.

Government of Alberta. (1995–2014). *Environmental Tools Guide*. Alberta:

Government of Alberta, retrieved from http://esrd.alberta.ca/about-esrd/environmental-tools-guide/default.aspx (accessed May 4, 2015).

Gunderson, L.H., Allen, C.R., and Holling, C.S. (2010). *Foundations of Ecological Resilience*. Washington: Island Press.

Gunningham, N. (2009). Environmental law, regulation adn governance: Shifting architectures. *Journal of Environmental Law*, 21(2), 179–212.

Gunningham, N., and Grabosky, P. (2004). *Smart Regulation: Designing Environmental Policy*. Oxford: Oxford University Press (Original work published 1998).

Hahn, R.W., and Stavins, R.N. (1992). Economic incentives for environmental protection: Integrating theory and practice. *The American Economic Review*, 82(2), 464–469.

Hessing, M., Howlett, M., and Summerville, T. (2005). *Canadian Natural Resource and Environmental Policy* (2nd edn). Vancouver: UBC Press.

Holley, C., Gunningham, N., and Shearing, C. (2012). *The New Environmental Governance*. Earthscan: New York.

Holling, C., and Meffe, G.K. (1996). Command and control and the pathology of natural resource management. *Conservation Biology*, 10(2), 328–337.

Holling, C.S. (1986). The resilience of terrestrial ecosystems, local surprise and global change. In W.C. Clark and R.E. Munn (eds), *Sustainable Development of the Biosphere* (pp. 292–317). Cambridge: Cambridge University Press.

Income Tax Act. (RSC 1985, c. 1 (5th Supp.) as amended (herein referred to as 'the Act'). Unless otherwise stated, stautory references in this article are to the Act).

Knudson, W.A. (2009). The environment, energy, and the Tinbergen Rule. *Bulletin of Science, Technology and Society*, 29(4), 308–312.

Kuhn, T.S. (1962). *The Structure of Scientific Revolutions*. Chicago: University of Chicago Press.

Määttä, K. (2006). *Environmental Taxes*. Cheltenham, UK and Northampton, MA, USA: Edward Elgar Publishing.

Milne, J.E. (2004). Environmental taxation: Why theory matters. In K.D. Janet Milne, Larry Kreiser and Hope Ashiabor (eds), *Critical Issues in Environmental Taxation, International and Comparative Perspectives*. London: Richmond Law & Tax.

Milne, J.E. (2012). This book's approach to environmental taxation. In J.E. Milne and M.S. Andersen (eds), *Handbook of Research on Environmental Taxation* (pp. 1–11). Cheltenham, UK and Northampton, MA, USA: Edward Elgar Publishing.

Milne, J.E., and Andersen, M.S. (eds) (2012). *Handbook of Research on Environmental Taxation*. Cheltenham, UK and Northampton, MA, USA: Edward Elgar Publishing.

Munda, G., Nijkamp, P., and Rietveld, P. (1994). Qualitative multicriteria evaluation for environmental management. *Ecological Economics*, 10, 97–112.

OECD. (2001). *A New Strategy for the Environment*. Paris: OECD.

Ostrom, E. (2009). A general framework for analyzing sustainability of social-ecological systems. *Science*, 325, 419–422.

Pigou, A.C. (1952). *The Economics of Welfare*. New Brunswick: Transaction Publishers. (2002, Original work published 1952).

Pindyck, R.S. (2007). Uncertainty in environmental economics. *Review of Environmental Economics and Policy*, 1(1), 45–65.

Porter, M.E., and van der Linde, C. (1995). Toward a new conception of the environment–competitiveness relationship. *The Journal of Economic Perspectives*, 9(4), 97–118.

Scheffer, M., Carpenter, S., Foley, J.A., Folke, C., and Walker, B. (2001). Catastrophic shifts in ecosystems. *Nature*, 413(6856), 591–596.

Senge, P.M. (1990). *The Fifth Discipline: The Art and Practice of the Learning Organization*. New York: Doubleday (Reprinted in 2006).

Sharpe, A., and Long, B. (2012). *Innovation in Canadian Natural Resource Industries: A Systems-Based Analysis of Performance, Policy and Emerging Challenges*. Ottawa, Ontario: Centre for the Study of Living Standards.

Sprohge, H., Tavallali, R., Kreiser, L., and Butcher, B. (2012). Lower cargon energy: The case of hydraulic fracturing for natural gas. In L. Kreiser, A. Yábar Sterling, P. Herrera, J.E. Milne and H. Ashiabor (eds), *Carbon Pricing, Growth and the Environment*. Cheltenham, UK and Northampton, MA, USA: Edward Elgar Publishing.

Stavins, R.N. (2003). Experience with market-based environmental policy instruments. In K.-G. Mäler and J.R. Vincent (eds), *Handbook of Environmental Economics [electronic resource]* (pp. 355–435). Amsterdam: Elsevier.

Sterman, J.D. (2000). *Business Dynamics: Systems Thinking and Modeling for a Complex World*. Boston: Irwin McGraw-Hill.

Tinbergen, J. (1952). *On the Theory of Economic Policy*. Amsterdam: North-Holland.

Turnpenny, J., Lorenzoni, I., and Jones, M. (2009). Noisy and definitely not normal: Responding to wicked issues in the environment, energy and health. *Environmental Science and Policy*, 12(3), 347–358.

Vollebergh, H. (2012). The role of environmental taxation in spurring technological change. In J.E. Milne and M.S. Andersen (eds), *Handbook of Research on Environmental Taxation* (pp. 360–376). Cheltenham, UK and Northampton, MA, USA: Edward Elgar Publishing.

Walker, B., Holling, C.S., Carpenter, S., and Kinzig, A. (2004). Resilience, adaptability and transformability in social-ecological systems. *Ecology and Society: A Journal of Integrative Science for Resilience and Sustainability*, 9(2), online.

Wallart, N. (1999). *The Political Economy of Environmental Taxes*. Cheltenham, UK and Northampton, MA, USA: Edward Elgar Publishing.

Index